Culture and Crisis in Britain in the Thirties

Culture and Crisis in Britain in the Thirties

edited by *Jon Clark, Margot Heinemann, David Margolies* and *Carole Snee*

LAWRENCE AND WISHART
LONDON

Lawrence and Wishart Ltd
39 Museum Street
London WC1A 1LQ

First published 1979
Copyright © Lawrence and Wishart, 1979

0853154198

Printed and bound in Great Britain at
The Camelot Press Ltd, Southampton

Contents

Acknowledgements

We are grateful to Faber and Faber Ltd for their kind permission to quote from *The English Auden* and from *The Collected Poems of Louis MacNeice*, and to Macmillan Publishers Ltd for their kind permission to quote from Martin Bell's *Collected Poetry*. We would also like to thank Christopher Cornford and Noreen Branson for permission to quote from the works of John Cornford and Clive Branson.

Foreword

Fifteen or twenty years ago, when it was widely accepted that the problems of material growth and stability in the West had been more or less solved, the radical art and literature of the nineteen-thirties must often have seemed overstated and remote. Today much of it feels startlingly relevant. Though many things have changed since the thirties, the responsibility and the challenge are in some ways comparable.

There has lately been a good deal of critical and scholarly writing about the period, especially its literature. Much of this, however, is uncomprehending and essentially unsympathetic to what artists and writers of the decade were trying to do. A rooted conviction that art and science should have as little as possible to do with politics — at any rate with left-wing politics — is disabling when it comes to recording and understanding the cultural history of the period. The authors of this volume, on the contrary, share the view that the culture of the thirties gained in strength and vitality by confronting instead of attempting to evade the profound economic and political crisis of those years. We believe that the commitment generated in the crisis was fundamental to the very real cultural achievement of the thirties.

The selection of essays in this volume is designed to give some idea of the richness and variety of culture in the decade. We do not want either to romanticize the period or to minimize and patronize its achievements, as so many recent commentaries have done — the diversity of age, approach and experience on the part of the authors will, we hope, help prevent this. The first-hand insights of the older generation (James Klugmann, André van Gyseghem, Ralph Bond, Betty Reid, Margot Heinemann and Arnold Kettle), who were themselves deeply involved in the cultural movement of the time, are complemented by the perspective of the younger contributors (Peter Widdowson, Bert Hogenkamp, Carole Snee, Iain Wright, David Margolies and Jon Clark), who write without direct personal experience of the period.

For those confronting the complex problems of the nineteen-seventies and eighties, the thirties stand out in retrospect as a time when the issues seemed relatively simple and the relation between culture and politics clear and direct. With two to three million unemployed and millions more undernourished, even the most privileged intellectuals might well feel guilty and outraged at the contrasts between rich and poor, while for many students finishing their education there was little hope of any but the most boring and routine job. The rise of Hitler intensified the general sense of instability and made real the threat of another world war.

For most intellectuals, however, to see themselves as allies of the workers and the labour movement was something altogether new. It must be remembered that as a group intellectuals were much more predominantly upper-middle and middle-class than now, since very few working-class children were educated beyond the age of fourteen. The universities were still dominated by Oxford and Cambridge and by fee-paying students, and the whole graduate body and the student movement were far smaller. Again, the living standards and way of life of professional and middle-class people – even in the humbler sectors like teaching – were much more sharply cut off from those of workers than they are today, in terms of security and leisure as well as housing and food. They had little contact with any culture or entertainment shared by working people. The talkies had just started (mainly, as Ralph Bond points out, with Hollywood dream films), but there was of course scarcely any television, and in films and novels of the early thirties little of the reflection of working-class tastes and life-styles that is commonplace in the modern media.

Moreover, while it is often assumed that it was a militant decade, the facts, as James Klugmann's essay points out, were not so simple. There was considerable rank-and-file militancy among the unemployed and in the old industrial areas, with hunger marches and mass demonstrations against the Means Test, and there was a broad mobilization of support for Republican Spain and anti-fascist struggles. On the other hand, the trade unions as a whole were far weaker and more divided than now, and there was widespread political demoralization after the débâcle of Labour in 1931. All this meant that while most intellectuals continued to acquiesce in the existing social system, many of those who did not were impelled to solutions and action well to the left of the official labour movement. If they came to the left at all, it was often to Marxism and Communism. T. S. Eliot noted the strength of this influence, especially among the young:

. . . no one who is seriously concerned can fail to be impressed by the work of Karl Marx. He is, of course, much more cited than read; but his power is so great, and his analysis so profound, that it must be very hard for anyone who reads him without prejudice on the one hand, or without any definite religious faith on the other, to avoid accepting his conclusions.   (*The Criterion*, XLIV, April 1932)

But to see the force of Marxist analysis was not necessarily to adopt it. For socialism and communism, much more directly than crisis-ridden capitalism, seemed to threaten the leisured, upper-middle-class existence which had been the main basis for traditional 'high culture'. Hence, for some, the survival of art became identified with the preservation and reinforcement of a class-divided, hierarchic society against the menace of egalitarian socialism. This attitude can be seen very clearly, as Arnold Kettle points out, in thirties poetry and in the critical writings of Eliot himself, and also in the works of Ezra Pound and Wyndham Lewis, not to mention Roy Campbell. This trend, which receives only passing treatment here, has been examined in depth by John Harrison in *The Reactionaries* (Gollancz, 1966).

The radical and left-wing cultural work – our main subject in this collection – is dominated, as James Klugmann stresses, by a sense of extreme urgency. This sense of urgency led many artists, scientists and writers to see their role in terms of direct service to the anti-fascist and working-class movement. But a wide gap had to be quickly bridged: if culture was to help the workers to give a new direction to history, the 'forces of culture' had to learn to communicate in forms and language clear and convincing to ordinary people. The effort to achieve this is discussed in the essays on the Left Book Club, film, and left theatre, as well as more generally in those on the working-class novel and poetry. This accessibility of thirties radical culture is perhaps its most important legacy.

It has become common in recent years to dismiss most of this work, often with no more than a cursory look, as simplistic, unimaginative and crudely propagandist. These judgements, we believe, are generally revealed to be inadequate when one goes back to the original works. Yet this is not easy to do when so much of the material is ephemeral, like live theatre, or buried in archives and specialist libraries. Thus we have devoted space to the detailed evolution of theatre and film, and to consideration of critical writing and periodicals like *Left Review*, as well as to the less widely available poets and novelists – even at the cost of important omissions elsewhere.

It would of course be quite wrong to see the impact of history only in terms of committed socialist and Marxist work. Thus Peter

Widdowson shows how the writing of already established novelists like
Virginia Woolf and Aldous Huxley confronts the crisis and is
profoundly influenced by it, as is that of the young Graham Greene. The
same is true of the whole critical enterprise of F. R. Leavis and *Scrutiny*,
dealt with by Iain Wright.

For reasons of space we have had to leave out a great deal, since it
seemed impossible to be comprehensive and at the same time detailed
enough to present first-hand material or to analyse any work in depth.
Most obviously, we have not given a factual record of the social and
political events, essential though this is for understanding the cultural
context. While much still needs to be done in this area, we would refer
readers particularly to *Britain in the Nineteen Thirties* by Noreen
Branson and Margot Heinemann (Panther, 1973), *Britain Between the
Wars* by C. L. Mowat (Methuen, 1956), and *Industry and Empire* by
Eric Hobsbawm (Penguin, 1968).

As in any historical period, most of the output of art and literature
probably ministered to the need for reassurance and escape. Even so,
we have not dealt with great areas of cultural production which
remained substantially unaltered, such as the West End musical
comedy and the romantic novel. The film, which was in a process of
particularly rapid development, is dealt with by Ralph Bond and Bert
Hogenkamp, and the theatre by André van Gyseghem and Jon Clark.
Apart from this we have not attempted to cover developments in
popular culture, radio, press, sport and recreation, then already
beginning to take their modern shape. A group at the Birmingham
Centre for Contemporary Cultural Studies is working on some of these
aspects for a projected book on the thirties, which will also include
studies of education and of a number of widely-read novelists not
discussed by us, writing largely in the nineteenth-century realist
tradition, such as J. B. Priestley, Winifred Holtby, Storm Jameson, A. J.
Cronin, Howard Spring.

Even within the field of radical and left-wing culture much has had to
be left out. A treatment of events in the visual arts, architecture and
music demands a separate volume on its own. Among writers, we have
again had to be highly selective to allow a meaningful discussion of
those we did treat. There is no special study of that complex and
contradictory writer, George Orwell: the best concise treatment of his
work is to be found in Raymond Williams's study *Orwell* (Fontana,
1971). There is also relatively little on Edgell Rickword, Randall
Swingler and Montagu Slater, for whose work the reader is referred to

the collection of essays edited by John Lucas, *The 1930s: A Challenge to Orthodoxy* (Harvester Press, 1978), Rickword's *Literature and Society. Essays and Opinions*, vol. 2, 1931–1978, edited by Alan Young (Carcanet Press, 1978), as well as Jack Lindsay's pioneer study *After the 'Thirties* (Lawrence and Wishart, 1956).

We hope that, despite the omissions, there is enough here to help correct some of the commoner misunderstandings and distortions — most notably, that thirties culture was just a small group of poets talking to one another, or that the whole radical and revolutionary impetus faded out in 1939, leaving not a rack behind.

Jon Clark
Margot Heinemann
David Margolies
Carole Snee

INTRODUCTION

The Crisis of the Thirties: A View from the Left

JAMES KLUGMANN

Editors' note: James Klugmann made the tape-recording from which the following article was taken in April 1977. Originally he was to have revised and extended it in collaboration with Margot Heinemann, but he died in September 1977 before this work could be completed. Even so, its value as a personal and political testament is such that we have decided to publish it in its present form.

James Klugmann was born in 1912 and educated at Gresham's School, Holt, and Trinity College, Cambridge, where he took a First in French and German. He joined the Communist Party in 1933 while doing research at Cambridge. Between 1935 and 1939 he was secretary of the World Student Association for Peace and Freedom, based in Paris, and travelled extensively in Eastern Europe, the Middle East, India and China. Called up as a private in 1940, he finished the war as a major attached to the British Military Mission to the Yugoslav partisans. From 1947 until his death in 1977 he worked full-time for the Communist Party of Great Britain, editing its theoretical monthly *Marxism Today* from 1962 to 1977.

James Klugmann was an outstanding lecturer and teacher, author of two volumes of the History of the Communist Party of Great Britain (and about to embark on a third, covering the period of this volume, when he died), and editor of two books on the Christian-Marxist dialogue. His erudition and wide experience gave him a perspective uniquely valuable for understanding the thirties.

The article was prepared for publication by the editors; the headings, sub-headings and notes are our own.

1. INTRODUCTION

There are in history some periods where things hardly move, which seem like plateaus, where, when you look back, having become older, it's hard to distinguish one moment from another. And there are periods of extreme change and struggle and storm. The thirties was definitely such a stormy period.

There is no iron law that history should occur, be written, by decades, and there are problems in the very thought of 'the Thirties'. But if you take it by and large, it was a period of storm and continuous event. Just think of the events in sequence: giant slump (1929); collapse of the Labour Government and election of the National Government (1931); Japanese invasion of Manchuria (1931); Hitler comes to power in Germany (1933); struggles against fascism in France; the 'five campaigns of annihilation' against the Chinese liberation movement and the great 'Long March' ending up in the North West with its capital at Yenan (1936); Italian invasion of Abyssinia (1935); establishment of Popular Front governments in France and Spain (1936); renewed Japanese invasion of Northern China (1937); Spanish Civil War (1936–9); betrayal of Munich (1938); invasion of Austria and Czechoslovakia by Nazi Germany (1938); outbreak of World War Two (1939). There can have rarely been a period in modern history with so many stormy events in so short a time.

In studying the decade it is economics that dominate, particularly in the first few years. But as you move into the thirties proper, the decade is dominated more and more by politics.

2. HISTORICAL BACKGROUND

(i) 'Poverty in the midst of plenty'

The decade begins with economic problems. A few years before, in 1928, was a period in which many boasts were made that now stability had come. The slogan of 1928 or thereabouts was 'Fordism, not Marxism'. Then in 1929 came the severest cyclical slump that the world had ever known! Extremely severe in the United States of America, where for three years production was less than half that of pre-1929. In Britain, by 1933, there were just under three million unemployed, or 23 per cent of all insured workers, with a slow process of recovery from 1934.

One of the slogans of the time was 'Poverty in the midst of plenty'. I think some of the present generation, looking back to the thirties, are almost offended by the over-simplicity of approach, and yet this 'poverty in plenty' seemed so simple and so ample a demonstration of the contradictions of capitalism, amidst the hunger, which made even advanced capitalist countries – like Britain and France – countries of great poverty and malnutrition. This was a period when, under an American scheme which went under the name of Agricultural Adjustment Administration, you could get high prices for signing on *not* to produce so much wheat, *not* to produce so much cotton, *not* to breed so many pigs. The standing joke of the time was the letter to the AAA – I paraphrase:

Dear Sir,
   Last year I not produced so much wheat and you gave me 5,000 dollars. I'm intending this year not to produce double the quantity, could you please send me 10,000 dollars by cheque?

This was a period when in Britain, under the heading of rationalization, there were cuts in the production of textiles, and reduction and even destruction of the equipment in the shipyards. Potatoes were being ploughed back into the land and coffee was being thrown in bags into the sea. When that was going on all around you, life seemed to demonstrate in an easy way the total bankruptcy of the capitalist system and shouted aloud for some sort of quick, rational, simple alternative. There was in this period a very strong feeling – and I think it's reflected in the culture and literature – of doom, doom that was not so very far off.

   The Labour Government was of course in deep crisis from the beginning of the period. There were the famous cuts in the dole and in the wages of teachers, civil servants, post office workers and the police. There was – and this itself spelled doom to the ardent patriotic supporters of capitalism – the mutiny of Invergordon (in 1931), the sacred navy. This was not really a political revolt, but a deep extension of the economic struggle into the navy, and it spelled doom in the headlines of the daily press. The symbol of Empire, the navy – *there* was strike.

   There was a feeling of threat also among the 'intermediary classes', between the working class and leading sections of the capitalist class, in short, the 'small people'. Small business people, smallholders in agriculture, felt doom very heavily oppressing them, pressing them down, and you could say, pressing them out – out of circulation, as, bit by bit, they became ruined. Chain stores were beginning to develop, and small shops felt the crisis deeply, particularly as in many areas their best customers, their essential customers – the workers – were unable to spend and there was a limit to the credit they could grant.

   This sense of impending doom, so strong in itself, sharpened the feeling of a need for an alternative. And therefore, in the realm of thought, of 'ideology', in the world of standards and morals, there was a dawning challenge to accepted sex morality, a challenge to widely taught standards of behaviour, and a broad challenge to the religious outlook. This, it's important to say, was not just an anti-religious challenge, but a challenge within religion that led to what was seen by many Christians as a return to earlier Christianity, where it had a social purpose and was linked essentially with the weak and with the poor rather than with the Establishment and obedience and the rich.

Harold Macmillan, later Conservative Prime Minister but then a back-bench MP, put it very clearly:

Now, after 1931, many of us felt that the disease was more deep-rooted. It had become evident that the structure of capitalist society in its old form had broken down, not only in Britain, but all over Europe and even in the United States. The whole system had to be reassessed. Perhaps it could not survive at all; it certainly could not survive without radical change. . . . Something like a revolutionary situation had developed, not only at home but overseas.[1]

(ii) *War and the threat of war – the influence of pacifism*

War hung over the decade like a shadow. The decade was in fact a sequence of wars. At the beginning (in 1931), the war between Bolivia and Paraguay led to the deaths of hundreds of thousands. Two rival imperialisms with two rival investments in two small Latin American states – to an outsider almost indistinguishable, speaking the same Spanish (although of course with great disparities of cultural and historical background); this was a typical reflection of imperialism's struggle for domination at the expense of two small countries. Then, into the thirties, the Japanese war, the Italian war in Abyssinia, German fascism expanding, calling for *Lebensraum*, the attack on Spain, on Austria, on Czechoslovakia, World War Two.

And so, not accidentally, it was a period of broadening pacifism and of deep anti-war feelings. Those of us who were youthful in the twenties were too young to remember World War One, but many of us remember how, as young readers or at school, we met with an intellectual bombardment of anti-war works of art that had arisen from it. Works by Henri Barbusse, Ludwig Renn and in particular Erich Maria Remarque's *All Quiet on the Western Front* (first published in England in March 1929 and reaching its twenty-first reprint (310,000 copies) in December of the same year) had a tremendous influence, and the great British war poets like Sassoon and Owen suddenly had a new lease of life amongst the youth of the middle and later twenties.

In the later twenties and the very beginning of the thirties, a number of organizations were founded, dedicated to informing people about the horrors of war. There was a movement called *Nie wieder Krieg!* (No more war!) that specialized in pictures of war horrors. There was, I remember, a photographic album of the wounded, with half a face or half a body, being hurried into hospital. This had a potent influence on many a writer and amongst the student movement. The Peace Pledge Union, founded in the 1934–5 period, commanded widespread support. Part of this was Christian-pacifist, the other part was labour-pacifist. There had traditionally been a strong pacifist stream inside the Labour Party and the Independent Labour Party (ILP). The Peace Ballot (1934–5), uniting thirty-eight organizations to carry it through, got eleven-and-a-half million signatures, which was one of the biggest signature-collecting campaigns that has ever been known in this country.[2]

In all sorts of places you found this spread of pacifism, this growing hatred of war. There was a public school revolt. I remember that, for my sins, I was put in charge of the Communist public school movement in the middle thirties, a new phenomenon in the Communist International. I was in Cambridge at the time, and small boys from all over the country used to run away from the public schools. One of the elements in this was the hatred of the compulsory Officer Training Corps (OTC). My job was to say that the line of the Communist Party was that they should go back to school, and I lost a whole number of willing recruits in the process of carrying out the party line!

One of the main motives that started me personally off on the road to Communism was the hatred of the compulsory OTC at my public school (Gresham's School, Holt), which incidentally was also W. H. Auden's school. The anti-OTC feeling was one of the ways of rebellion that I think you find in Auden and a whole number of other people. The struggle against war, which developed throughout the decade, was certainly one of the main roads to socialism and to Marxism, and this applied to both working-class people and intellectuals.

(iii) *The rise of fascism and Spain*

If the economic motive and the war motive hung heavy on the decade, so of course did the rise of fascism. At first, at the beginning of the decade, there were still many illusions and much confusion with regard to the nature of fascism. In Germany (party comrades used to argue that the same standpoint was just as dangerous in Britain, and I would say it still is today) it was argued right up to the beginning of the thirties that 'it can't happen here'. Fascism was linked with Mussolini and Italy, where it had come relatively quickly and, to people outside, for relatively obscure reasons. Still in 1933, the full extent of the difference between fascism and other forms of bourgeois rule was not yet clarified inside the Communist movement.

Hitler's victory in January 1933 was a bombshell for revolutionaries and progressive people. It's perhaps hard for people who weren't alive or politically thinking people then to realize what it meant. You have to realize that, for all revolutionaries and for most left-wing people, it was almost taken for granted that, after the October Revolution of 1917 in Russia, the next great revolution was to be in Germany. And the large size of the German Communist Party, but also the much greater influence of Marxism around the Communist Party and in the left wing of the Social Democratic Party and in cultural circles, meant that the journey to Berlin, study in Germany, the cultural visits and so on, were second only to the journey to Moscow. After seeing the results of the revolution in Russia, you went to Germany to see the preparation of the next one. The ideological influence of the revolutionary or rebel culture was very deep and wide, whether it was in painting, drama or other fields. Names like Brecht, Tucholsky, Kaiser and Toller I remember especially, because I had studied German at university and was a great addict of German expressionist theatre. There was a little theatre club down Villiers Street by Charing Cross station, the Gate Theatre, where I used to go, and then there was the Festival Theatre in Cambridge. These were things we hung on to, which influenced us tremendously, and warmly and well.

Then, with January 1933, there came a real, agonizing reappraisal throughout the revolutionary movement. It was a fairly devastating event. It should be remembered what German fascism did, the *internal* destruction, step by step, of everything progressive, starting with Communists, proceeding to Socialists, trade unions, Centre Party, liberals, radicals, the Church (or at least anything in any sense Christian), killing en route, imprisoning, torturing millions of Jewish people, burning books, ranking as 'cultural bolshevism' most of German culture from the Middle Ages onwards. One needs to be reminded of this. And *externally*, also, the external outlook and war threat and the internal policy of fascism went together. And so this agonising reappraisal meant that millions of people, in Britain as in other countries, became drawn into the struggle against fascism, or this or that aspect of fascism, in one or another form.

Immediately after January 1933 the next main point of struggle moved to France, because the Fiery Cross (*Croix de Feu*) and other similar movements were growing very strong. Stormy demonstrations in 1934 brought really rapid advances in unity between Socialists and Communists first, and later between Radicals, Socialists and Communists. By 1936, there were Popular Front governments in both France and Spain.

The Spanish struggle, beginning in July 1936, became the symbol and focus of world anti-fascist resistance. It's not by chance that, of all the great struggles of the last forty years, one has lived in the minds and hearts of the British progressive movement and working-class movement more than any other, and that is the Spanish struggle. So deep are those feelings that, to an extent, they have been passed on even to generations who never knew the struggle in Spain.

It was the focus because it was clear that this was not a civil war in the accepted sense, this was an attack of fascism from outside, led by German fascism and supported by Italian fascism, linking up with all that was most reactionary inside Spain. It was a focus because of the character of the resistance, not just its heroism, but its unity and foresight, its ideological outlook, its culture. People felt that the Spanish Civil War was a war for us, it wasn't just a war for them, that victory in Spain could prevent the start of a new world war. This isn't just hindsight, this was often and openly said.

The struggle in support of the Spanish Republic took place on a number of different levels. There was a level, extraordinarily broad, of support for the Spanish Peoples' Republic on the basis of foodships, medical equipment, medicine, the sending of doctors, the adopting and looking after of refugees and Basque children. It involved people of all political opinions, including many, many Tories, people of all religions. It was an extremely broad, humanitarian movement.

Then there was a sort of middle level of political support for Republican Spain, calling on the French and British Governments to intervene on the side of the legal Spanish government, to send arms to Spain, to recognize the Republican Government and to fulfil the commitments which go with full diplomatic and political recognition. This was strong inside the TUC and the labour Party after 1937, and involved of course the Communist Party in political support.

Then at the highest level – the level of the International Brigade – there were people so utterly committed that they were ready to go and actually fight in Spain. This was a movement of left Labour, militant trade union and Communist people. There were some 2,000 British members of the International Brigade, of whom some 500 were killed and 1,200 wounded, about 80 per cent working class, about half of them members of the Communist Party and the Young Communist League.

Alongside the struggle against foreign fascism was the problem of the growth of fascism inside Britain itself. The fight against the British Union of Fascists (the BUF), the blackshirts, led to many well-known struggles. The greatest of the anti-fascist demonstrations was in Hyde Park on 9 September 1934: 150,000 people demonstrated against about 2,500 blackshirts, surrounding them; then there was the famous Cable Street struggle against fascism in the East End of London in the autumn of 1936, adopting the Spanish slogan 'They shall not pass'.

(iv) The significance of the Soviet Union for the Left in Britain

The Soviet Union was advancing economically and socially at a time that corresponded to the deepening of the crisis in the advanced capitalist countries. I said earlier that the feeling of impending doom led to a demand for an alternative, and the fact of the contrast between what was taking place in the Soviet Union and in the capitalist world naturally enough helped many people to see their demand for an alternative embodied in socialism as developed in the USSR.

The first Five Year Plan was completed in four years, at the very time when production was falling most sharply in the capitalist world. Literature, art, the whole culture of the Soviet Union, was dominated by construction, great buildings, great dams, great schemes. The novels were full of it, the hero was the hero of construction, the villain, the saboteur. And this contrasted with 'Poverty in the midst of plenty', the destruction of wealth that was taking place under capitalism in its crisis.

Moreover, the end of the twenties and early thirties was a period when some of the best cultural achievements of the Soviet Union were either being brought to Britain or translated into English and becoming known to British people. My generation at least (I joined the Communist Party in 1933, I began to call myself a sort of Marxist in my last term at school at the very end of the twenties) came to see the films of Eisenstein and Pudovkin. The film societies themselves were quite important politically, because, to the best of my memory, the official distribution apparatus rejected Soviet films. You had to join some film club or other in order to see Soviet films, and political battles were fought around them.[3] (One of the great physical battles of fisticuffs in Cambridge was fought with a tough rugger and boating squad awaiting the exit from one of the Russian films. This became one of the high points in the history of the left!) Similarly the novels, Sholokhov's *Quiet Flows The Don* in translation, Alexei Tolstoy's trilogy, works sometimes written earlier, but now translated and being spread. Such literature and films and theatre seemed to contrast with what we would have said at the time was the 'decay' or 'crisis' of culture under capitalism. Particularly I think it was the optimism and hope within them which gripped us so strongly.

As the Soviet Union was the first country to make the revolution, and as *all* were attacking it constantly, we revolutionaries, as it were, had a genuine historic task of rallying to the defence of this first revolution, the accomplishment of which was, I think, the greatest event in world history to date – of untold significance. However, we tended to leap over directly into communist society with the vision splendid, we tended psychologically to identify what took place in the Soviet Union with the establishment of a communist, faultless, final type of society. And it shone before us. Everything that we wanted and desired in the new social system, we 'read into' Soviet society. Thus, if there had been in our faith (I use the word advisedly) in the Soviet Union a utopian element, it was easy to see how for many, when the awareness arose much later that it wasn't a perfect society – that it was a society that had known many errors and in which crimes had been committed in the name of Communism – that the sum, a socialist faith with some illusions, could turn into disillusion.

(v) *The Labour Party and the trade unions*

Contrary to what is often thought, the thirties was not on the whole a period of great strikes. Posthumous legend grew up, I think, to create the impression that it was such a stormy period: in reality it was not.

The period started, it is true, with the great struggle against the cuts. Throughout this period, but particularly in the first half, the unemployed movement, by now called the National Unemployed Workers' Movement (NUWM), was in struggle, under fairly direct Communist political leadership, but unchallenged in the sphere of the unemployed and very strong.

The occupational structure in industry was shifting. Manual wage-earners made up something like three-quarters of the working population, but there was a shift taking place from heavy to light industry, from highly-skilled to semi-skilled. The TUC membership, which had been something like six-and-a-half million in the boom after

World War One, was only 4·3 million by the eve of the General Strike,
3·75 million by 1930 and only 3·3 million by 1934.

In the post-General Strike period, there was a considerable
movement, under the title of 'Mondism' or 'Mond/Turnerism',[4] of class
collaboration, and many of the great working-class struggles of the
middle and later thirties took place under the leadership of unofficial,
rank-and-file, left-wing movements, very often under Communist Party
leadership. Examples of such movements were the London Busmen's
Rank and File Movement and the Clyde Apprentices' Movement.
There was also a considerable movement against rationalization,
against the speed-up, intensification of labour and time-and-motion
study.

The Labour Party was still under deep reformist influence. In the left
of the Labour Party, however, were organizations like the Socialist
League, and there were a number of left-wing constituency parties.
There were struggles in the Labour Party on economic and social
issues, and particularly in the fight against fascism. Despite very great
resistance throughout from the right-wing leadership, who always
opposed, both in the TUC and the Labour Party, any organized form of
unity with Communists, unity grew very strongly.

3. THE COMMUNIST PARTY – 'FROM CLASS AGAINST CLASS' TO
THE POPULAR FRONT

It's very important, I think, to understand the Communist Party if you
want to understand the decade. Many of the books which have been
written about the thirties have been by people who want to write a
history of the decade without the Communist Party, or by people who
have for a short time been partly or wholly identified with the party and
have been disillusioned, expressing their view of the thirties as a shade of
anger against Communism.

At the beginning of the decade the CP was in a particularly weak
position, but by the end of the thirties it was exercising an
extraordinarily large influence in some sections of the working class and
in some industries like mining, and a very wide influence amongst
students and intellectuals and in the field of culture. This involved a
move from an extraordinarily difficult period, a bad period if you like, in
the life of the Communist Party at the end of the twenties and early
thirties, to an extremely fruitful period in the middle and later thirties –
from 'Class against Class' to the 'United Front' and 'Popular Front'.

The years following the General Strike of 1926 were very difficult for the labour movement as a whole, both as a result of the strong move to the right in the official labour movement and the sectarian attitude of the CP on many issues. When the history is written, it will show that, against the class conciliation and defeatism that followed the defeat of the General Strike, the small Communist Party did play a very courageous and positive role in many ways, continuing the fight and putting heart into it. But nevertheless it did make a number of very profound errors of approach, of practice, which I think have to be discussed, and were of course closely linked to the mistakes in the Communist International of the period.

What kinds of mistakes? There was a tremendous overestimate of the political meaning of the economic crisis and of the reaction of the workers to the crisis. Every demonstration against poverty was interpreted as a symbol of the new revolutionary period, and therefore between 1928 and 1930 every action was interpreted as a revolutionary action needing a revolutionary tactic and strategy. There was a confusion of all types of struggles with revolutionary struggles, and the putting forward therefore of revolutionary slogans that isolated the revolutionary left from the mass of the workers.

Then there was the refusal to distinguish in tactics and strategy between the Labour Party and the Conservative Party, and the belief that the official trade unions were so bureaucratic that it was not possible to change them. The CP fought the General Election in May 1929 on a programme entitled *Class Against Class*, which stated among other things:

Class is against class. The Labour Party has chosen the capitalist class. The Communist Party is the party of the working class – the Labour Party is the third capitalist party.

This approach was taken to its extreme in the theory of 'social fascism', which argued that right-wing reformism or social democracy is social fascism because it leads directly to fascist rule. Bourgeois democracy, the rule of a right-wing Labour government or the rule of fascism, were seen just as different forms of capitalist rule, and you couldn't distinguish one as more dangerous to the working class than the other.

Without going into the argument about this any further, the effect on the party was a tremendous isolation, a tremendous fall in numbers. In France the membership of the Communist Party fell from over 80,000 in 1925 to 28,000 in 1933, in Britain from 12,500 in January 1927 to about 2,500 in 1930–1. During the early thirties, slowly and gradually, step by step, not fully consciously at first, the process of correction of these wrong approaches began to be made, both externally within the international Communist movement and the Comintern and internally within the British Communist movement. Of course, the agonizing reappraisal after Hitler came to power in 1933 was a big factor, and there had always been a substantial section of trade union militants in the party who had rebelled against the 'Class against Class' policy. (There was the famous 'deviation' of *Hornerism*, for instance, associated with the name of the Welsh miners' leader, Arthur Horner.)

This reappraisal achieved its most important expression at the Seventh Congress of the Communist International in July/August 1935, and no political appreciation of the background of the thirties would be complete without a reasonable study of the findings and arguments of this Congress, a Congress that was sounding the alarm that fascism was something qualitatively different and more dangerous than normal bourgeois rule and calling for a United and Peoples' Front against fascism.

The theory of the United Front which Georgi Dimitrov put forward in his opening speech at the Seventh Congress started from an analysis of the levels of consciousness of the working class and of the broader mass of working people. It explained that people, working people, come to fight the effects of capitalism often before they come to fight capitalism itself, which is the cause of these effects. The revolutionary must find him- or herself at the heart of all these movements, therefore with the people, fighting against every type of injury and harm they are receiving from capitalist society – the fight on wages and hours, fighting on liberties, fighting in solidarity, fighting against fascism, and so on. And therefore there had to be a policy of united front of the working class and popular unity of the whole working people at all levels, on all issues. The platforms of these movements were not to be abused by revolutionaries, to seize them and use them for their own revolutionary ends. The united front was open, public, sincere, and not a manoeuvre. Hence the whole concept and organization of the United Front of the working class and, along with the middle sections of the community, the broader Popular Front or Peoples' Front – the development of Peoples' Front governments, something new in the history of the working class.

On two other ideological as well as practical points the Seventh Congress, which was the result of debates and concrete developments in a number of countries during the preceding years, was of unsurpassed importance. First, it put the struggle for democracy back into the centre of the fight for socialism. In the 1927–32 period democracy was considered almost a dirty word in the Communist movement, something that needed to be exposed as an ideology of the bourgeoisie. It was of enormous importance for us to develop a concept of socialist democracy, to be achieved through the winning of power, taking over all that had been won in the struggle for democracy under capitalism, and qualitatively extending and expanding it. Every liberty that concerned the people became of concern to a revolutionary, to a Marxist, and in this way the working class could take the lead in the whole community in the fight for democracy.

The second type of issue that arose from the Seventh Congress was the re-establishment of a Marxist and Leninist concept of patriotism and internationalism. It seems to me that in the late 1920s and even later, one of the major errors of Communists in Germany was to hand over deep and wounded national feelings to the fascists on a plate, and to equate internationalism and anti-nationalism, instead of seeing that genuine, progressive national feelings and patriotism were the other side of the medal of popular and proletarian internationalism. And the more the working class emerges as the leader of the defence of such national feelings, the more it can carry out its international duties.

In relation to democracy, the French again gave us much in the 1934–5 period. They retook possession of the French Revolution, they repossessed the tricolour, the colours of France. They put the red flag side by side with the tricolour, and at the end of their meetings sung the *Marseillaise* and the *International*. It wasn't always easy for us. I remember trying to explain to French comrades that it wasn't so easy: 'Il y a une toute petite différence entre *La Marseillaise* et le *God Save The King*.' However, you see what it did: it repossessed for the Marxist revolutionary of today his or her cultural heritage of the past. We became no longer just the critics of the insufficiencies of Wat Tyler seen through the eyes of a card-holding peasant, or of the 1790 Jacobins, or of the moralistic limitations of Chartism. We became the inheritors of the Peasants' Revolt, of the left of the English Revolution, of the pre-Chartist movement, of the women's suffrage movement from the 1790s to today. It set us in the right framework, it linked us with the past and gave us a more correct course for the future.

However, there were, in this Stalin period, a number of aspects of the particular approach of Stalin which bedevilled our work. It wasn't just that we idealized or idolized the Soviet Union, which in fact, as with all idealization and idolization, always weakens rather than strengthens the fight. Apart from the fact that we therefore saw every critic of the Soviet Union as a class enemy, and quite probably a conscious agent of capitalist society, there were a number of more generalized ways in which the Stalinist influence weakened our work.

Firstly there was an approach I would characterize as 'inevitabilism' – this categoric conception that there were laws of history that would grind themselves out as inexorably as laws of natural science; that it was all fixed, it was all certain. My experience is that better than certainty is the understanding of laws of history as laws of trend. Marxism can show you that opportunities arise in history – whether or not those opportunities are taken depends on us, depends on the working class, on the Communists, on their consciousness, on their struggle: on *that* depends the outcome. If you're certain and it doesn't happen, it can easily lead to disillusion. If it depends on you, you can take your part in it, and you can see where you've succeeded and where you've failed. Inevitabilism was in fact very much like Jansenism or Calvinism; it had to happen, you were sure it would happen, you had grace, you were the elect. When I studied Jansenism as a student of French history, we used to say about grace: 'Either you had it, or if you hadn't had it, you'd had it.' And there was a phenomenon rather like that about being a member of the Communist Party.

A second problem was the over-simplification of complex situations, and often the slurring over of contradictions within reality, and the development of stereotypes – what I would call 'compartmentalism'. It seemed at first super-revolutionary. You developed categories of how things would proceed, then tucked reality neatly into them. However, this is really doing very much what bourgeois ideology does. Life is incredibly complicated, and however much we systematize our theory into compartments (and you couldn't think if you didn't), reality, life, always has the trick of being that much more complex. And each stage of reality, each new period of history, finds new complexities with which to confront us. What we needed to do was develop an approach which didn't confuse Marxism and magic, which allowed us to develop categories without insisting prophetically that the future would conform with what we as a national or international organization or as a people had conceived in our minds.

A third weakness came I think through what philosophers have often called 'voluntarism' – that it was sufficient to will things. 'There is nothing a Bolshevik cannot do,' we used to say, and therefore we would 'will' things. But alas, there are certain things that Bolsheviks can't do, such as to defy the laws of nature and – often– trends in society. It's not sufficient to will things. Voluntarism gives you a kind of arrogance which can isolate you, the promotion of great schemes that often end in ruin.

A fourth weakness is what I think I would call the 'conspiracy theory'. When you were thwarted, it was due to a great conspiracy. We had too easy a conception of the bourgeoisie *always* meeting and making firm decisions and conspiring. There was a danger that we saw agents everywhere, that wherever we saw people with whom we disagreed, we saw agents who had been actively promoted by the bourgeoisie to act consciously in their interests.

These are some of the weaknesses in our work in this period. The fact that I've dealt with them at some length shouldn't in any way be used to denigrate or belittle the achievements of the communist parties in the thirties. They led the movement against fascism and war, they developed the national liberation movements in the most appallingly difficult conditions, they led the movements that became the basis of the resistance to fascism during World War Two, they developed the movements in countries like Spain that became the precursors of the type of unity of the democratic, revolutionary, anti-monopoly alliance that is with us in the world today.

And so, in the thirties, the communist parties, which started from positions of great weakness, developed positions of relative strength. (In France, the PCF increased its membership from 28,000 in 1933 to well over 300,000 by the end of 1937.) The CPGB grew from the depth of around 2,500 in 1930 to 11,500 in 1936 and 17,500 in 1939 (reaching 56,000 in 1942). Both in sections of the working class and amongst cultural workers and students, the CPGB had an influence many times its own membership and size.

4. INTELLECTUALS AND COMMITMENT

(i) *Professional and cultural workers*

One of the reasons why it is necessary to identify the thirties with commitment is that professional people, cultural workers, people in all types of creative activity, of different class origins, became conscious of the class nature of Britain, and committed to that class – the working class – whose destiny it was to replace capitalist Britain by a socialist Britain. The class nature of Britain rose to the surface, as it were, in many ways, partly because of the economic crisis, partly because of skilful propaganda, explanation, education and writing. Important sections of the middle class, professional people, intellectual people, came to understand, to sympathize, to want to help, then to struggle with and alongside the working class.

Perhaps I am speaking too much from personal experience, but I suppose the unemployed struggle was one of the struggles that most exposed the class nature of Britain. Many people who would not normally have thought of such things became involved, often at first almost in a sort of charitable, philanthropic way, and then step by step becoming more actively conversant with the real class nature of British capitalism – the meaning of the dole, the anomalies, the torture of the Means Test, the almost barbarous arrangements by which, when the dole was being considered, the wages of the other earning members of the household were taken into account, when war pensions were held against you, widows' pensions, a life-time of saving, a father's pension or a child's earnings were counted against a household.

When I was first sent, after a few weeks' membership of the Communist Party in 1933, to a South Wales mining town, I met people (I was then twenty-one) older than me who had never worked at all, didn't know what work was. I saw empty houses furnished with bits of wood and orange boxes, children without shoes, rickets everywhere; small shopkeepers ruined because their customers couldn't buy; illness, tuberculosis (TB in those days was a dread word rather like cancer is now – it often signified that you were waiting for the end); emigration, either to other countries or anyway out of South Wales. And yet, in utter contrast to that, I experienced the humanity, wisdom, logic and dignity of the hunger marchers.

The hunger march was a very imposing thing, because it was a form of planned operation. People would set off from different parts of Britain and, after marching for so many days with accommodation arranged sometimes against great odds, they would converge at a given date in London. It needed a desperate amount of self-discipline to be a hunger marcher, not just because of the hardship of the march (people were undernourished, insufficiently clothed and marching long distances). People had to resist police provocations as they marched and as they slept, when they would be turned out of halls and corn exchanges by police squads early in the morning. Ideologically it needed a remarkable firmness, with meetings and contact with the civilian population at each place.

If you just take the student movement, I remember the marches through towns like Oxford and Cambridge, the fraternization of students with the hunger marchers and, be it said, of hunger marchers with the students, which wasn't so easy, going into these centres of the children of the rich. These were quite traumatic elements in the birth and growth of the student movement and broke down many resistances. We, an extraordinarily erudite and arrogant generation of Cambridge students, who thought that we were the best intellectuals, and that the intellectuals were the wisest of the community, we were still lost at the beginning of the thirties, often with immense knowledge but no philosophy, immense mental effort and activity but no purpose. And then we suddenly met up with people who knew where they were going, knew what they were doing, who could discuss a problem in a clearer, more coherent, more logical way than the most advanced 'double first' amongst us. And do so with a resilient humanity absent from the typical intellectual of the time, where there was a constant kind of internal strife, deep introspection, a not uncommon suicide.

However, these intellectuals were not just what the French call *fils de papa*; they were utterly sincere, willing to give everything for something if they could find that something. And then they came across this new species, the British working man, in action and in struggle, not the British working man in inverted commas, but the working man and working woman in reality. This might be a short episode in their lives, but it was something of a symbol of the awakening of real culture, of the acceptance by people devoted to study and art of a degree of social responsibility. This was not in the purely philanthropic abstract, but led to a shedding of some of the arrogance, to a certain modesty which was almost 'revolutionary' for an intellectual.

For example, health and class became linked in people's minds. There was a stirring amongst nutrition workers, there was a whole literature on nutrition, on the class-incidence of health. People were starting projects like Dr Julian Tudor-Hart has been doing in recent times from his general practice in a mining area. Such activity became very widespread in this period. Infant mortality was 42 per 1,000 in the Home Counties, 114 per 1,000 in Jarrow: the incidence of TB and rickets was totally different in the depressed areas from the 'sweet south'. You could see two nations in one when you looked at the medical statistics. There was also the great debate of the middle thirties, what was a minimum on which people could live? – it's a horrible thing, anyhow, how do you fix a minimum on moral and physical standards? Could you live on 15s 3d or 15s 9d? This involved Dr McGonigle, who made his revolutionary study of Poverty and Public Health (because it *was* revolutionary to see diet in class terms); the very progressive role of John Boyd-Orr, who made his survey of Food, Health and Income in 1936; the Committee against Malnutrition headed by the blind doctor Frederick le Gros Clark; the Children's Minimum Campaign Committee campaigning for family allowances (Eleanor Rathbone's name is closely connected with this). Then there was the debate about the class character of education and housing, the statistical study of chronic overcrowding, the private builders' boom, the growth of tenants' associations and the fight against the landlords, great rent struggles as in the East End of London in 1938 with new fighters for tenants like Father Groser and Tubby Rosen. Then there was the birth of the first Old Age Pensioners' Association in 1938–9. All this ripened, developed this growing feeling of commitment.

Like all things, you have to see it as a process. People became committed in different ways, some more rapidly, some by classic slow stages. For some it started as a feeling of guilt: you could have upper-class people, public-school people, Church people, orthodox Christians, philanthropic people, finding these conditions, feeling guilt and wanting to help. And then came a process of being drawn in to active help in one or other sphere – nutrition, against war, medical aid for Spain, the unemployed, collections, demonstrations, posters. And then, in the process of struggle, came the first meetings with the working class and the closer identification with the heart of the struggle. Then the understanding of the relationship to capitalist society, of the causes of the issues on which you were struggling, and then finally the commitment to belong to this or that organization, in the last analysis a revolutionary organization implicit in the need to change society.

(ii) *Marxism and the student movement – personal reminiscences*

In the early 1920s the Marxist student movement had been largely one of individuals. The Communist movement of the time saw the students by and large as a reactionary force out of which, if you remember *The Communist Manifesto*, a few individuals will betray their own class and pass to the working class. In 1926, alas, the students were known essentially as strike-breakers and scabs.

The late twenties are hard to summarize, it seems to me. Using my own language, it represented very much a 'revolt in the superstructure'. There were small groups of people who were deeply in revolt against this or that aspect of the superstructure, of morality, attitudes, ideas. They were against the sexual customs, against institutional religion, against their parents, against academic arts in the sense of the Royal Academy, against academic poetry and institutional drama. They were often known in some universities as aesthetes, used as a pejorative word. You could tell them by their clothing and hairstyles, their attitudes, their habits – they were angry, they were rebellious. Some of them were extremely powerful intellectually, but few of them could relate their own personal rebellion with the situation in society. They were more individual rebellions, and you could see this of course in poetry, in drama. *Experimental* was the word: there were experimental journals, there was complex art against oversimplistic art and so on.

The early thirties represented a period of transition towards something like a student *movement*, a movement of student Marxists. A number of those who were rebels in the superstructure advanced to the position of social revolutionaries. The difficult passage was made from rebel to revolutionary, and began to be made in an organized way. The history has yet to be written: you will find precursors in the famous debate in 1933 in the Oxford Union when the motion that 'This House refuses to fight for King and Country' was carried.

By 1933 more people were joining the Communist Party in the universities; it began to develop into something like a movement. The channels we've already seen. For some it was 'misemployment' (as distinct from unemployment), for some anti-fascism, for others anti-war. The Communists began to win something like a majority in socialist societies, or to develop their own organizations such as the October Club at Oxford. They began to become something of an influence, though still marked by some quite deep sectarianism. Their class composition was mainly middle and upper because the universities concerned were in the first place Oxford, Cambridge and the London School of Economics.

It was symptomatic that many of those coming to revolution wanted to break with their own past, their families, the student movement, to become 'workers'. It was plain in their clothing and hairstyles and language, which had to strike a blow at officialdom. There was a mixture of very deep, very genuine determination to break with the past and become part of what was new, which was not just a joke, which for many people involved total changes of their lives and giving up fortunes, but also contained within it a streak of romanticism. I remember demonstrating with John Cornford, a lonely personal demonstration, shouting our private slogan 'Keep culture out of Cambridge!', which represented our attitude to Auden, Spender and others at the time. There was a tremendous commitment linked still with a certain sectarianism and a certain sort of romanticism.

Moving into 1934, the movement begins to shed some of the romanticism and sectarianism. I suppose one of the dramatic moments was the visit of the Clydeside Communist Willie Gallacher to Cambridge University, which had the largest student group at that time. Gallacher was offended to a degree – and correctly – by the sort of language, clothing and attitude of the comrades who wanted to leave the university and denigrated their own academic work, although he was impressed by the growth and size of the movement and the calibre of the people who were coming into it. Out of this meeting came the slogan, I remember, 'Every communist student, a good student'. He said; 'We want people who are capable, who are good scientists, historians and teachers. It doesn't follow at all you'll be good workers. We need you as you are: if you have a vocation, it's pointless to run away to factories. One or two of you may become full-time revolutionaries, but this is a thing that only a few of you will be able to do. We want you to study and become good students.'

Out of that and other meetings of the same sort came greater clarity in expressing the 'organic', the integral, proper relationship between the middle sections – the professional sections, the students – and the working class. A real student revolutionary has as his or her duty to bring his or her people to the side of the working-class movement, not to opt out of that movement and find an individual niche inside the working class. This represented a very great change indeed.

When you studied all the facets that were involved in student life, it became clear that on this or that issue (except for a tiny minority that went up to universities like Oxford and Cambridge for purely social reasons, because their ancestors had), all those who studied were affected adversely by capitalism in one or other way. Therefore, there could be a perspective of winning the overwhelming majority of the student movement to the side of the working class. This was a turning point in the attitude of revolutionary students to the students' unions, to the NUS, to the union societies at Oxford and Cambridge that weren't in the NUS, to the broad student movement.

You can see here how important was the conception of this relation to the working class for intellectuals and students. I've mentioned already the hunger marchers and their influence. Now, in the movement against Mosley and the fascists, in the various demonstrations, students and workers marched side by side. The support of strikes also became a fairly regular phenomenon of the student movement. Students in London would support the busmen's strikes, for instance, selling the *Busman's Punch* at the bus garages. I remember Cambridge students going in groups to garages during the busmen's strike, others supporting the Pressed Steel strikes in Oxford, and so on. Students also went to Spain. In my own group, the Trinity College group of the CP, three comrades were killed in Spain and one was wounded. This illustrates the fact that, whatever the element of romanticism or upper-class constituency, for those who belonged it was eminently a serious thing that they were doing.

One aspect of this thought and practice was the relation of vocation to revolutionary activity. Capitalism hit at study, you could say very roughly, in two ways. One was the aim of study. After all, you studied medicine to become a doctor, but what future was there as a doctor if you were essentially a doctor for the rich, and at the same time there was all the rickets and tuberculosis? You were going to be a scientist, but was science to be for profit or for people, was it to be for destruction, war, or was it to be for construction? It was very difficult even then to get scholarships to continue scientific research that was separated from war research. Capitalism thus hit at your vocation, at what you meant to become, and pushed you, or gave you a kick in the right direction, to come to the side of the class who, by changing society, could make medicine and science worthwhile.

Secondly, capitalism distorted and narrowed the philosophy and approach of all the theoretical disciplines. I knew it by the way in which teaching was carried on in the history of French and German literature, which varied from *Geistesgeschichte* (the history of idealistic concepts like Romanticism and Classicism) to the gossiping chronicles of French literary history, where you learned all about Racine's mistresses but little about the relation of literature to society. The reciprocal relationship of literature and society opened up a solution to so many problems, and so with history. Suddenly the dull historical lectures became challenging through a whole new concept of history. The relation of society to natural science, to philosophy, to history, to the history of literature and art – in all spheres totally new perspectives were opened.

Goethe was a great subject for research workers in German, and you could get a three-volume book about books and articles on Goethe – thousands of pages! Was there anything on Goethe that hadn't been written? 'The influence of Goethe's seventh mistress on the first scene of *Faust Part 2*' was one of the themes. What was there left to do as a researcher? And then, suddenly, there was nothing done, there was hardly a book about Goethe that was worth reading. Suddenly you realised that everything still had to be done. From feeling stilted, cynical, fed up, you saw that the whole of intellectual life had to be restudied. Once you had the social approach, research became infinitely harder, because you were dealing with the influence of everything on everything, the interrelations and movement of everything. It meant work, hard work.

The slogan 'Every communist student, a good student' led to a phenomenal change in Tripos results. I remember at one stage 60 per cent of CP students got Firsts in Cambridge, whereas the average previously would have been about 3 to 5 per cent. The same energy that drove you into the revolutionary movement drove you to probe in your subject, made a good student of you. Marxism made everything rich. Although it didn't do the work, it opened you to do more work than you'd have done with a bourgeois philosophy. The basis was set for a very great growth in the student movement. One mustn't exaggerate, but it was the beginning for many of the transition from rebel to committed revolutionary.

(iii) *The establishment of a Marxist tradition in Britain*

Thus, the climate was set in the thirties for the entry of Marxism. The basis was laid for a generation which came to see how powerful Marxism could be to the study of all the various disciplines and, as I've just mentioned, in order to defeat the bourgeois superiority, the situation demanded that people work very hard to develop Marxist approaches.

In this period, unlike today, Marxism was not accepted as an -ism, as a philosophy, and therefore this generation of Marxists had to do an appalling amount of work in order, as a first stage, to establish the Marxist approach to literature, history, philosophy and science as a genuine part of the discipline. In philosophy there was Maurice Cornforth, David Guest, John Lewis, T. A. Jackson; in political economy Maurice Dobb; in history Leslie Morton, Dona Torr, Christopher Hill, later Eric Hobsbawm, George Rudé, Hymie Fagan;

in labour history Dona Torr, Allen Hutt; in literature Ralph Fox, Alick West, Jack Lindsay, Edgell Rickword, Montagu Slater, a little later Christopher Caudwell, then Arnold Kettle; in classics George Thomson, Ben Farrington; in the history of art Francis Klingender; in the study of the British imperialism Palme Dutt; T. A. Jackson studying Ireland, Ben Bradley India; in natural science J. B. S. Haldane and J. D. Bernal, and many others. Altogether this was something like a period of Marxist creativity and philosophical study.

One has to admit that, more at the beginning than at the end, there were elements of sectarianism and dogmatism throughout. However, I think that the Marxism of the period was overall very creative because it was battling. You never stopped battling. Therefore you were constantly being confronted by new situations in which you or your movement or your group had to make your own decisions virtually without reference. You were always having to think out problems anew. It's very different from a period when you're living on a plateau, where there are no great things happening and you can get locked up in conceptual reasoning, getting further and further from reality.

5. CONCLUSION – THE THIRTIES: A DECADE OF COMMITMENT

It is correct, I think, to call the decade a decade of commitment, because of the extent to which so many people of the working class and middle sections of society and intellectuals were deeply connected, deeply personally and collectively committed to struggle, linking their own individual professions and trades and activities with collective struggle, seeing themselves, if they came from the middle sections, as finding their future alongside, and under the leadership of, the working class. This is what I think, when you look back on the decade as a whole, is so impressive.

It was a decade in which one had much experience of allies and alliances, of relationships between the working class and its allies, and their operation in all sincerity on different levels of consciousness. It was a decade in which people in the cultural field and intellectuals and students, coming closer to the working class, learned very often to speak in a way that was comprehensible, and to a degree to shed their own specific, more jargonistic and conceptual way of talking. It was a decade in which Marxism made quite a large advance as an alternative to reformism, penetrating as a formative influence into every intellectual field.

It seems to me that Marxism should never demand of each intellectual, each creative artist, that he or she express wholly and directly in their painting or music or writing the political propaganda, the teaching of Marxism. Such a compulsory demand can kill art instead of inspiring it. But genuinely committed professional workers, intellectuals and artists can make a tremendous contribution to revolutionary struggle. In periods of great struggle – and the thirties was such a period – it seems to me inevitable that significant sections of intellectuals will commit themselves to the working class, to the struggle for democracy against fascism and to the struggle for socialism, although they will do so in a multitude of different ways.

The thirties has therefore left its mark. Today, the decade is the target of much hatred, and it's a great compliment to it that people who are reactionary fear it so much. So much has been written to disparage it, to distort it, that it is of very great importance for the period to be studied by those who can appreciate it, but at the same time in a critical way.

Perhaps in different forms, at different levels of commitment, in these late 1970s, there is again a development in intellectual and creative circles of a period of commitment. There are new dangers. In the thirties there were few Marxists: Marxists had to gain their place by hard work. Now we could say that everybody is a Marxist, Marxism is profitable. There is developing what the Germans used to call *Kathedermarxismus*, academic Marxism. You can see within Marxism the struggle taking place today: it's very different in this way from the thirties. However, it seems to me that the study of the thirties and its commitment can offer us substantial help in finding our bearings in the more complex period today.

NOTES

1. Harold Macmillan. *Winds of Change*, London, 1966, p. 283.
2. The Peace Ballot was centred on the idea of collective security, which the majority endorsed. It was thus not 'pure pacifism'.
3. For more details on the reception of Soviet films in Britain in this period, see Ralph Bond's article, 'Cinema in the Thirties', pp. 241–56.
4. In 1928 senior industrial and trade union leaders held joint discussions at top level with the aim of promoting industrial co-operation and efficiency. This 'co-operative' approach to trade unionism came to be known as 'Mond/Turnerism' after the leaders of the two delegations to the talks, Sir Alfred Mond, Chairman of ICI, and Ben Turner, TUC Chairman in 1928.

F. R. Leavis, the Scrutiny Movement and the Crisis

IAIN WRIGHT

The *Scrutiny* movement was one of the most powerful but paradoxical intellectual groups to emerge from the thirties crisis. Its influence, both on literary criticism (and hence, indirectly, on literature itself) and on educational and cultural thought generally, has been extensive and persistent. *Scrutiny* itself, a quarterly review, ceased publication in 1953, and the *Scrutiny* sect has long ago formally disbanded. F. R. Leavis, its chief instigator and ideologist, saw to that personally, casting off and anathematizing his collaborators one by one, formally proclaiming the failure of the whole enterprise,[1] and then dedicating the last years of his life to a set of generalized denunciations of modern civilization so wild and misanthropic that only the movement's lunatic fringe[2] stayed loyal. Yet if the Leavisites have gone, Leavisism lives on. Its influence can be traced not only in the literary and social criticism of an impressive range of individual writers, from Raymond Williams, Richard Hoggart and the 'old New Left' on one wing to the Black Paper editors on the other, but in a subtler, more pervasive form in the very structures and presuppositions of English teaching in schools and colleges throughout Britain and the Commonwealth.

The odd thing is, that because the *Scrutiny* movement's influence has been so diffuse and indirect, because it has always refused explicitly to defend its general positions in public debate, and because Leavis himself was always so savagely effective in demolishing his critics, there has been no attempt to make a comprehensive study of the movement or to draw up a balance sheet of its positive and negative effects.[3]

What were the *Scrutiny* movement's main achievements? In the field of textual criticism, it redrew the map of English poetry, expanding on hints in T. S. Eliot's early essays to launch a frontal assault on Romanticism and its Victorian aftermath, and to elevate the early seventeenth century as the great age of English verse.[4] It courageously defended Eliot and other modernist poets against the conservative academic establishment, and proclaimed that a poetic revolution had taken place, overturning outmoded Victorian conventions and establishing a style adequate to the modern world – 'New Bearings in

English Poetry'.[5] Later, as the new bearings failed to live up to expectations, *Scrutiny* turned its attention to fiction, fighting an equally vigorous campaign for the recognition of D. H. Lawrence as a major artist, and (according to Leavis) establishing 'a new idea of the history and traditions of the novel in English'.[6]

But *Scrutiny*'s achievement cannot be assessed entirely – or even primarily – as literary criticism. It was fundamental to the movement that 'a real literary interest is an interest in man, society and civilization, and its boundaries cannot be drawn'.[7] Literary criticism was not to be regarded as a 'circumscribed' activity. On the contrary, it had a 'high function' in the state, providing 'the best possible training for intelligence – for free, unspecialized, general intelligence . . . which we are peculiarly in need of today'.[8] It was, in fact, no more than the base-camp from which to launch a national campaign of cultural renewal. It is as such a campaign that *Scrutiny* asks to be judged and as such that I have chosen to discuss it in this essay. In this field it had two main successes. First, it initiated a debate on the social function of literature and a critique of 'mass civilization' (the term sarcastically used by Leavis to denote pulp fiction, commercialized journalism and manipulative advertising) which provided the impetus and vocabulary for much later work, such as William's *Culture and Society* and *The Long Revolution* and Hoggart's *The Uses of Literacy*. Second (and I put the strongest stress on this achievement, although it is harder to define or to quantify), it established an ideology and a *raison d'être* for a new and highly insecure social group – the professional teachers of English, who, demoralized simultaneously by scientists' attacks on the value of the humanities and by the growing social crisis, were oppressed by a sense of their own ineffectiveness. *Scrutiny* told them, not simply that their work was socially useful, not simply that English was the most important subject in the school and the English department the very centre of the life of every university, but that upon them, quite literally, the future of humanity rested:

The minority capable not only of appreciating Dante, Shakespeare, Donne, Baudelaire, Hardy (to take major instances) but of recognizing their latest successors constitute the consciousness of the race (or of a branch of it) at a given time. . . . Upon them depend the implicit standards that order the finer living of an age, the sense that this is worth more than that, this rather than that is the direction in which to go, that the centre is here rather than there. In their keeping . . . is the language, the changing idiom, upon which fine living depends, and without which distinction of spirit is thwarted and incoherent.[9]

It is this article of the *Scrutiny* creed which has been most pervasive and most deadly in English thinking about literature and education since the thirties. It was this, together with the doom-laden and diabolized analysis of 'the crisis' from which it originated and the defeatist cult of D. H. Lawrence's socio-sexual theories to which it retreated, that led to the hair-raising elitism and the arrogant attitude of moral superiority that is so often the mark of the Leavisite teacher. It was this that led to the proud refusal to engage in open dialogue with other disciplines and positions, and the contemptuous dismissal of practical politics and of those who are 'eaten up with caring about Fascism or Leagues of Nations'.[10] (After all, if you have taken upon yourself the lonely and terrific task of maintaining the 'consciousness of the race', you cannot allow yourself to be distracted by transitory trivia like the Fascist take-over of Europe.) It was this, in the years after the Second World War, when the movement had palpably failed to achieve its major goals, that led to a growing narrowness and defensiveness, and to Leavis's own persecution-mania, his increasingly self-sustaining and self-defeating pessimism, his tendency to squander his energies in battering the stuffing out of straw targets like C. P. Snow as if the future of western civilization depended on it.

How was it that this group of Cambridge dons, with their small-circulation journal,[11] was able to generate such a powerful and emotion-laden movement? To understand that, we need to understand the emotional and intellectual satisfactions – or compensations – that *Scrutiny* offered, and to understand those in turn within the context of the history of the English literary intelligentsia in the late twenties and early thirties.

Donald Davie provides us with a starting-point when he writes that, for his generation, Leavis was 'the god that failed':[12] the phrase aptly suggests the ways in which the *Scrutiny* movement was able to function both as a substitute-religion[13] and, above all, as a *substitute politics* in the thirties.[14] This is my main contention in this essay. Leavis was always and primarily a political writer, most of all when he claimed not to be. His work is all of a piece and serves one end – a sustained half-century's propaganda campaign for an idiosyncratic and pessimistic version of classical nineteenth-century liberalism – and it provides the material for a fascinating case-study of the intolerable contradictions and the inevitable self-destruction of that ideology between the wars.[15] It was those very contradictions which gave it such a broad appeal in the early thirties. Leavis was stridently anti-Marxist, yet he articulated a sense of the crisis of capitalism as deep and sincerely-held as any Marxist's. He sounded a clarion-call *simultaneously* for 'drastic social change' and for 'continuity' and 'tradition', and he was able to conceal the inconsistencies of this position from his disciples (and, one suspects, from himself) by his refusal to theorize. *Scrutiny* could thus offer its supporters a warming sense of commitment without ever making it quite clear what they were committing themselves *to*. Theorizing was 'abstract', according to the *Scrutiny* doctrine, and abstraction was the work of the devil, the very root of the malaise which the movement aimed to extirpate. Thus Leavis's curious incapacity for self-reflection, his stubborn pretence that, of all modern ideologies, his alone was incapable of systematic exposition.[16] Thus the peculiar blend of candour and evasiveness in his prose style, the impression which it gives of continually circling its own main contentions without ever stating them explicitly for fear of being 'abstract'. Thus too the circularity of his critical vocabulary, a closed dance of certain key-terms – 'Life', 'realized', 'actual' – whose meanings are merely self-referential, a private code. And thus the strange thwarted violence of the whole *Scrutiny* enterprise, a violence of repression, issuing from the fact that Leavis's refusal to make theoretical statements leads him instead, as Pamela McCallum puts it, to 'reproduce them through his engagement with other critics or texts', so that he is obliged 'to recreate and preserve his own (unstated) identity in each critical engagement'.[17]

It is precisely this circularity of critical language and this wilful refusal to say what he means, systematically, which makes it both so difficult and so necessary to lay bare the movement's underlying world-view. Leavis has taken care to cover his ideological tracks, never reprinting those early articles and editorials which reveal *Scrutiny*'s positions most nakedly, so that now the literary world has almost forgotten that the journal was the product of a highly specific moment of English cultural and political history,[18] and that what it articulated was not 'the tradition' of English culture (an entirely mythical beast in any case) but the dilemmas of a certain variety of literary liberalism at its moment of crisis.

The roots of that crisis run back into the twenties and as far as the First World War. Leavis himself, unlike many leading literary intellectuals of the period, had been at the front, as a stretcher-bearer. He was deeply affected, both physically and mentally (both his sleep and his digestion were permanently impaired), and although he rarely refers to these years in his writings, they clearly provided one of the decisive experiences of his life. The trauma was more than a merely personal one, of course. For Leavis, as for most liberal intellectuals of his generation, the war was above all a rupture – 'the great hiatus', he called it once. It had broken the 'continuity' of national life, irreversibly, and had made history alien and meaningless: it was like 'a dead object', as E. M. Forster put it, 'fallen across the page, which no historical arts can arrange, and which bewilders us as much by its shapelessness as by its size', and it had turned the postwar world into 'a planetful of scraps'.[19]

'A planetful of scraps': the same image haunts Leavis's own writings. Disintegration, fragmentariness, things falling apart as the centre ceases to hold; the loss of firm shapeliness and hierarchical order in both society and literary language, each exacerbating the other:

Here we have the plight of culture in general. The landmarks have shifted, multiplied and crowded upon one another, the distinctions and dividing lines have blurred away, the boundaries are gone, and the arts and literature of different countries and periods have flowed together . . .[20]

. . . more and more does human life depart from the natural rhythms, the cultures have mingled, and the forms have dissolved into chaos . . .[21]

. . . the contemporary plight . . . – the lack of form, grammar, principle, and direction.[22]

. . . 'one must speak for life and growth, amid all this mass of destruction and disintegration.'[23]

Everywhere, the images of atrophy and decline. Leavis, like Forster, seems to have lost all faith in historical progress as a result of the war.[24] His first published works show the strong influence of Oswald Spengler, whose *Decline of the West* has been described as 'the classic summary of the now familiar pessimism of the twentieth century West with regard to its own historical future'.[25] The book had had a phenomenal success in Germany in the early twenties, with its cheering message that it was Western civilization as a whole and not just Germany which was on the verge of final disintegration, and it enjoyed a certain vogue in England too: it was introduced to the English public as a 'decisive challenge to belief in progress', a book which had proved beyond doubt that 'there has been no continuity of progressive development'.[26] It is not difficult to reconstruct what the impact of such a work, with its vast apparatus of (mainly spurious) historical scholarship, would have been on a group of literary intellectuals who

considered that Eliot's *Waste Land* was the definitive statement of the
modern condition. Leavis told the readers of his first pamphlet, *Mass
Civilization and Minority Culture* (1930) that 'A good account of some
aspects of the modern phase may be found in *The Decline of the
West*',[27] and in his second pamphlet, *D. H. Lawrence*, published in the
same year, he quoted a long passage in which Spengler describes
modern man as an intellectual nomad, a 'rootless intellect . . . separated
from the power of the land', and remarked that 'One can, without
endorsing the Spenglerian idiom or philosophy, recognize the felicity of
this as an account of the present situation'.[28] The qualification is crucial,
and provides the key to the whole *Scrutiny* enterprise: Leavis accepted
Spengler's description of 'the Decline', but fiercely rejected the fatalistic
attitudes, 'the proud philosophic indifference', which it fostered, turning
instead to Lawrence as the representative of 'the splendid human
vitality, the creative faith, and the passionate sense of responsibility that
make Spengler's fatalism look like an arduously mean exercise of self-
importance'. The words read like a slogan for the decade. 'Spenglerism
plus resistance': that would be an accurate description of the ideological
roots of the whole *Scrutiny* enterprise. A passionate crusading zeal
plus, at root, a haunting conviction that all effort was in vain and the
disease incurable.

Where had Leavis and his collaborators to turn for allies, or more
hopeful alternatives? The great Victorian cultural sages, with their
optimistic confidence in the power of Culture against Anarchy, now
seemed distant and simplistic. Leavis had an enormous admiration for
Matthew Arnold – indeed, his work may be seen as a set of variations
on Arnoldian themes – but the modern situation was 'a nightmare
intensification of what Arnold feared'.[29] The Victorian commentators
had not been wrong but insufficiently prescient. They had not warned
their successors of the scale of the catastrophe. Leavis would have
sympathized with Forster's feeling that 'Arnold's "bad days" are
Halcyon compared with our own. . . . And if we look back into the past
for comfort, we see upon the faces of its great men a curious mixture of
comprehension and of blankness'.[30]

On the other hand, Leavis was too young to have had any share in the
revived cultural optimism of the decade before the war, when a new
variety of progressive Liberalism had emerged, providing an ideological
basis for the work of men like Forster, Maynard Keynes, Goldsworthy
Lowes Dickinson and Leonard Woolf, the so-called Bloomsbury
Group. These ideas too must have seemed already anachronistic to the

young Leavis when he returned from the trenches, and in any case Bloomsbury was soon to be denounced as the antithesis of Lawrence, and therefore, of course, of Life. And the left? The struggling young Labour Party was too busy keeping its head above water and coping with the immediate economic consequences of the war to have much time to spare for Leavis's gloomy contemplation of the Waste Land: Ramsay MacDonald was hardly the ally with whom Leavis would have chosen to ride into battle against the philistines. The new, Marxist left had yet to emerge, and anyway, as we shall see, all socialism for Leavis meant machine-worship, and 'machinery', after 'abstraction', was the chief minister of the forces of destruction in *Scrutiny*'s infernal pantheon.

It was a desperately isolated position for anyone with so strong and sincere a sense of the terminally critical state of society to find himself in; and it was not – in the early stages – entirely a wilful and self-imposed isolation. As Perry Anderson has argued, we ought to see Leavis's extravagant claims for literary criticism 'not as a reflection of megalomania on the part of Leavis, but as a symptom of the objective vacuum at the centre of the culture'. Very few English social scientists, philosophers or economists were showing any interest in 'totalizing' their own situation – that is, in attempting a general diagnosis of postwar English society. Leavis had some excuse, in the opening years of the thirties, for feeling that most of his fellow-intellectuals were refusing to face the responsibilities of being 'fully alive in their time'.[31]

The most damaging result of his intellectual isolation, for Leavis himself and for the whole *Scrutiny* movement, was his tendency to hero-worship the few allies or models who did offer themselves. As the thirties crisis deepened, and the contradictions of the *Scrutiny* position became more intolerable, it was Lawrence who was posthumously to play the role of guru. But in the formative years Lawrence had not been so highly rated – his primitivism seemed to Leavis 'a refuge from the general malady rather than a cure'[32] – and the chief influences were T. S. Eliot, I. A. Richards and his own wife, Queenie Leavis. It will be useful to examine in some detail the contribution made by each of these critics, for between them they provided the basic components of the movement's creed, a creed already fully-formed when *Scrutiny* itself was launched and to which no major modifications were made during the thirties.

In the general torpor of English cultural thought in the twenties, T. S. Eliot and his friend and admirer I. A. Richards seemed to many

young intellectuals the only two writers who offered a new start and
were truly 'alive . . . to the exciting strangeness of the present phase of
human history'.[33] How many critics make a real difference to how one
actually reads, Leavis asked, in an essay entitled 'What's Wrong with
Criticism?'

> At least two of them are of our time: Mr Eliot and Mr Richards; it is a very
> large proportion indeed of the total. Mr Richards has immensely improved the
> instruments of analysis . . . Mr Eliot has not only refined the conception and
> the methods of criticism; he has put into currency decisive re-organizing and
> re-orientating ideas and valuations. The stimulus of these two very dissimilar
> forces has already made itself felt, and there is no reason to suppose that Mr
> Empson's book *Seven Types of Ambiguity* will prove to be the only important
> critical work produced by their juniors.[34]

That remark occurs in the opening paragraphs of *Scrutiny*'s second
number, and it is clearly a manifesto: the *Scrutiny* writers are
themselves the 'juniors' who will consolidate Eliot and Richards's work.
Leavis's own early publications are in effect restatements and
extensions of his masters' key-ideas.

Eliot was the most powerful influence. Leavis's first book, *New
Bearings in English Poetry*, described itself as 'largely an
acknowledgement . . . of indebtedness to a certain critic and poet'
(clearly Eliot) and was an extended celebration of Eliot as the first
writer 'fully alive in our time', the man who had made the 'fresh start' for
both poetry and criticism. Leavis's claims for Eliot were enormous – he
expected a poet of Eliot's stature to be 'the most conscious point of the
race in his time', [35] and was proportionately embittered and
disappointed when Eliot failed to live up to his extravagant
expectations. They were also strikingly paradóxical, and they take us to
the heart of the paradoxes of the *Scrutiny* ideology.

Leavis, like most zealots, had tried to mould his god in his own image.
He presented Eliot as the archetype of that peculiarly representative
English intellectual type, the revolutionary conservative. Eliot had
created an authentically modern poetic, but he had done so, according
to Leavis, not by embracing modernity but by rejecting it in disgust: his
was 'a world in which the traditions are bankrupt, the cultures uprooted
and withering, and the advance of civilization seems to mean death to
distinction of spirit and fineness of living'.[36] Similarly, if Eliot had made
the revolutionary fresh start, he had done so by a mighty leap
backwards into the past, to re-establish both an idea of tradition and

communications with a specific tradition, that of the early seventeenth century, the last historical moment (according to *Scrutiny*) when English culture had been whole and unalienated, reason and emotion in balance with one another; the last moment before scientific rationality and capitalist economic organization had combined to rupture continuity. 'Tradition': this (together with its synonym 'continuity') was the first key-term of the *Scrutiny* position. It was repeated with talismanic insistence in almost every essay produced by the group, and it was from Eliot that it derived: it was the chief 'decisive re-organizing idea' which he had put into circulation for them. In his essay 'Tradition and the Individual Talent' Eliot had argued that for a writer to achieve true individuality and true contemporaneity, he must engage in 'a continual surrender of himself as he is at the moment to something which is more valuable', namely 'the mind of Europe', or 'tradition', which the poet can only acquire by an immense labour of research.[37]

This notion appealed to Leavis, first because it chimed in with his own puritanical dislike of romantic individualism, and second because in Eliot's grand conception of 'the tradition' as a vanished wholeness which only the scholarly work of a dedicated band of poets and critics could keep alive, and which could thus compensate for the fragmentariness of postwar Europe, the young Leavis glimpsed an alternative to 'Spenglerian fatalism' and a crusade worth devoting his life to.

Unfortunately, Eliot himself was not much interested in leading the charge, and was deeply sceptical of literary education as moral rearmament. William Empson has described how Eliot soon became badly rattled by Leavis's demagogic style:

how *disgusting* the behaviour of Leavis was, what mob oratory his arguments were, couldn't something be done to stop him? – and then, with cold indignation, 'Of course, I know it's going to be me next.'[38]

He was right. Leavis soon parted company with his first begetter, especially when he discovered that Eliot had gone Anglo-Catholic and turned against Life (i.e. criticized Lawrence). Leavis the outlaw (as he liked to style himself) became disgusted with Eliot's capitulation to literary and social conservatism – 'Mr Eliot has become a public institution, a part of the establishment'[39] – and from its earliest days Eliot appears in the pages of *Scrutiny* as the Lost Leader. Indeed, the decision to launch the journal was in part a direct result of Leavis and his friends' 'final depression'[40] with the decline of Eliot's own critical review, *The Criterion*, which they had seen as the only serious review to survive the twenties. Leavis's first editorial expresses 'the general regret that the name of *The Criterion* has become so dismal an irony and that the Editor is so far from applying to his contributors the standards we have learnt from him'.[41]

Here was the former disciples' dilemma in a nutshell: Eliot had given them their key ideas, but would offer no help in applying them. They would need to find other allies to help them recast the notion of 'tradition', in ways which Eliot had never intended and as the basis of a political campaign. This was where *Scrutiny*'s second key-term, 'sensibility', together with the ideas of I. A. Richards, came in. In one of the propaganda pamphlets launched at the same time as *Scrutiny*, Leavis wrote

Everything must start from and be associated with the training of sensibility. It should . . . be enforced . . . that everything worth saying in criticism of verse and prose can be related to judgments concerning particular arrangements of words on the page.[42]

Now this statement is evidently either tautologous or untrue (of course all discussions of literature 'can be *related* to' the details of expression; does he mean 'must be exclusively confined to'?) and even Leavis seems to have realized that he has gone too far. He adds:

Literary history and knowledge of the background, social and intellectual, remain, of course, indispensable. They should, and associated with this criticial training they can, be made to serve an essential end: the understanding . . . of what a literature is and what a tradition.

This is another shorthand way of saying that the new movement must be based on a synthesis of Eliot and Richards, the cultural theory of the one and the instruments of analysis of the other. The 'training of sensibility' mentioned is the one which Leavis and his friends had received from Richards at Cambridge, when they took part in the seminars which formed the basis for their teacher's most influential book, *Practical Criticism* (1929).

Richards was indeed the founder of the method still called 'practical criticism' in English departments all over the world and thus, in a real sense, the founder of the dominant ideology of twentieth century Anglo-American literary studies. He was mainly responsible for launching the idea that literary criticism was nothing else but the art of reading, an art not innate but only to be acquired by an immense labour of personal self-discipline, and that the business of the critic was the closest possible attention to the words on the page and the determined exclusion of 'irrelevant associations'. No one would deny the positive benefits which this approach has brought to literary studies. But in *Scrutiny*'s case, as in American 'New Criticism', it led to excesses and oddities. If you confine your attention exclusively to what we can call the 'lexical' aspects of literature, to its immediate textures, you will find it very difficult to give an adequate account of the ways in which that 'background, social and intellectual' penetrates every detail of a literary text, for language is always part of history, and the meanings of words change as their contexts change. You will find it difficult to devise a way of discussing either the larger structures of literary works (*Scrutiny* never found a critical language appropriate to long poems nor, despite many attempts, to the novel), or non-verbal literary structures: plays were always discussed in *Scrutiny* as if they were poems, with little sense of the specific qualities of drama as performance. More seriously, such an approach will tend, as *Scrutiny*'s did, to a peculiarly fetish-ridden kind of linguistic theory, not only overstressing texture against structure, but overvaluing 'concreteness', 'particularity', 'immediacy', 'muscularity' against what is dismissed as 'abstraction'. Leavis once went so far as to *define* a poet as one who 'should evoke the concrete particulars of immediate experience' – a peculiarly limiting description – and went on to proclaim that the criticism of '*all thinking* . . . likely to interest those of us who are preoccupied with the problems of living' (it is not quite clear who this category is intended to exclude) 'concerns its fidelity to concrete particulars'.[43]

Richards's own language-theories did not lead him into this extreme fear of 'abstraction'. Quite the reverse in fact: he became so absorbed in the pleasures of theory-building that he often seemed to lose all contact with actual literature, actual society – and this was precisely why Leavis eventually rejected him, accusing him of evading 'the motor-buses and other difficulties and dangers in his theoretical path, slipping into the empyrean by something very like the Indian rope-trick'.[44] Nevertheless, it was Richards's project for a new art of reading intended to solve 'the communication problem', both socially and individually, which provided the Scrutineers with their basic methodology as well as their conception of the academic literary critic as national saviour. Here we come to Richards's second main contribution. It was he, more than any one else, who was responsible for the Matthew Arnold Revival Movement in the twenties and thirties, and for the sudden resurgence of

the creed that literary culture offered the only hope for new growth amid
'this mass of destruction and disintegration', modern Europe. He
prefaced his own most visionary sermon,[45] *Science and Poetry*, with
Arnold's prediction that, as all creeds were shaken and all traditions
dissolved, and even religion 'materialized' itself, it would be in poetry
that 'our race, as time goes on, will find an ever surer and surer stay'.
Despite (or because of) his absorption in abstruse researches into
semantics and semiology, he had an even more lurid and apocalyptic
vision of 'the crisis' than his pupils the Scrutineers: 'the Hindenburg line
to which the defence of our traditions retired as a result of the
onslaughts of the last century will be blown up in the near future', he
solemnly predicted: 'if this happens a mental chaos such as man has
never experienced may be expected'.[46] By the mid-thirties the more
level-headed Scrutineers had begun to see these as 'very bourgeois
bogies',[47] and at last even Leavis turned with savage scorn on Richards's
proposed remedy, his claim that 'poetry . . . will remake our minds and
with them our world'.[48] But the scorn is partly self-punishment. In the
early days Richards had been regarded as an infallible oracle, and his
grand dream of poetry's future gave *Scrutiny* its very *raison d'être*: its
ideologists never seem to have tired of quoting Richards's claim that the
poet 'is the point at which the growth of the mind shows itself',[49] and
Leavis's even more extravagant paraphrase of it, his conviction that the
poet is 'the most conscious point of the race in his time'.

We can see now how the basic components of the *Scrutiny* ideology
were assembled. Take T. S. Eliot's notion of tradition (created for quite
a different purpose). Narrow it by abolishing Eliot's European
perspective, and confine it to a highly chauvinistic preoccupation with
'our race'. Narrow it further by grafting it onto I. A. Richards's newly
created discipline of 'practical criticism', with its reduction of criticism
to 'close reading' and its conviction that only by the extension of such
reading skills can the Decline of the West be averted. Tradition can
now be crampingly equated with *literary* tradition, and the state of the
nation may be measured solely in terms of its linguistic health. All those
other elements which might plausibly be thought to play their part in its
culture – its philosophical traditions, its laws, political theory,
architecture, music, crafts – or to have some relevance to an assessment
of its state of health – levels of unemployment and infant mortality,
distribution of wealth, social welfare provision, civil liberties,
democratic decision-making – all these can be relegated to an inferior
status. Do all this, and the logic broadens again irresistibly into

megalomania. The poet is the most conscious point of the race. But, as Matthew Arnold had taught, his health in turn is dependent on the existence of a healthy literary criticism, and in the modern age responsible criticism has withered away, a victim of the commercialization of the press. It can no longer flourish in the wider society and must therefore be cosseted in the only sanctuaries left, the new university English departments – and of these, only Cambridge is guaranteed germ-free. Thus, on a tiny band of Cambridge dons devolves the awesome task of resisting 'the universal reductive process'[50] as Leavis dubbed it, the last words of Pope's *Dunciad* echoing grandly in his mind.

Having established the broad ideological basis, the next step was to reformulate Richards's rather nebulous account of the cultural decline in more precise terms, backed up by detailed analysis, in order to provide the platform for a political campaign. This was the function performed by F. R. Leavis's early pamphlets and, above all, by Q. D. Leavis's *Fiction and the Reading Public*, a book which rapidly became the canonical text of the movement. Mrs Leavis's book, published in 1932, is essentially an extrapolation of I. A. Richards's key ideas into what the author calls an 'anthropological' study of the contemporary situation, plus an investigation of its historical roots. Richards had been her research supervisor, and she describes the work as having been encouraged by 'certain hints thrown out by Mr I. A. Richards in *Principles of Literary Criticism*'[51] about the need to study the general decline in mass culture, especially 'best-sellers'. The first part of the book accordingly analyses how popular novel fiction is promoted and distributed, records how the authors of *Tarzan* and *The Sheik* had responded to a questionnaire about their attitudes to their readers, and so on. Mrs Leavis claims that her 'anthropological' approach means that she will confine herself to presenting bare facts ... without involving value-judgments ... I have not set out to state a case'.[52] But this statement is only another example of the Scrutineers' often comic inability to perceive how passionately aprioristic their analyses were: in fact, her book is a blisteringly vituperative and splendidly biased assault on what she calls the 'manure heap' of contemporary pulp-fiction, plus a very useful analysis of the growth of manipulative advertising and the commercialized newspaper press. It is hair-raisingly snobbish of course, and comically puritanical (at one point she lashes out at 'the lascivious syncopated rhythms of the twentieth-century song- and dance-records'), but no matter: it is first-rate destructive pamphleteering. The real difficulties – both for Mrs Leavis and for the campaign which her book validated – was that she felt compelled to explain how all this had come about. The mistakes of this part of *Fiction and the Reading Public* are as impudent and spectacular as the successes of the other.

It was of course axiomatic for all Spenglerians and Richardians that no one else had ever lived in such an awful age, and that modern history lay at the nadir of a long decline from a state of perfection. The whole position was based, as we shall see, on a deep nostalgia for a Golden Age (the first full-length article published in *Scrutiny* argued that 'Complete absence of nostalgia in a modern writer is suspect, suggesting complacent fellowship with the main commercial group').[53] Thus, for Mrs Leavis to bring home to her readers the full awfulness of the present state of literary culture, she had to establish that once upon a time there had been something called the 'homogeneous reading public', a time of vanished wholeness without class-divisions, 'in 1760, for example, when any one who could read would be equally likely to read any novel, *or every novel*, published'.[54]

Now this notion is of course pure fantasy, and it is very hard not to accuse Mrs Leavis of deliberate intellectual dishonesty here: it is true that she did not have access to subsequent research on popular literature, but she would not have had to dig very deeply, even in 1932, to uncover the evidence for the large quantities of pulp fiction consumed by the eighteenth century reading public. Her obsession with atrophy also leads her into some extraordinary critical judgments, which were in their turn to have a distorting effect on *Scrutiny*'s map of the great tradition. One of the reasons why Dickens, for example, was long neglected and disparaged by the movement (only to be inconsistently rehabilitated in 1970 as one of the greatest geniuses of English literature) was surely that *Fiction and the Reading Public* had dismissed him with contempt as a mere symptom of the cultural disease, a writer who 'stands primarily for a set of crude emotional exercises . . . uneducated but also immature'.[55] Mrs Leavis *has* to argue this absurd position, of course, if her main thesis is not to fall apart. For in her over-simplified historical model there is a direct correlation between the spread of popular literacy and cultural decline. Dickens was a popular nineteenth century novelist. Therefore, by definition, his novels are no more than 'the painful guesses of the uninformed and half-educated writing for the uninformed and half-educated'. Once concede that it might be precisely his 'popular' qualities, his ability to draw from and speak to the deepest levels of the Victorian popular imagination, which were the very source of his extraordinary creative vitality, and the theory collapses and puts not only the historical existence, but also the desirability of a 'homogeneous reading public' severely in doubt. How many of the major works of world literature have been genuinely the products of such a public? Is it not the case that many, even most, of the greatest works celebrate or confront human society in its heterogeneity, that they arise from and articulate schism and contradiction?

The homogeneous reading public had a close and equally mythical cousin, the 'organic community'. Here we arrive at the true taproot of *Scrutiny*'s ideology, and 'tap-root' is the appropriate metaphor: the phrase 'rooted in the soil' recurs again and again in *Scrutiny*, signifying the highest praise that can be given a writer. Shakespeare's greatest asset, for instance, was that he could draw on 'a genuinely national culture. . . . A national culture rooted in the soil . . . the popular base of culture was agricultural.' The later work of James Joyce, by contrast, is no more than 'a characteristic symptom of dissolution', an embodiment of the rootless 'cosmopolitan' culture which surrounds him: modernist experiments like *Finnegans Wake* are 'a flimsy consolation for our loss'.[56] That loss is dwelt on obsessively in the early numbers of *Scrutiny*. For its fullest statements, one should turn to the numerous articles by Denys Thompson, one of the editors, and to *Culture and Environment*, which Leavis and he wrote jointly. Just back round the last bend in the road, just out of sight over the last hill, there had apparently been a sort of happy Hobbit-land, the organic community, a golden rural world without class-conflict or exploitation, in which labour was unalienated and fulfilling: 'at the core of this beautifully sufficient culture there throve a life-giving tradition. . . . The lives of the peasants were fulfilled . . . in touch with the seasonal rhythms . . . delight in the work itself . . . numerous exciting crafts. . . .'[57] Was it retrievable? No, on the whole the Scrutineers did not think that it was: mechanization was irreversible. All one could do was to create a substitute. What possible substitute could there be? Why, literary criticism of course. This may sound like a parody of *Scrutiny*'s logic, but it is stated perfectly explicitly on the first page of *Culture and Environment*, a book designed to be the basic weapon in the *Scrutiny*-teacher's propaganda arsenal:

. . . literary education, we must not forget, is to a great extent a substitute. What we have lost is the organic community with the living culture it embodied. Folk-songs, folk-dances, Cotswold cottages and handicraft

products are signs and expressions of something more: an art of life . . .
growing out of immemorial experience, to the natural environment and the
rhythm of the year.

The most astonishing thing about the idea of the organic community,
this keystone of the whole *Scrutiny* enterprise, was that Leavis and his
collaborators never showed the least interest in establishing whether it
had actually existed. George Sturt's highly coloured autobiographical
reminiscences of *The Wheelwright's Shop*,[58] Stuart Chase's
sentimentalized accounts of the harmonious lives of illiterate Mexican
peasants, Adrian Bell's rhapsodies over the beauty of Suffolk labourers'
dialect – these were eagerly cited as sound proofs of its reality. There is
not the whisper of a hint in the pages of *Scrutiny* that any of its
contributors had looked for a moment at the figures for the incidence of
infant mortality, malnutrition and illiteracy among these happy
peasants, nor that they had any notion of the economic mechanisms
whereby the urban market economy had penetrated and exploited this
'beautifully sufficient culture'. This was of course why *Fiction and the
Reading Public* so quickly became a sacred text for the Scrutineers: it
was their only work which even pretended to base its cultural theory on
detailed social-historical research (although it did not actually produce
any of the evidence: that was all to be published, Mrs Leavis promised,
in a 'pendent study', which never appeared). The Scrutineers clearly
regarded it as having established beyond doubt that there had been a
homogeneous culture, now on the point of disappearing even as a
memory. No need to spend more time investigating the past: the present
pressed too urgently. On with the crusade, under the slogan of 'criticism
as the New Organic Community'.

Fiction and the Reading Public was the trigger for the whole
movement. F. R. Leavis has said that it lay in *Scrutiny*'s 'immediate
background . . . with its documentation and analysis of the
developments that had left our culture in the plight that disquieted and
challenged us'; that its influence was 'pervasive and potent'; and that it
established a new 'sociological' approach to literature, providing a
model for 'taking the literary intelligence to non-literary fields'.[59] That
last phrase is the crucial one. It reminds us again that *Scrutiny* was a
part of the widespread attempt in the early thirties to make literature
and the study of literature more relevant to the social crisis.

That attempt took a variety of forms as the essays in the present
volume show. Many intellectuals were attracted into the new pacifist

movement. Some moved on rapidly from pacifism to an identification with Marxism and membership of the Communist Party. Some were temporarily seduced by the New Party, an apparently progressive breakaway from the Labour Party which soon transformed itself into the British Union of Fascists. Others again, following T. S. Eliot's lead, joined the religious revival and took refuge in a peculiarly reactionary brand of Anglo-Catholic High Toryism.[60] But for many writers the collapse of traditional reformist politics – 'the impotence of the practical mind to do anything essential in practice'[61] – resulted in a disillusion with politics as such, and a return to the gloomiest moments of the early twenties when history seemed meaningless and all hope of historical progress had been lost. Thus E. M. Forster, who had campaigned vigorously for the Independent Labour Party's policies in the mid-twenties and was now emerging as the representative figure of left liberalism, wrote sadly and nostalgically of the death of political idealism. All parties, he wrote, had sold out to 'mechanization' and did nothing but 'organize, organize, organize'.[62]

That was precisely *Scrutiny*'s view. Leavis agreed that 'few will be inclined to deny . . . the need for political action',[63] but his wife was simultaneously writing that 'it is no longer possible for an intelligent man to make politics his career'.[64] It was a paradoxical position, and the Scrutineers took the paradoxes to their extremes. What Matthew Arnold had predicted, Queenie Leavis's 'social anthropology' had confirmed: apart from those slit-trenches where the guerrillas of Sweetness and Light still held out, all classes and institutions in English society had been 'mechanized', and nothing met the eye but 'cultural disintegration, mechanical organization, and constant rapid change'.[65] All political action, by definition, was therefore also 'mechanical': 'political programmes have not sufficient ends: they are preoccupied with machinery merely', Denys Thompson told his readers.[66]

One can see quite clearly what is happening here, as the logic of sincere and socially committed teachers collapses under the pressure of the crisis. What Thompson *means* is that he and his friends are fed up with the National Government and do not see much hope in the alternatives either. What he *says* is that *all* politics is a matter of mere 'machinery', tinkering with externals. This is the characteristic *Scrutiny* reflex. Bewildered by the aftermath of the war and by the Depression, out of touch with the industrial centres and with practical politics, saddled with their oversimplified diagram of English history and their nostalgic dream of a lost Golden Age, the Scrutineers were incapable of taking an objective overview of their own situation. They consistently portray it in histrionically absolute and apocalyptic terms, seeing themselves as lonely heroic figures silhouetted against the lurid glow of the Last Days. Because D. H. Lawrence is dead and T. S. Eliot has turned to Rome, English literature faces extinction. Because they cannot see a way out of the immediate political impasse, all political action (except their own of course) is doomed and futile. This style of argument has a marked tendency towards circularity and self-reinforcement, and an equally marked tendency to close itself to alternative points of view. One would suppose, for instance, that *Scrutiny* would have had to exempt Marxism from its generalization that all existing political creeds were ostriches, and only concerned to tackle the superficial symptoms of the social disease. Not at all. Marxism too, it transpires, has fallen victim to machine-worship: Trotsky, in this regard, 'like all Marxists, becomes indistinguishable from Mr Wells'.[67] Marxism is 'too bourgeois',[68] and its class-analyses are merely 'a characteristic product of our "capitalist" civilization'[69] rather than a transcendence of it. *Scrutiny* will reject all that and strive instead, like Matthew Arnold, to create a force beyond and above all social classes – a new kind of culture, 'an autonomous culture, a culture independent of any economic, technical or social system as none has been before . . . a rootless culture'.[70]

This is a curious and desperately circular syllogism, and it seems tragic, in retrospect, that the combination of Leavis's arrogance and the raw state of much English Marxist cultural theory prevented the genuine dialogue between Leavis and the left from which both could have gained so much, and which would have helped Leavis to escape the bitter trap of his own isolation. For the gap which divided them was not really so great, and in the early days many of the other Scrutineers tried to bridge it. Denys Thompson argued that the capitalist system was 'better ended' and that no economist who assumed its continuance was worth serious attention.[71] L. C. Knights, another editor, warned his colleagues against accepting right-wing caricatures of Marxist theory – ' "the materialistic view of life" . . . does not necessarily mean "the worship of the machine" '[72] – and made a serious attempt in his own work to apply insights from historical materialism to literary history.[73] Herbert Butterfield, in a long and balanced investigation of 'History and the Marxian Method', said that it had now been 'satisfactorily explained' that to be a Marxist was not to be a 'crude economic determinist', and went on to argue that, on the contrary, 'this economic approach to history . . . will better help us to construct a mentality that can squarely set itself to the lines of the modern world'.[74] Even Leavis himself, in an essay which, not surprisingly, he never reprinted, wrote in 1933 that 'I agree with the Marxist to the extent of believing some form of economic communism to be inevitable and desirable . . . and only by a deliberate and intelligent working towards it can civilization be saved from disaster.'[75]

On their side, the left seemed for a time to be eager for an alliance, understanding the importance of *Scrutiny*'s campaign against the growing power of the advertising industry, the commercialization of the press, the cynically exploitative machinery of the new mass entertainments industry:

Scrutiny is too valuable a weapon against the Philistines to be left permanently in the position of the two heroes who 'wept like anything to see such quantities of sand',

as A. L. Morton put it.[76] But it was to no avail. Leavis refused to listen to those Marxists who, as David Margolies shows in his essay in the present volume, were patiently trying to demonstrate that the theory of base and superstructure need not lead to 'crude economic determinism'. He consistently chose as his targets the most naïve and reductive examples of Marxist cultural thought and literary criticism (there were many to hand), and therefore never engaged with those aspects of historical materialism which might have helped him to clarify his own analysis as they were helping Knights and Butterfield to clarify theirs. The pages of *Scrutiny* soon began to fill with the parody 'Bolsheviks of the penny paper cartoons' which Knights had warned against, and eventually Leavis persuaded himself that resisting the Red Threat had been *Scrutiny*'s prime purpose from the very start:

We were anti-Marxist – necessarily so (we thought) . . . Marxist fashion gave us the doctrinal challenge . . . Cambridge, then, figured for us civilization's recognition of its own nature and needs – recognition of that, the essential, which Marxian wisdom discredited, and the external and material drive of civilization threatened, undoctrinally, to eliminate. It was our strength to be . . . representatives of that Cambridge. We *were*, in fact, that Cambridge . . .[77]

This is Leavis rewriting history, of course, and it is characteristic of the Manicheanism of his later career, his tendency to present complex issues in crudely over-polarized terms. It is nevertheless true that soon after its inception the '*Scrutiny* movement in education' began explicitly

to offer itself as a substitute for radical politics: its programme, claimed
L. C. Knights, was 'of greater importance than . . . direct action by
teachers in favour of a collectivist society'.[78] Leavis agreed: 'The
teaching profession is peculiarly in a position to do revolutionary things
. . . and by a bold challenge there, perhaps the self-devotion of the
intelligent may be more effectively enlisted than by an appeal to the
Class-War.'[79] *Scrutiny*'s front-line cadres, according to Thompson,
'would be more deeply revolutionary than many propagandists for the
economic revolution which is urgently desirable, in that they would
have a more radical insight into the ills of megapolitan civilization'.[80]
The movement was even to have a kind of quasi-Leninist form of
political organization. A meeting was held in Cambridge in the summer
of 1933 to discuss whether 'the education movement that *Scrutiny*, with
the associated books and pamphlets, in any case represents might now
be profitably made more explicitly a "movement"', and although it was
decided not to 'formulate a political programme and start to stump the
country with it', and that 'any elaborate machinery of organization was
to be avoided' ('machinery', was of course, by definition, always to be
avoided) the editors hoped that an organization would 'develop
spontaneously – in local "cells", so to speak – with a minimum of
incitement.'[81]

Not altogether surprisingly, these hopes for the spontaneous growth
of a national political organization did not come to very much. It is not
my intention here to chart in detail the movement's development
throughout the decade. That would be material for a different and much
longer study. My aim has simply been to uncover and locate historically
the main components of *Scrutiny*'s theory of cultural crisis. In fact, that
theory underwent surprisingly little modification in the thirties (or
later): *Scrutiny*, always essentially regressive, remained fixated on its
original dilemmas, closed off by the very terms of its ideology from the
possibility of registering the complex historical shifts of the decade, and
the movement therefore followed a sadly predictable course.

This 'entirely fresh approach to the essential problems of politics – an
approach that circumvents old obstacles and impasses', which the
editors had promised with the kind of innocent arrogance so
characteristic of the movement,[82] turned out to be as comically
impractical and as unaware of the 'motor-buses and other difficulties' in
its path as I. A. Richards's schemes when it came to proposals for
concrete educational action. Mere 'machinery' was beneath *Scrutiny*'s
notice of course, so 'We have nothing to offer in solution of the

problems discussed in educational journals. . . . Our case is more fundamental',[83] and it would not insult its readers' intelligence by basing its case on arguments 'of the wearisome statistical kind'.[84] It was unperturbed by the objection that many of the aspects of the educational system which it wished to reform (such as the excessive reliance on formal examination) had been designed to serve the needs of a specific economic system, and were therefore incapable of being changed from within by teachers' pressure groups: if, for example, right-minded examiners got together to express their disapproval of the examination system, 'it is a fair chance that that bogey, "the requirements of the business world", would disappear, leaving the field clear for a new start in education'.[85]

When such bogies obstinately refused to disappear at the touch of *Scrutiny*'s arguments, the faithful began to get restless, and their unease must have been increased by the fact that the suggestions for practical educational action which *were* made all seemed to amount to turning schools into propaganda-machines for 'the tradition' or for the 'organic community' and its substitute: 'since English traditional culture is dead, it is of the first importance that tradition should be sustained through literature'[86] – that is, through feeding children a strong diet of Sturt, Chase and company, backed up with 'practical criticism' of a set of texts preselected to validate *Scrutiny*'s cultural theory.[87] 'Slight indoctrination may be incident', conceded Thompson in a breath-taking understatement, [88] and so many readers began to find. 'To revive or replace a decayed tradition is a desperate undertaking,' Leavis frankly admitted.[89] It certainly is, and doubly so when your audience begins to realize that it was a tendentious fiction in the first place.

Scepticism grew, even among *Scrutiny*'s own contributors. Goldsworthy Lowes Dickinson, the grandfather of the Bloomsbury Group and Forsterian left-liberalism, had warned the Scrutineers in their first number that it was an illusion to believe that they could keep clear of politics in 1932: 'war and capitalism' were the great issues of the day, and: 'You young men may or may not agree with [my] view but you ought at least to have a view; for, if you are indifferent, you will pay the price of indifference with your lives.'[90] Others soon took up the same point. Campaigns for educational reform are all very well, wrote W. H. Auden in the second issue, but 'Dearie, you can't do anything for the children till you've done something for the grown-ups.'[91] And the militant pacifist H. L. Elvin, biting the hand that commissioned him, put the matter even more bluntly: war could now only be avoided by collective political action, which in turn meant commitment to a political party. 'To refuse to be partisan is such a matter is to be futile . . . it is only by a constant and direct concern with action, to make his opinions effective, that the Intelligent Man's intelligence is likely to be anything more than his own private diversion.'[92] The remark was ostensibly aimed at the fence-sitting contributors to Leonard Woolf's *The Intelligent Man's Way to Prevent War*; but every reader of *Scrutiny* would have known that 'intelligence' was one of Leavis's favourite terms – 'Intelligence has an active function' was the slogan of *Scrutiny*'s 'Manifesto' – and realized who the real target was.

Scrutiny at first made some effort to answer these demands for it to 'show our colours', as Leavis put it,[93] and even made some self-criticisms: the first editorial of 1934, for example, confesses that 'we know that we have not made such a direct approach to the problems of economics, social order and international relations as their terrible urgency might seem to demand of us'.[94] But as the European crisis deepened, Leavis and his collaborators became more and more rattled by their critics. Auden, Elvin, Edgell Rickword, A. L. Morton, Herbert Butterfield and company disappear from *Scrutiny*. It makes less and less effort to find a 'direct approach' to social issues, and becomes more and more a literary critical journal in a narrowing sense. It becomes not only stridently anti-political (as well as anti-philosophical, anti-anthropological, anti-sociological and anti-Freudian), but unprepared even to argue. The less it seeks dialogue, and 'the common pursuit of true judgement' with other positions, the less it is offered them, the more defiantly isolated it becomes,[95] and the more its melodramatically exaggerated sense of itself as an embattled élite is encouraged, until all mention of the grand scheme for a nation-wide '*Scrutiny* movement in education' is dropped and Leavis retreats to his conception of the Cambridge English Faculty as a lonely moral lighthouse in the encroaching darkness.

It is one of the saddest and most quixotic stories in modern English intellectual history. Leavis began from a deep and genuine sense of the magnitude of the interwar crisis, of the ways in which the individual consciousness 'may be profoundly affected by the "economic process"',[96] and of the fundamentally social – even communal – nature of literature. Yet he ends, prisoner of his own historical myths and after the consequent failure of his attempt to create a new kind of political movement, by retreating to the most extreme cultural individualism, positing a transcendentalized literary critical sensibility,[97] possession of a tiny minority and to be tended only by initiates: the 'consciousness of the race', miraculously unviolated by the universal reductive process: the desperate and impossible dream of an 'autonomous culture'.

NOTES

1. 'The promise that might have seemed to be inherent in it has been defeated . . . Cambridge is no longer a centre of life and hope . . . the actuality is an accelerating drift (which will become a drive) of Americanization' (F. R. Leavis, *English Literature in our Time and the University* (1969), pp. 19, 24).

2. See, for example, the now defunct journal, *The Human World*, described by Tom Nairn (in a phrase which says as much about the *New Left Review* as its enemies) as a 'damp spiritual *cul-de-sac* [which] represents, surely, the last gasp of élite conservative pseudo-humanism' (*New Left Review*, 75 (September–October 1972), p. 14).

3. The only full-length study of F. R. Leavis, by Ronald Hayman (1976), is trite, gossipy and entirely unanalytic. Useful commentaries on aspects of Leavis's work can be found in John Casey, *The Language of Criticism* (1966); Perry Anderson, 'Components of the National Culture', *New Left Review*, 50 (July–August 1968), pp. 3–57. The most searching analysis of Leavis's cultural thought known to me is a Cambridge University doctoral dissertation by Pamela McCallum, which, when published, will provide a theoretical basis for future research on the *Scrutiny* enterprise. Francis Mulhern's *The Moment of 'Scrutiny'* appeared as the present volume went to press.

4. See F. R. Leavis, *Revaluation* (1936), a collection of essays originally published in *Scrutiny*.

5. The title of F. R. Leavis's first full-length book, published in 1932.

6. See F. R. Leavis, *The Great Tradition* (1948), essays reprinted from *Scrutiny*.

7. F. R. Leavis, 'Sociology and Literature', *Scrutiny*, vol. XIII, no. 1 (Spring 1945), p. 78. Reprinted in his *The Common Pursuit* (1952).

8. F. R. Leavis, in the first essay which he published in *Scrutiny*, 'The Literary Mind' (*Scrutiny*, vol. I, no. 1 (May, 1932), p. 24). He has just quoted Ezra Pound's statement that literature's 'function in the state . . . has to do with maintaining the very cleanliness of the tools, the health of the very matter of thought itself' – one of *Scrutiny*'s favourite aphorisms.

9. F. R. Leavis, *Mass Civilization and Minority Culture* (Cambridge, 1930), pp. 4–5; reprinted in his *Education and the University: A Sketch for an 'English School'* (1943), substituting 'Conrad' for 'Hardy'. Reviewing *Scrutiny*'s achievements, Leavis later said bluntly that 'It was essential to the conception of *Scrutiny* to demonstrate that . . . a key community of the *élite* [could be] . . . formed and held' ('"Scrutiny": A Retrospect', in vol. XX of the 1963 reissue of *Scrutiny*, p. 6.)

10. F. R. Leavis, 'D. H. Lawrence and Professor Irving Babbitt', *Scrutiny*, vol. I, no. 3 (December, 1932), p. 275. The phrase is Lawrence's, who claims that such people 'never live on the spot where they are'. Leavis approvingly comments: 'Lawrence always lived on the spot where he was. That was his genius.'

11. 750 copies of each issue were printed throughout the thirties.

60 IAIN WRIGHT

12. Donald Davie, 'A Voice in the Desert', *The Times Literary Supplement*, 1 October 1976, p. 1233.

13. Note, for example, the ambiguously religious language to be found in many of Leavis's essays, especially when he is genuflecting towards Lawrence, and the emphatic but evasive use of the word 'spiritual' at pivotal points of his argument. The notion of culture as a religion-substitute derives directly from Matthew Arnold's *Culture and Anarchy* (1869), one of the movement's sacred texts, which sets out 'to recommend culture as the great help out of our present difficulties' since religion (which is said to have the same 'great aim' as culture) has failed to cope. The Scrutineers seem to have been divided among themselves on the issue, however. L. C. Knights explicitly warned against the plethora of 'religion-substitutes at all levels' which were a symptom of the 'disorder of contemporary thought' (*Scrutiny*, June 1933, p. 94). Leavis seemed equally clear that, while most *Scrutiny* readers would 'find the possibility of adhesion to any formal religion a remote one' (*Scrutiny* vol. I, no. 4, p. 319), it was simultaneously the case that 'recovery of religious sanctions in some form seems necessary to the health of the world' (*Scrutiny*, vol. I, no. 3, p. 213). Given two such premises, what else could his campaign logically be but a surrogate-religion?

14. *The God that Failed* was the title of an influential anthology of recantations by ex-Communists and fellow-travellers of the thirties, edited by Arthur Koestler and published in 1950.

15. For Leavis's roots in nineteenth-century liberalism, see his edition of *Mill on Bentham and Coleridge* (1950).

16. See, for a classic instance of this, the correspondence between René Wellek and Leavis published in *Scrutiny* in 1937 (vol. V, no. 4, pp. 375–83; vol. VI, no. 1, pp. 59–70). Wellek, while admiring the powers of critical insight shown in *Revaluation*, wishes that Leavis had stated his 'assumptions more explicitly and defended them systematically'. Leavis declines, and replies by arguing an altogether different point, that philosophy and literary criticism are different kinds of intellectual procedure, and that a critic's judgements should not be based on 'a theoretical system or a system determined by abstract considerations'.

17. P. McCallum, unpublished Ph.D. dissertation, Cambridge University. See note 3 above.

18. '. . . We were very conscious of being in a particular place at a particular time, and the cue, we should have said, was to make the most of the advantages the accidents of the place and the time offered' (F. R. Leavis, '"Scrutiny": A Retropect', loc. cit., p. 4).

19. E. M. Forster, reviewing H. G. Wells, *The Outline of History* in *The Athenaeum*, 2 and 9 July 1920, pp. 8–9, 42–3.

20. F. R. Leavis, *Mass Civilization and Minority Culture*, p. 19.

21. F. R. Leavis, *D. H. Lawrence* (Cambridge, 1930), p. 28.

22. F. R. Leavis, *New Bearings*, p. 129.

23. F. R. Leavis, quoting Lawrence, in 'Restatements for Critics', *Scrutiny*, vol. I, no. 4 (March 1933), p. 319.

24. Again like Forster, Leavis reserved his bitterest scorn for the H. G. Wellses of the day – those who naïvely equated the advance of science with progress. Science was in fact the Destroyer: 'the tradition of literary culture is dead, or nearly so', Leavis proclaimed in his first *Scrutiny* article. '. . . it was Science that killed it . . . by being

the engine of the social changes that have virtually broken continuity' ('The Literary Mind', *Scrutiny*, vol. I, no. 1 (May 1932), p. 21).

25. H. Stuart Hughes, *Oswald Spengler: A Critical Estimate* (New York, 1952), p. 165.

26. E. H. Goddard and P. A. Gibbons, *Civilisation or Civilisations: An Essay in the Spenglerian Philosophy of History* (1926), p. 2.

27. F. R. Leavis, *Mass Civilization and Minority Culture* (Cambridge, 1930), p. 5.

28. F. R. Leavis, *D. H. Lawrence*, pp. 27–8.

29. F. R. Leavis, *English Literature in our Time and the University*, p. 33.

30. E. M. Forster, 'Notes on the Way', *Time and Tide*, 9 June 1934, p. 723.

31. Perry Anderson, 'Components of the National Culture', *New Left Review* 50 (July–August 1968), p. 50. Specifically, Anderson suggests that 'when philosophy became "technical", a displacement occurred and literary criticism became "ethical".' This seems to me to make good sense in the light of Leavis's own pronounced antagonism to philosophy (see note 16). Not long before he died he wrote 'I call myself an "anti-philosopher"' ('Mutually Necessary', *New Universities Quarterly*, vol. 30, no. 2 (Spring 1976), pp. 129–51).

32. F. R. Leavis, *D. H. Lawrence*, p. 18.

33. F. R. Leavis, reviewing William Empson, *Seven Types of Ambiguity* in *The Cambridge Review*, vol. LII, no. 1275 (16 January 1931), p. 186.

34. F. R. Leavis, 'What's Wrong with Criticism?', *Scrutiny*, vol. I, no. 2 (September 1932), p. 132.

35. F. R. Leavis, *New Bearings*, p. 19.

36. F. R. Leavis, ibid., p. 165.

37. T. S. Eliot, 'Tradition and the Individual Talent', *The Egoist*, vol. VI, no. 4 (September 1919), pp. 54–5, and vol. VI, no. 5 (December 1919), pp. 72–3. Reprinted in *Selected Essays* (1951), pp. 13–22.

38. William Empson, 'The Hammer's Ring', in R. Brower et al. (eds.), *I. A. Richards: Essays in his Honor* (New York, 1973), p. 74.

39. F. R. Leavis, 'Retrospect 1950', *New Bearings* (reprinted, 1950).

40. F. R. Leavis, 'Reminiscences of D. H. Lawrence', *Scrutiny*, vol. I, no. 2 (September 1932), p. 190.

41. F. R. Leavis, 'Under which King, Bezonian?', *Scrutiny*, vol. I, no. 3 (December 1932), p. 214. On the positive side, *Scrutiny* hoped to fill the gap left by the disappearance of *The Calendar of Modern Letters*: 'Of what a serious critical review might be we had an example before us in *The Calendar*. . . . The name of our new quarterly was itself thought of as a salute and a gesture of acknowledgement – an assertion of a kind of continuity of life with *The Calendar*, whose "Scrutinies" . . . it overtly recalled' (F. R. Leavis, '"Scrutiny": A Retrospect', p. 3). *The Calendar*'s joint editor, Edgell Rickword, was a Marxist, and was soon to re-emerge as one of the editors of *Left Review* – another instance of the ambivalence of *Scrutiny*'s relations with the left at this time.

42. F. R. Leavis, *How to Teach Reading: a Primer for Ezra Pound*, (Cambridge, 1932), p. 25.

43. F. R. Leavis, 'The Literary Mind', *Scrutiny*, vol. I, no. 1 (May 1932) p. 22 (my italics). Realizing perhaps that this ruled out of court the greater part of European philosophical and theological thought, Leavis hurriedly went on to argue, with convoluted but characteristic logic, that, 'Of a good prose, in so far as it is abstract

and general, it may be said that its virtues are a matter of the negative presence of the concrete and particular; it is not merely absence, but exclusion, an exclusion felt as a pressure.'

44. F. R. Leavis, 'Dr Richards, Bentham, and Coleridge', *Scrutiny*, vol. III, no. 4 (March 1935), p. 392.

45. 'Sermon' is the right word here: Richards once admitted that his main theoretical statement of the period, *Principles of Literary Criticism* (1924), was 'a sermon disguised in the fashionable scientific language of the day'.

46. I. A. Richards, *Science and Poetry* (1926), p. 82.

47. D. W. Harding, 'I. A. Richards', *Scrutiny*, vol. I, no. 4 (March 1933), p. 337.

48. 'Clearly there would be no point in asking for – what would nevertheless be very interesting – a little specificity here; there may be three times as many modern poets, and poets three times as promising, as any I know of, but that would not make Dr Richards's optimism regarding their influence critically respectable. In fact, Poetry in general for Dr Richards – and for him it is always in general – is, it becomes impossible in these places to doubt, a myth . . . a large private myth . . .' (F. R. Leavis, 'Dr Richards, Bentham, and Coleridge', loc. cit., p. 392).

49. I. A. Richards, *Principles of Literary Criticism* (1924), p. 61.

50. 'Cambridge . . . exemplifies rather than resists the universal reductive process' (*English Literature in our Time*, p. 24).

51. Q. D. Leavis, *Fiction and the Reading Public* (1932), p. xiv.

52. op. cit., pp. 207 and xvi.

53. D. W. Harding, 'A Note on Nostalgia', *Scrutiny*, vol. I, no. 1 (May, 1932), p. 12. Harding goes on to say that 'permanent, unresolved nostalgia is a failure too', and the remark reflects ironically, perhaps deliberately, on its context. Was he sounding a warning to his fellow-Scrutineers here, at the beginning of their campaign, when he argued that intellectuals often use literature as a substitute for 'the sense of security given by membership of an adequate social group' – a means of easing their own isolation and constructing a substitute-solidarity with the past? 'The contemporary flank-rubbing herd that highly-developed people can form at any one period is naturally small,' he wrote, 'but it has the advantage of a tradition extraordinarily rich and accessible compared with that of the main community. And though the flank-rubbing herd is a necessity, yet the recorded feelings and attitudes of people no longer living are remarkably effective in sanctioning and confirming one's own ways of living.' This seems to me to come very close to suggesting that the idea of 'the tradition' is a reflex of the intellectual's inability to live fully in his own present. But if Harding was issuing a warning here, it went unheeded and *Scrutiny*'s flank-rubbing continued. Compare the complex ironies of this essay with Leavis and Thompson's naïve recommendation of literary education as a 'substitute' for the organic community.

54. Q. D. Leavis, op. cit., p. 33 (my italics).

55. ibid., pp. 156–7.

56. F. R. Leavis, 'Joyce and "The Revolution of the Word"', *Scrutiny*, vol. II, no. 2 (September 1933), pp. 198–200.

57. Denys Thompson, 'A Cure for Amnesia', *Scrutiny*, vol. II, no. 1 (June 1933), pp. 2–11. Thompson's article was, in effect, the editorial to the journal's second volume.

58. 'It is part of *Scrutiny*'s policy to make Sturt's work known' (Denys Thompson, loc. cit., p. 10).

59. F. R. Leavis, '"Scrutiny": A Retrospect', loc. cit., p. 2.

60. Some of the leading Scrutineers seem to have regarded resistance to the new obscurantism as one of *Scrutiny*'s main ideological functions. See, for instance, L. C. Knights's attack on reactionary Catholic propaganda in *Scrutiny*'s fifth issue: 'Such criticism seems particularly necessary since the attitude represented by the Essays is at present fairly common – even those who are not professing Christians find it intellectually *chic* to be "influenced by T. E. Hulme," to flirt with St Thomas . . .' ('Quicunque vult . . .', *Scrutiny*, vcl. II, no. 1 (June 1933), p. 100. Knights is reviewing *Essays in Order* by Jacques Maritain and others.)

61. 'Scrutiny: A Manifesto', *Scrutiny*, vol. I, no. 1 (May 1932), p. 3. The Labour government, having failed altogether to contain the economic crisis, had fallen a few months before this was written, and the National government which replaced it was proving no more successful. Cf. Leavis's remarks about 'The problems of contemporary civilization, before which statesmen and politicians look so depressingly impotent' in 'Why Universities?', *Scrutiny*, vol. III, no. 2 (September 1934), p. 132 – another reminder of the extent to which *Scrutiny* issued from a specific political impasse in the early thirties, and was in essence the expression of a kind of deflected radicalism.

62. E. M. Forster, 'Some Memories', in G. Beith (ed.), *Edward Carpenter: In Appreciation* (1931), p. 78. Forster is paying tribute to Carpenter's libertarian socialism, recalling how he had 'dreamed like William Morris that civilization would be cured' by the union of manual work and fresh air. However, Forster laments, 'The Labour movement took another course'.

63. F. R. Leavis, 'What's Wrong with Criticism?', *Scrutiny*, vol. I, no. 2 (September 1932), p. 135.

64. Q. D. Leavis, *Fiction and the Reading Public*, p. 191.

65. F. R. Leavis, 'Joyce and "The Revolution of the Word"'. loc. cit., p. 200.

66. Denys Thompson, 'The Machine Unchained', *Scrutiny*, vol. II, no. 2 (September 1933), p. 186.

67. F. R. Leavis, 'Under which King, Bezonian?', *Scrutiny*, vol. I, no. 3 (December 1932), p. 207.

68. F. R. Leavis, 'Restatements for Critics', *Scrutiny*, vol. I, no. 4 (March 1933), p. 322.

69. F. R. Leavis, '"Scrutiny: A Retrospect', loc. cit., p. 4.

70. F. R. Leavis, 'Under which King, Bezonian?', loc. cit., p. 210.

71. Denys Thompson, 'The Machine Unchained', loc. cit., p. 186.

72. L. C. Knights, 'Quicunque vult . . .', loc. cit., p. 96.

73. See L. C. Knights, 'Shakespeare and Profit Inflations' (*Scrutiny*, vol. V, no. 1 (June 1936), pp. 48–60), reprinted in his *Drama and Society in the Age of Jonson* (1937). Knights's book, conceived in the form of a kind of dialogue with English Marxists like Strachey, Fox and Charques, set out to 'map the social and economic bases of Elizabethan-Jacobean culture and make some profitable correlations' with the drama of the period.

74. Herbert Butterfield, 'History and the Marxian Method', *Scrutiny*, vol. I, no. 4 (March 1933), pp. 339, 346. Butterfield is contrasting the Marxian method with the characteristic form of British political science which he believes has 'the chief part

in forming a discrepancy between our mentality and the contemporary situation'.

75. F. R. Leavis, 'Restatements for Critics', loc. cit., p. 320. In the previous issue (p. 206) Leavis had written that 'there seems to be no reason why supporters of *Scrutiny* should not favour some kind of communism as the solution of the economic problem'.

76. A. L. Morton, 'Culture and Leisure', *Scrutiny*, vol. I, no. 4 (March 1933), p. 326. Morton is replying to Leavis's 'Under which King, Bezonian?'.

77. F. R. Leavis, '"Scrutiny": A Retrospect', loc. cit., p. 4.

78. L. C. Knights, 'Good Intentions in Education', *Scrutiny*, vol. II, no. 2 (September 1933), p. 218.

79. F. R. Leavis, 'Restatements for Critics', loc. cit., p. 323.

80. Denys Thompson, 'What Shall We Teach?', *Scrutiny*, vol. II, no. 4 (March 1934), p. 386.

81. *The 'Scrutiny' Movement in Education*, a leaflet dated August, 1933 and distributed with *Scrutiny*, vol. II, no. 2 (September 1933).

82. *The 'Scrutiny' Movement in Education*.

83. L. C. Knights, 'Scrutiny of Examinations', *Scrutiny*, vol. II, no. 2 (September 1933), p. 137.

84. Martin Crusoe, 'English Work in the Public School', *Scrutiny*, vol. I, no. 4 (March 1933), p. 368.

85. L. C. Knights, 'Scrutiny of Examinations', loc. cit., p. 160.

86. Denys Thompson, 'A Cure for Amnesia', loc. cit., p. 6.

87. See, for instance, the section entitled 'Positive Suggestions' in F. R. Leavis's *How to Teach Reading*. The 'Scheme of Work' Leavis proposes centres, not merely on critical comparisons, but on comparisons whose outcome has already been decided by the teacher: 'Do comparisons between representative poems of the seventeenth and nineteenth centuries *in order to bring out* the advantage the seventeenth-century poets enjoyed in being in the "tradition of wit"' (my italics). See also F. R. Leavis's 'A Sketch for an "English School"' in *Education and the University*; and, to see *Scrutiny*'s educational propagandism at its comic extreme, the sample school exercises listed at the end of *Culture and Environment*. e.g. '. . . examine the common assumption that we have "progressed" in the last century'; 'Work out the life of a person who responds to the advertisements he or she reads. Compare it with the lives of the Villagers in [Sturt's] *Change in the Village*'; 'Compare *Tarzan* with *She* (see *Principles of Literary Criticism*, p. 36.)'.

88. Denys Thompson, 'What Shall We Teach?', loc. cit., p. 384.

89. F. R. Leavis, 'The Literary Mind', *Scrutiny*, vol. I, no. 1 (May 1932), p. 31.

90. G. Lowes Dickinson, 'The Political Background', *Scrutiny*, vol. I, no. 1 (May 1932), p. 43.

91. W. H. Auden, 'Private Pleasure', *Scrutiny*, vol. I, no. 2 (September 1932), p. 194.

92. H. L. Elvin, 'War: Can the Intelligent Stop It?', *Scrutiny*, vol. II, no. 3 (December 1933), pp. 327 and 329.

93. 'It would be very innocent of us to be surprised by the frequency with which we are asked to "show our colours"'. F. R. Leavis, 'Under Which King, Bezonian?', loc. cit., p. 205 [opening words].

94. Unsigned editorial, *Scrutiny*, vol. II, no. 4 (March 1934), p. 331.

95. 'We, of course . . . repudiated altogether the suggestion that, for responsible minds, it could be a matter of "showing colours", or that there were any relevant "colours"

to be shown. We did indeed reject Marxism and we had no use for any proposed antithesis, Fascistic, Poundian, Wyndham-Lewisite or Criterionic' (F. R. Leavis, '"Scrutiny": A Retrospect', loc. cit., p. 17).

96. F. R. Leavis, 'Restatements for Critics', loc. cit., p. 323.

97. 'A culture expressing itself in a tradition of literature and art – such a tradition as represents the finer consciousness of the race and provides the currency of finer living – can be in a healthy state only if this tradition is in living relation with a real culture, shared by the people at large' (F. R. Leavis, 'Under which King, Bezonian?', loc. cit., pp. 207–8). The catch, of course, as Leavis goes on to say, is that 'real culture' (by definition agricultural) is irretrievably lost, since 'the nineteenth century . . . destroyed . . . the organic community' and the remnants survive 'in spite of the rapidly changing "means of production"'. Therefore the only recourse is to attempt to create an 'autonomous' culture; 'if there is to be a culture, it must be independent of whatever economy is in operation, and its continuity be preserved by conscious effort' (Denys Thompson, 'What Shall We Teach?', loc. cit., p. 385). And that in turn can only be done by a dedicated and sequestered élite. The unreal dilemmas created by the theory of the organic community thus convert a strikingly 'communal' cultural theory into a strikingly élitist one at a single stroke.

Left Review *and Left Literary Theory*

David Margolies

1. LITERATURE AND POLITICS IN LEFT REVIEW

The crisis of the thirties made traditional notions of literature and criticism irrelevant. It was not so much that they were 'wrong' or even decadent as that they had no relation to the overwhelming issues of the day. The notion that culture was 'above the struggle' was obviously false for the left, as it was for the *Scrutiny* movement (as Iain Wright has shown in the preceding article). In a society so fundamentally divided, even refusing to take a political position was itself a position – literature was political. This recognition of literature's political nature was the starting point of left literary theory. Writers on the left rejected the notion of literature as passive contemplation and generally saw it as an active participant in social issues. Michael Roberts in his preface to *New Country* (1933) said the novelist must choose sides (Stephen Spender, however, in 'Poetry and Revolution' in the same volume, said that poetry and politics do not mix), while other writers went further and said literature had a job to do. In the words of Dimitrov, 'Literature must serve the great revolutionary ideal of millions of workers.'[1] Literary criticism, too, was politically important, '. . . for the more we realize that these "works of imagination" are governed by social conditions', said Edgell Rickword, 'the sooner shall we change our social conditions in accordance with what our "imaginations" tell us. they could be'.[2]

Thus the recognition of literature's political role not only provided a basis for judging works of literature in the present; it also offered a perspective for examining writings of the past. But it was not just that literature was pressed into service for the period of crisis; an active and political character was eventually seen by many left critics to be part of the essential nature of literature.

Left Review was the journal of Left cultural discussion from October 1934 to May 1938. Set up to bring letters into the revolutionary struggle, it began with an explanation of the threat to letters from fascism and the crisis in capitalism, and most of its contributions dealt with such immediate questions for literature rather than directly with literary theory. Contributors had no tradition of Marxist literary

criticism to fall back on – there was no such tradition – so they made
their literary theory indirectly as they argued other issues.

The contributors to *Left Review* may have lacked the guidance of a
Marxist critical tradition, but their experiments in theory were
unrestricted by a 'line'. 'I hate capitalism,' Lewis Grassic Gibbon said;
'all my books are explicit or implicit propaganda. But because I'm a
revolutionist I see no reason for gainsaying my own critical
judgment. . . .'[3] A great diversity of literary viewpoints was expressed
under the anti-fascist umbrella. Real controversy, often hot, took place
in its pages; and, since it appeared monthly, discussion had an
immediacy quite foreign to the theoretical quarterlies of today. Thus,
for example, F. D. Klingender, explaining that revolutionary criticism
was more difficult in bourgeois society than in the Soviet Union, said:
'That is why any tendency – however deeply buried in the innermost
recesses of the subconscious – of silently assuming that a Soviet artist
"can do no wrong" is the worst possible crime';[4] and he was sharply
attacked in the next issue by Ralph Fox who called him 'Colonel Blimp-
Klingender' and suggested the best way to help him 'would be to deprive
him of pen and ink for the rest of his life'.[5] Although Fox's attack seems
to have missed the significance of Klingender's point, the principles on
which it is based are sound: Fox dismisses the argument because, he
says, Klingender wants from a work only an explicit message, a line. In
the following issue Klingender continued the argument with a highly
rational discussion of generalization and abstraction. While
controversies may not often have been settled in the pages of *Left
Review*, such continuing, genuine argument fostered exploration of
ideas rather than adherence to a fixed line.

Even though *Left Review* had no clear line, there seemed to be three
basic assumptions on which almost all critical contributions were
based. The most general was the premiss that all art is class art. That is,
art is not neutral or disinterested or above the battle. While Eric Gill
actually argued the premiss and concluded that 'all art is propaganda',[6]
most contributors took it for granted, although some also explored the
extent and significance of art's class character. Thus Edgell Rickword
says:

What bourgeois education teaches us to call the best art is, I am prepared to
agree, what has proved the most successful propaganda at some date in
history; and the most successful propaganda is, naturally, that which exemplifies or deodorizes the ideology of the ruling class

but adds that this 'does not exhaust the functions and achievements of art'.[7]

It followed logically that, if art was involved in the class struggle, art could be judged in class terms. The second assumption was that social value is the proper criterion of art. F. D. Klingender wrote:

There can be only one standard for the assessment of any ideological phenomenon, whether of the present or of the past: its relevance in terms of social reality.[8]

But there was considerable disagreement about how to employ such a criterion. It was accepted that sound politics was not sufficient to ensure good art, even though occasionally very narrow judgements were made – such as Elizabeth Coxhead's rejection of Chaplin's *Modern Times* because it 'will shake the world, but only with laughter'.[9] But there was also considerable refinement of social criteria. Edgell Rickword, reviewing C. Day Lewis's *Noah and the Waters*, accepts Day Lewis as an ally rather than a committed revolutionary because his insistence on the contemplative role of the poet confines the work 'to being one more statement of the inability of the capitalist system any longer to use its poets productively, but prevents it being a revolutionary poem'.[10] A. L. Lloyd, attacking surrealism for having no bearing on proletarian problems and as 'a particularly subtle form of fake revolution', is careful to say that surrealism is *not* fascist-leaning art.[11]

The third assumption was a corollary of social criteria, the premiss that art is active (i.e. that it *does* something, rather than being merely a passive reflection). The fact of crisis demanded action. Art was important, not because it was pure reflection, but because of its potential for serving revolution. John Lehmann said writers could be useful as writers without going outside their art.[12]

Literature should help 'to mould the young revolutionary leaders', Dimitrov said in his speech before the Soviet Writers' Association, printed in the June 1935 *Left Review*:

'Where, in our literature, are the heroes of the proletarian movement . . . Where are the examples to be imitated by millions of workers?'[13]

Others saw the usefulness of art in terms of 'directed' realism. Arthur Calder Marshall said:

'The most important function of the revolutionary novelist, to my mind, is to portray the whole scene as it is . . .'

which means doing more than presenting accounts of militancy,[14] and Charles Madge wrote:

If the novelist has any function in our age, it is to delineate the relationship of an individual to his class, on the basis of scientific materialism.

The novel that does not exercise this function, he said, is only a drug.[15] Jack Lindsay connected realism directly with class struggle, quoting a letter he received from a worker:

It is no use describing life on the dole to an unemployed man; he appreciates all this sympathy, but he wants to see the way out, to have the fundamentals of the class-struggle constantly underlined.[16]

The link between realism and usefulness was reinforced by what was often presented as a parallel between art and science. The notion of experiment and scientific accuracy informed the notion of art. In the first issue of *Left Review* Amabel Williams-Ellis presented literary technique as comparable to scientific technique and C. Day Lewis presented them as parallel, calling the poet 'the scientist of words', who also experimented and needed minute accuracy. Poetry 'discloses for us emotionally, as science does intellectually, the hidden links in nature'.[17] In the field of criticism, rather than imaginative creation, Douglas Garman praised Caudwell's *Illusion and Reality* as 'not just another essay in aesthetic appreciation. It is an attempt to give a scientific account of the origin of poetry. . . .'[18]

Most of the statements of literature's function, however, were not supported by any developed notions of what art is. As Montagu Slater pointed out, there was a notable lack of theory,[19] and Edgell Rickword attributed the 'present contemptible level of literary criticism' to 'empiricism' and 'contempt for theory'.[20] The idea of an art-science parallel, even if it was no more than a convenient method of explanation, encouraged more rigorous examination of literature. C. Day Lewis's 'Revolutionaries and Poetry' (one of the articles that drew the parallel) examined seriously the nature of literature in order to approach the question of whether poetry was of any value to the revolution. He warned against 'literary sentimentality' that would accept verse only on the basis of its revolutionary standpoint. 'Poetry was one of the chief instruments through which primitive man, by expressing his emotions, gained strength to fight against the economic conditions which gave rise to those emotions.' The same function for poetry exists in the modern world, he said; poetry helps us to feel our motives 'more keenly and get them in perspective'. But it achieves this effect, not through direct propaganda, the statement of a line; the poem must be technically competent to achieve its effect, and the first qualification of a poem is that it should be a good poem technically; the poem is essentially propaganda but it must be effective as poetry to be effective as propaganda.[21] (In the 'Postscript' to the 1936 edition of his *A Hope for Poetry* he offered the corollary, that social commitment can revitalize poetry.)

Alick West, in the same fashion, stressed the need for an understanding of the dialectical unity of form and content for successful criticism. The mode of literature is concrete, he said, and demanded that criticism take that concreteness into account. Thus in a review he criticizes one Marxist interpretation of Shakespeare because it makes Shakespeare into an abstraction and misses what is creative in the plays. If his content is separated from his poetic and dramatic form, Shakespeare's effect and value cannot be understood.[22]

Most of the literary theory advanced in *Left Review* was, of course, not up to the standard of West or Day Lewis. There were also some classically crude judgements, such as Alec Brown's 'Literary English from Caxton to us is an artificial jargon of the ruling-class; written English begins with us',[23] and a prescriptive tone, with phrases such as 'quite rightly', occurs with some frequency. But it certainly does not deserve the low reputation most left criticism of the thirties suffers four decades later.

That reputation seems to have little basis except in a few writings of left sympathizers – such as Edward Upward's 'Sketch for a Marxist Interpretation of Literature' in *The Mind in Chains* – and, in fact, writers in *Left Review* regularly attacked crude, mechanical, abstract responses to literature. Rickword, for example, wrote that Philip Henderson's *Literature* would not convince anyone who doubted it of the social character of literature; it would fail because it is all cut and dried – abstract and metaphysical – and lacking in historical perspective.[24] He criticized David Daiches' *Literature and Society* on similar lines, saying:

Mr Daiches' failure is not due just to these incidental lapses (which in a survey of seven hundred years would be excusable), but to an insufficiently concrete appreciation of the works themselves and the conditions under which they were produced.[25]

The criticism is not mere hostile dismissal; it is a constructive analysis of errors that criticism trying to be Marxist must overcome. If literature and criticism could be weapons in a revolutionary struggle, then defective weapons must be taken seriously and their inadequacies noted.

Considering that the intention of *Left Review* was cultural journalism – it never attempted to be a theoretical journal – it published a surprising quantity of excellent literary theory. Rickword, West, Day Lewis, Garman and Fox all made genuine contributions to theory in its pages. The full literary vitality of the journal can be seen in the ability of most of its contributors to distinguish almost intuitively between works that merely played on political symbols, and literature of social and aesthetic integrity. A. L. Lloyd, for example, speaks of the sad spectacle of 'politically left artists preoccupied with painting academic pictures of muscle-bound workers with a hammer and sickle appearing in the sky above them',[26] and A. L. Morton of the 'new and rather disgusting cant of sensationalising poverty and unemployment'.[27] However excellent it may be, the theory in *Left Review* appeared entirely in articles too short to allow much development. Yet, even though they were never integrated into a unified theory in the pages of the journal, they laid the foundation for the more developed theory which appeared in the books of Fox, West and Caudwell.

Nineteen thirty-seven saw the publication of Ralph Fox's *The Novel and the People*, Alick West's *Crisis and Criticism*, and Christopher Caudwell's *Illusion and Reality*, an extraordinary outpouring of Marxist literary theory at one time, and all in one way or another responding to the crisis, especially as it was reflected in literature – in the dislocation of literary values, the lack of direction of the novel or poetry, and the abdication of criticism.

2. RALPH FOX

Fox begins his work with the idea of crisis: his limited aim is to look at the English novel's present and its future prospect and 'to try to understand the crisis of ideas which has destroyed the foundation on which the novel seemed once to rest so securely'.[28] The crisis can be understood only through Marxism, and through Marxism the novel can once again be significant, says Fox. 'It is the aim of this essay to show that the future of the English novel . . . lies precisely in Marxism. . . .'[29]

Fox addresses a reader doubtful that Marxism is the appropriate philosophy for dealing with imaginative literature, and tries to convince him of the contrary, reassuring him that economic determinism is indirect and explaining at length the fundamental Marxist notion on cultural production, that social being determines consciousness. He tries to allay the reader's fears of Marxism, that it is, for example, hostile to individuality, saying it gives the fullest value to the individual but also sees him in a social context:

So that each man has, as it were, a dual history, since he is at the same time a type, a man with a social history, and an individual, a man with a personal history. The two, of course, even though they may be in glaring conflict, are also one, a unity, in so far as the latter is eventually conditioned by the former, though this does not and should not imply that in art the social type must dominate the individual personality. Falstaff, Don Quixote, Tom Jones, Julien Sorel, Monsieur de Charlus, are all types, but they are types in whom the social characteristics constantly reveal the individual, and in whom the personal hopes, hungers, loves, jealousies and ambitions in turn light up the social background.[30]

The novelist 'must understand how his final result arises from the individual conflicts of his characters' and also see the pattern of life. Marxism gives him 'the key to reality when it shows him how to discern that pattern and the place which each individual occupies in it'.[31]

Fox offers a sound background of Marxism to the reader, but it is something preliminary to literary theory rather than the theory itself. The nature of *Left Review* precluded much elaboration of theory or example in argument; Fox, writing a book, follows the same style without the apparent necessity. His insights are often suggestive – for instance, 'The essence of the creative process is the struggle between the creator and external reality, the urgent demand to master and re-create that reality'[32] – but are given no development. Thus they lose much of their value as theoretical illumination and become slogans. He is also too full of prescription, even going so far as to call for a particular novel about Dimitrov, leader of the Communist International:

Few would disagree with the view that in our time there is one example of moral grandeur and courage worthy to stand beside the greatest in our human history, the defence of Dimitrov against the Fascist court in Leipzig.[33]

Dimitrov's own similar suggestion appeared in the June 1935 *Left Review* – he said he was astonished that his Leipzig trial had not been utilized in literature.[34] Fox was himself a novelist and recognized what was probably excellent material (he points out that Dimitrov was not born a hero – 'Yet Dimitrov, the man, was forged in this very struggle which I have just described'[35]), but to prescribe it seems out of place.

Fox's critical judgement is good and his few chapters on the history of the novel say enough to be interesting and useful. He does not just categorize but characterizes each age's relation to the real world. Thus, instead of discussing *Robinson Crusoe*'s documentary significance, he is concerned with its heroic grandeur. Similarly, he makes heroes of Rabelais and Cervantes, giving very little information – nothing for the student to underline – but recreating attitude and making judgements: Rabelais and Cervantes 'were universal geniuses and no work equal in stature to theirs has since been written in that variegated prose fiction which we call the novel'.[36] His statements on the attitude of Rabelais and Cervantes make credible his directives for literature:

The revolutionary task of literature to-day is to restore its great tradition, to break the bonds of subjectivism and narrow specialization, to bring the creative writer face to face with his only important task, that of winning the knowledge of truth, of reality. Art is one of the means by which man grapples with and assimilates reality.[37]

The Novel and the People does not have much importance in terms of the objective development of theory, for its principles are not elaborated in detail or integrated into a rigorous system. But even if they cannot withstand sustained theoretical probing, Fox brings his principles to life and endows them with a significance that sound logic alone could not achieve – he makes literature's subjectivity *feel* important.

Fox's great strength, then, is that he gives an attitude to literature, rather than abstracted principles. He is a big man, comfortable in the notion that men make their own history. The great writer, regardless of his politics, says Fox, must engage in a revolutionary battle with reality, 'revolutionary because he must seek to change reality. For him, his life is always a battle of heaven and hell . . . a fight for the soul of man'.[38] He presents literature as an imaginative mastering of the world which can, in turn, if sufficiently energetic, help master the world in reality. The novel for Fox is part of man making his own history.

3. ALICK WEST

Alick West presented no unified theory, no single structure, but his theoretical statements have a richness based on a wide experience of close reading of literature. He was more obviously a practising critic than Fox or Caudwell and his conclusions are more fully argued and supported than theirs. His great strength in *Crisis and Criticism*, from which all the other virtues of his theory seem to derive, is a full sense of literature as a social phenomenon. He understood literature as social in its very essence – in deriving materials from the life of community, in employing a social medium, and in having a social use. To ignore this and treat works of literature as things separate from living society – the 'interpretation of literature in terms of isolated mental states' that he termed 'abstract criticism' – distorts their nature and lessens the reader's response, he said.[39]

West's most important contribution to left literary theory is not his specific literary conclusions but his finding a different source of value for literature. He was able to recognize the genteel bias of literary values – the understood antithesis of work and culture – and root it out of his own criticism, finding instead the source of all cultural value in labour and production. The 'value of literature,' he says in *Crisis and Criticism*, 'always consists in its organising social energy in a particular activity.'[40] Thus literature has a clear social, even economic, value.

But West goes beyond the question of ultimate value to find in work a source for literature. Work, he says, determines emotion:

... the basis of all emotion is the activity of society in keeping itself alive and changing the means of doing so; and that the basis of the emotion of each one of us is our share in that activity.[41]

Work also puts subject and object into relation:

Through the work of production the world in itself is made into a world for us; and through this work we see the world as it is in itself and in terms of our aim of making it a world for us, a human world.[42]

This 'world for us', reality seen in terms of our own desires, is the basis of our finding emotional significance in culture:

Literature shows both the natural and social world in terms of the actual and desired relation to them and of their objective reality . . . the presentation of the world as our world and as itself awakens the feeling of social energy because it is a repetition of our own activity in making the world human through work.[43]

Literature is an outgrowth of community and the social labour process, and helps to assist social progress. For West, as for Fox, literature helps men to make their own history.

This function for literature leads West to functional aesthetic criteria. All literature is part of the movement of society, he says:

But it does not follow from this that Marxist criticism only aims at discovering the economic and social forces at work in any piece of literature, while it ignores its aesthetic value. It aims at judging its aesthetic value in terms of its relation to the movement of society.[44]

Bourgeois idealist aesthetics are not the only kind. West draws a revolutionary conclusion:

the criticism of our lives, by the test of whether we are helping forward the most creative movement in our society, is the only effective foundation of the criticism of literature.[45]

While this criterion is politically generated and overstated, in essence it accords well with the coolly-reasoned, less rhetorical parts of his theory. West stresses that judgement is not made on the basis of adherence to abstract principles – the social effects of art exist only through concrete effects on individual wills and desires:

The relation of literature as art, distinguishable from other literary matter, to the social and economic development that determines all literary production, good, bad and indifferent, is through the fact that the economic basis is not an automatic machine, but living men and women, whose energy has to be organised. Good literature contributes to that organisation and to the changing of it; bad literature consumes its products, and debases them.[46]

West is not simply playing with slogans. He supports his conclusions with concrete and detailed discussion of literature, using at times works thought quite intractable to a Marxist approach, such as Eliot's poetry and Joyce's *Ulysses*. Thus West treats Joyce's style and, as well as showing the novel to be a product and reflection of his age, he can explain the kind of *effect* it has – he can see it in practical terms. And he could, then, judge the novel in the light of its effect.

West also considers at length difficult general problems that too often are avoided with abstract formulas, such as the problem of form. Again, he does not base his discussion on exceptional works peculiarly shaped to his own needs, but on a Shakespeare sonnet, and shows that form is not merely something produced mechanically by content, or something that serves merely to reflect content; through examination of actual examples he shows that it also has an effect. But the social energy that literature organizes is not aroused through form apart from content.

Form and content together excite it and direct it. The relation of form and content in literature is similar to that already noted in regard to language itself: the form of the words and sentence expresses and appeals to the previous experience of the social organism; the content of the particular act of speech indicates a particular activity; the excitement of energy is the result of both processes.[47]

Content is of prior importance in the unity, says West, because it involves the writer's response to his immediate situation, his social decisions.

The continuing, dialectical, relation of form and content is illustrated by West with reference to Shakespeare:

This, of course, does not mean that the particular decision represented by the content of Shakespeare's sonnet determines its sonnet form; but it modifies the previously existing sonnet form. And the form which Shakespeare finds ready to his hand is itself the result of an endless number of new contents slightly modifying the form in which previous contents had been embodied. In this sense, content, the particular action, determines form, the result of previous action.[48]

Clearly West did not arrive at final answers in regard to the problem of form and content (though he continued to write and to define the questions until his death thirty-five years after he wrote these lines – see *A Good Man Fallen among Fabians*, *The Mountain in the Sunlight*, and the previously unpublished essay on D. H. Lawrence in the 1975 reissue of *Crisis and Criticism*). What he did achieve was to locate within a Marxist framework a problem that has always proved very difficult for Marxist critics, and he was able to do this through taking seriously, and exploring in detail, the understanding that literature is social and active.

4. CHRISTOPHER CAUDWELL

Christopher Caudwell was the most important, and is today the most widely known, left literary theorist of the thirties. His *Studies in a Dying Culture* (1938) combined the cultural sweep of West with the revolutionary ardour of Fox, while *Illusion and Reality* was the only lengthy work directly to elaborate a theory of literature.

Caudwell had no formal connection with literary tradition – he had not been to university and had in fact left school before he was fifteen. Killed in Spain at twenty-nine, he experienced his entire development as a Marxist during the period of crisis and it could be said that his attitude to literature was shaped by social struggle. A sense of crisis, of excitement and struggle, pervades all his writing.

Caudwell has the freshness of discovery, which often gives to his prose a thrilling quality and makes everything he says seem momentous; whereas West, older and seeing in longer perspective, could make points as significant as Caudwell's (sometimes even the same points) that seemed in his scholarly, well-balanced, mature prose quite unremarkable. West was seldom carried away by his own argument and probably made fewer errors than Caudwell, but his judgements never came together in a unified theory of literature. Caudwell, with enormous energy, forged from diverse concepts a single theory that covers all cultural production. Certainly it contains many weaknesses and is muddy, incomplete, sometimes even juvenile; but it has the strength of a whole theory and the excitement of seeing all human endeavour in a single vision. It seems to provide the reader with not just an intellectual understanding, but a complete orientation in a crisis-torn world. It offers the same challenge of men making their own history that marks Fox's work, and at the same time a durable theory for analysing cultural productions.

Caudwell's perspective in *Studies* is revolutionary but his narrow consideration of political effect leads sometimes to superficial judgements. Thus, while his essay on D. H. Lawrence offers some brilliant insights into Lawrence's work and the role of the artist, his conclusions are far too narrow: 'But it is Lawrence's final tragedy that his solution was ultimately Fascist and not Communist.'[49] Similarly, his essay on Freud reveals with striking clarity how Freud's mythology embodies the basic illusions of bourgeois consciousness and, although he presents Freud reasonably as an outstanding pioneer in an as-yet-primitive science, he can also say:

By a strange irony, Freud becomes the apologist of the Fascist philosophy which rejects him, which burns his books, and seems repugnant to him. Yet this is the irony of all bourgeois culture, that because it is based on a contradiction, it gives rise to the opposite of what it desires. It desires freedom and individual expression, but, because it believes freedom is to be found in abolition of social organisation, it gives rise to all the tyrannies and blind crippling necessities of the modern world. Freudism, attempting to cure civilisation of its instinctive distortions, points the way to Nazism.[50]

Illusion and Reality has the same revolutionary vigour but it also has more balance. Douglas Garman, in *Left Review*, wrote that it is 'specifically revolutionary' because of the way Caudwell apprehended Marxism, 'firstly as an essentially dynamic view of life, capable not only of explaining but of changing it; and secondly, as a consistent method, applicable to all functions of living, all modes of knowledge'.[51] It has the important addition of serious consideration of how literature achieves its effects, fusing a revolutionary view of the world with a grasp of literature as a specific kind of activity, and this is the basis of Caudwell's theoretical achievement.

Central to Caudwell's revolutionary thinking was Marx's Eleventh Thesis on Feuerbach – 'The philosophers have *interpreted* the world in various ways; the point however is to *change* it' – which summed up the whole of his theory and offered him a functional view of cultural products. All man's activity, he said, not just revolutionary activity, is directed to changing the world. He changes the world to make it better accord with his desires:

The conflict between man's instincts and environmental reality is precisely what life is, and all the products of society – hats, art, science, houses, sport, ethics and political organization – are adaptations evolved to moderate and cure that conflict.[52]

Literature is simply one part of this process. Caudwell has taken the demand that literature do something in the crisis situation and generalized it: the *essential* nature of all literature is to do something.

In saying what literature does Caudwell seems to draw heavily on C. Day Lewis's 'Revolutionaries and Poetry' in the July 1935 *Left Review*, using his idea of the parallel between science and poetry and building from his explanation of poetry's function in regard to the economics of primitive life. Men are not instinctively economic, Caudwell says, and therefore:

It is necessary to harness man's instincts to the mill of labour, to collect his emotions and direct them into the useful, the economic channel.[53]

Poetry is such an instrument, creating a collective spirit and an ordering of social values.

Literature in the modern world also fulfills its function through a reorganization of values. It offers a projection of values onto reality, a picture of reality distorted in its objectivity in order that it may be more true subjectively – what Caudwell means by 'illusion'. The values of the 'illusion' remain with us in reality and thus motivate us to change reality to accommodate the illusion. Literature, then, like science, is a guide to action – science by showing us how to get what we want; literature by telling us what it is that we want.

As art tells us the significance and meaning of all we are in the language of feeling, so science tells us the significance of all we see in the language of cognition.[54]

Literature is an emotional guide to action; not providing information merely, nor serving passively as a signpost, but moving us in relation to reality and, through changing our emotional organization, changing the world.

Caudwell's theory of the function of literature has also the importance of providing a theoretical justification for judging literature in relation to reality. Both West and Fox were eloquent in saying that criticism of our lives is the only basis for criticism for literature, but it was an emotional, rather than a logical, conclusion of their arguments.

Elaborating on Marx's Eleventh Thesis on Feuerbach, Caudwell says that the purpose of all man's activity is to increase his freedom. Art and science are social products 'and the social product whether material or ideological can have only one goal, that of freedom. It is freedom that man seeks in his struggle with Nature.'[55] Literature functions as a guide to action in that context, and thus it is good or bad as it guides us toward or away from greater freedom. The criterion cannot be applied directly – judgement based on the explicit politics in a work disregards the complexity of the literary experience – and Caudwell does not show how to apply it through detailed criticism such as West practised. His achievement, however, is of enormous theoretical importance: he shows that the demand that literature serve social progress is not an extra-literary, political criterion imposed in time of crisis, but is fundamental to the essential nature of literature.

The immediate pressure on the critical practice of the thirties is often used to excuse its crudities. There was in fact remarkably little crudeness but, more important, the pressure may have been responsible for the achievement. It was not distant scholarship that produced the excellences of left literary theory, but the demand for something practical, for a literature that would be active in a world of conflict, and a theory that could link art and struggle. Crisis produced revolutionary thinking in literary theory – the rejection of the view of literature as passive decoration for a view of it as active.

For the Marxist [wrote Edgell Rickword], culture is not a mass of works of art, of philosophical ideas, of political concepts accumulated at the top of the social pyramid by specially-gifted individuals, but the inherited solution of problems of vital importance to society.[56]

It was understood that although literature was not practice, neither was it passive reflection. Viewed in the dialectical interaction of theory and practice, it was seen as a guide to practice; and thus literature, too, could change the world.

NOTES

1. *Left Review*, vol. I, no. 9, p. 346; 2. II, 9, p. 418; 3. I, 5, p. 180; 4. II, 1, p. 39; 5. II, 2, p. 81; 6. I, 9, p. 342; 7. I, 2, p. 45; 8. II, 1, p. 40; 9. II, 6, p. 274; 10. II, 7, p. 340; 11. II, 16, pp. 897–8; 12. II, 16, p. 883; 13. I, 9, 345; 14. II, 16, p. 876; 15. III, 3, p. 183; 16. III, 3, p. 179; 17. I, 10, pp. 400, 397; 18. III, 6, p. 352; 19. I, 9, p. 364; 20. I, 11, p. 479; 21. I, 10, pp. 399, 401, 397, 399; 22. II, 16, pp. 906–9; 23. I, 3, p. 77; 24. II, 1, p. 41; 25. III, 14, p. 890; 26. II, 16, p. 896; 27. II, 13, p. 721.

28. Ralph Fox, *The Novel and the People* (Lawrence and Wishart, 1937; reprinted 1944 and 1948; paperback reprint 1979), p. 19 (page references to 1979 edn).

29. ibid., p. 26.

30. ibid., p. 34.

31. loc. cit.

32. ibid., p. 28.

33. ibid., p. 121.

34. *Left Review*, I, 9, 344.

35. Fox, op. cit., p. 121.

36. ibid., p. 56.

37. ibid., p. 37.

38. ibid., p. 38.

39. Alick West, 'On Abstract Criticism' in *5 on revolutionary art*, ed. Betty Rea, Lawrence and Wishart, 1935, pp. 81, 85–6.

40. Alick West, *Crisis and Criticism* (Lawrence and Wishart, 1937; reprinted, minus one chapter, in *Crisis and Criticism and Selected Literary Essays* (Lawrence and Wishart, 1975), p. 85.

41. ibid., p. 64.

42. ibid., pp. 85–6.

43. ibid., p. 88.

44. ibid., p. 75.

45. ibid., p. 102.

46. ibid., p. 99.

47. ibid., p. 98.

48. loc. cit.

49. Christopher Caudwell, 'D. H. Lawrence: A Study of the Bourgeois Artist', in *Studies in a Dying Culture* (Bodley Head, 1938; reprinted in Christopher Caudwell, *The Concept of Freedom*, Lawrence and Wishart, 1977), p. 19.

50. 'Freud: A Study in Bourgeois Psychology', ibid., p. 125.
51. *Left Review*, III, 6, p. 352.
52. Caudwell, *Illusion and Reality. A Study of the Sources of Poetry* (Macmillan, 1937; paperback reprint, Lawrence and Wishart, 1973), p. 187.
53. ibid., p. 35.
54. ibid., p. 241.
55. ibid., p. 173.
56. Edgell Rickword, 'Culture, Progress and English Tradition', in C. Day Lewis (ed.), *The Mind in Chains. Socialism and the Cultural Revolution* (Frederick Muller, 1937), p. 254.

W. H. Auden: Poetry and Politics in the Thirties

ARNOLD KETTLE

Since this is by no means an exhaustive or 'authoritative' essay, I had better start by mentioning the limits of what I want to say in this piece, which is chiefly about Auden and the young middle-class poets who were involved in left politics and the anti-fascist movement of the thirties. I am not interested in claiming that they were or ought to have been more or less 'political' than they actually were. I am not much interested in assessing precisely how 'Marxist' Auden or his poems were. Nor am I concerned to propose some impregnable general 'theory' about the relation of poetry and politics. I *am* interested in considering what can be learned from the experiences of the thirties (for better and worse) about the ways in which writers can become more involved in the needs and struggles and issues of their time, the time of the transformation of a basically bourgeois society into a basically socialist one, and how the socialist movement can profit from the insights and experiences of writers who use language in a creative way because their perceptions penetrate to truly important aspects of reality.

The case *against* the young middle-class poets of the thirties, made with varying emphases but considerable regularity over the subsequent decades, is, essentially, a political case emerging from the Cold War and the brainwashing which was one of its aspects. This is not to say that none of the hostile criticism has anything in it. But the cold-war element is so powerful that unless the literary critic is conscious of it from the start he stands little chance of coming up with a reasonably objective assesssment of the literature of the period.

It is now quite the thing, for instance, to quote Auden's description of the thirties (from the poem 'September 1, 1939')[1] as 'a low dishonest decade', as though it referred indiscriminately to left and right and to see his withdrawal from political commitment in simple terms of 'disillusionment'. It is not nearly so simple as that. 'September 1, 1939', which begins:

> I sit in one of the dives
> On Fifty-Second Street
> Uncertain and afraid
> As the clever hopes expire
> Of a low dishonest decade . . .

is indeed a kind of farewell, not just to the thirties but to the English Auden. And no doubt among the clever hopes and dishonesties evoked are errors and sillinesses and deceptions of the left in general and of Auden and his friends in particular.* The poem does indeed mirror the poet's own movement from a more generous commitment to popular causes to the flickering affirmation of one who sees himself as an ironic point of light in a doomed world. But the general tone and burden is not anti-left or indeed anti-political at all. The 'love' which is a keyword is not clearly or primarily a socio-political concept, but neither is it an alternative to politics. To read the poem as though it chronicled the escape of Auden from the spider's web of left-wing politics, with Stalin as the spider, is, simply, to misread it.

When Auden wrote (of New York):

> Into this neutral air
> Where blind skyscrapers use
> Their full height to proclaim
> The strength of Collective Man,
> Each language pours its vain
> Competitive excuse . . .

he had certainly not entirely forgotten or rejected what he had learned from Marxism. And the final lines of the same stanza:

> Out of the mirror they stare,
> Imperialism's face
> And the international wrong.

may not be the last word either in poetry or political analysis; but they are not the words of a writer overcome by revulsion against the horror of Left-Book-Club politics.

Of course the situation is complicated by the fact that the later Auden himself not merely connived at but went out of his way to encourage such misreading of his earlier poems, this one in particular.

---

* Including the kind of thing referred to in the lines beginning 'Our hopes were still set on the spies' career' which Auden himself expressed in 'August for the people . . .', a poem of 1935 dedicated to Christopher Isherwood.

By pretending that the words 'we must love one another or die' were rubbish (because we will die anyway) and revising the poem in ways that shatter its coherence, he paid his own peculiar grotesque tribute to the potency of cold-war attitudes. But fortunately the poems had already appeared and are irrevocably a part of the thirties, as the editor of *The English Auden* very sensibly and properly recognizes.

I have started with 'September 1, 1939' not because it is one of his best poems but because, while full of moving resonances for the reader steeped in Auden's poetry, it is also a good point for the new reader to come in at, with its simple relaxed diction, its relatively straightforward allusions (you have to connect Hitler with Linz), and its clear historical context. Written a few months after Auden and Isherwood had decided to settle in America it is rightly included by Edward Mendelson in his *English Auden* volume, for it is indeed a kind of 'Envoi' and Auden's own later mutilations of his poems can only underline the nature of the crisis he and his generation faced.

The mutilations also raise the complex yet necessary question as to how far any of Auden's poems (some would say the poems of anyone) can be treated as directly autobiographical anyway. I have referred to 'September 1, 1939' as though the 'speaker' of the poem were, necessarily and simply, the poet himself. But obviously it isn't quite like that. Many of Auden's poems are more like dramatic monologues, spoken by a 'persona' who isn't necessarily to be identified with the poet himself, any more than you can identify Macbeth with Shakespeare. Some of them have strong elements of parody in them. 'Brothers, who when the sirens roar,' sometimes entitled 'A Communist to Others', is one such; and indeed it is always naïve, not to say dangerous, to assume that any sentiment or opinion in the poems is the author's own, just like that.

Yet it is equally naïve to treat the poems, or Auden's revisions of them, as though they wrote themselves or operated on the basis of some pure, autonomous aesthetic principle. In *some* sense, even if it's often an elusive and deliberately cagey one, they 'reflect' his own journeys and choices. History and ideology get into them all.

'September 1, 1939' can be read, quite properly, as a vital step in Auden's movement away from political poetry. But, again, it is not a simple story. Auden and Isherwood went to America not just because they were disillusioned with European politics (though, of course, like everyone else they were depressed and fearful about the advances of fascism and the growing likelihood of a new world war). They also went to America for personal reasons connected with their search for satisfactory homosexual relationships. Isherwood has made this quite clear in the last pages of *Christopher and His Kind*[2] and when Auden explained to his friend, Professor E. R. Dodds, in a letter (dated 11 March 1940, and made public in the 'Young Writers of the Thirties' exhibition at the National Portrait Gallery in London in 1976) why he stayed in America, he did not mention politics but wrote: 'For the first time I have a happy personal life.'

In emphasizing this point I do not want to play down the importance of political events like the defeat in Spain, the Moscow purges and the Soviet-German Non-Aggression Pact of 1939 in striking at the hopes and self-confidence of the British left of the thirties. Nor, of course, do I want to gloss over the failure of the left to build a movement strong enough to defeat fascism without a second world war and all that involved. But to see this failure and the collapse of the left – including left poetry – after 1939 primarily in terms of the wickednesses of the international communist movement and 'disillusionment' with the Soviet Union (communism as the God that failed) strikes me as hopelessly superficial and inadequate and is precisely what I mean by cold-war brainwashing.

The gains of the thirties – including the appearance of a body of poetry more wide-ranging, democratically relevant and humanly progressive than the bulk of British twentieth-century poetic production – were not in some total sense negated either by weaknesses within them or by the Cold War that followed them. On the contrary, the experience of the thirties – including the Seventh World Congress, the forging of weapons of corporeal and mental fight against fascism, the poetry of W. H. Auden – was an important contribution to all the gains made since. It was presumably because he realized this that Auden, when he became positively anti-political, spent so much of his time revising the poems he thought the most politically effective. An interesting point here is how generally and poetically disastrous the revisions were. I do not see how any reasonably objective assessment of his revision of, for example, 'Now the leaves are falling fast' (not a particularly 'political' poem at all) could prefer the revision to the original. And I can only draw the conclusion that the position of the later Auden involved an all-round retreat.

Though the British left in the thirties was undoubtedly very ignorant, sometimes in a dangerously self-induced way, about what the Soviet Union was really like, it is also true that blind faith in the Soviet Union was never the principal basis on which the Communist Party – let alone the left movement as a whole – built its campaigns, its thinking and its hopes. That there was a powerful element of 'the Soviet Union right or wrong' in communist thinking it would be idle to deny; but this certainly wasn't the principal motive-force of the move to the left of millions of people, including the young writers. The Soviet Union or hopes about it entered very little into the poetry of the period. The shock and fear of fascism, contempt for the British ruling class, a sense of solidarity with people battling against poverty and exploitation, were far more basic ingredients. The Soviet Union was, it is true, seen sympathetically and hopefully by most people who became involved in the left movement. And there was good reason for this. It was the *only* part of the world not dominated by the drives and needs of the capitalist system; it was a struggling socialist country (not regarded by anybody as a 'great power') which had resisted the attempts of the surrounding powers to smash its revolution; and it had the only government consistently trying to achieve collective resistance to fascist aggression. The principal role of the Soviet Union in much left thinking in the thirties was therefore as a kind of 'opposite' – the opposite of capitalism and of fascism whose very existence proclaimed the possibility of a different and better way. Of course such an attitude did, and was probably bound to, involve a good deal of self-deception and utopianism: but it was nothing like as unrealistic, or unhelpful, as the outlook which saw 'Communism', embodied in the Soviet Union, as the enemy and blinded people to what was going on, not in another very different and complex part of the world, but under their noses.

The left-wing poets of the thirties were primarily interested neither in the Soviet Union nor in Communism in the abstract but in the problem of making sense of their own dilemmas and of the society and the world into which they had been born. It was the First World War, its consequences and, above all, its *meaning*, that lay behind their lives and consciousness. The differences between the Britain of 1907, when W. H. Auden was born, and that of 1931, when he was twenty-four, were so great that no one could be unaware that he or she was living through some sort of deep social and political crisis: yet at the same time, because there had been no invasion, no occupation, and 'victory' rather than 'defeat', it was surprisingly easy to pretend that nothing much (except the slaughter, softened into the word 'sacrifice') had really happened. The Empire remained, the City of London remained, the General Strike failed, only the Liberal Party seemed to have taken an irrevocable knock. The death of liberal England was something that writers, especially the middle-class writers with their traditional education and most of their traditional privileges intact, had to discover. They discovered it in their poetry.

> Our hunting fathers told the story
>   Of the sadness of the creatures,
> Pitied the limits and the lack
>   Set in their finished features;
> Saw in the lion's intolerant look,
> Behind the quarry's dying glare,
> Love raging for the personal glory
>   That reason's gift would add,
> The liberal appetite and power,
>   The rightness of a god.
>
> Who nurtured in that fine tradition
>   Predicted the result,
> Guessed love by nature suited to
>   The intricate ways of guilt?
> That human ligaments could so
> His southern gestures modify,
> And make it his mature ambition
>   To think no thought but ours,
> To hunger, work illegally,
>   And be anonymous?

Auden's poem,[3] written in 1934, is one such exploration into the strange death of liberal England. It opens with an evocation of imperialism – images of big-game hunting and the individualist ethic – and finishes with a quotation from Lenin. It does much more than that of course, playing on words like 'hunting', 'finished', 'intolerant' and 'liberal' with a marvellous sense both of their ambiguities and their historical and anthropological dimensions. I can think of few short poems of the post-1945 period (Ted Hughes' 'Pike' would be one) with so much that is stimulating and imaginative to say about the changing condition of England.

Auden's poem doesn't merely offer us an apprehension of the contradictions involved in the exposure and overturning of the liberal tradition; it does so with a peculiar note and energy characteristic of the best poetry of the thirties and in marked contrast to the note which T. S. Eliot, in *his* exploration of the death of liberal England, had sounded in the twenties. To Auden and his friends Eliot's poetry had indeed been a

kind of revelation (C. Day Lewis in his essay *A Hope for Poetry* saw
Hopkins, Eliot and Wilfred Owen as the main immediate poetic
ancestors of the left poets). But in the later twenties and thirties Auden
moved left while Eliot, reacting to the same crisis in a different way,
went steadily to the right.

Eliot shared with the left poets a sense of the inadequacies of
bourgeois-democratic society. In 1932 he was writing

The present system does not work properly, and more and more people are
inclined to believe that it never did and that it never will: it is obviously neither
scientific nor religious. It is imperfectly adapted to any purpose except that of
making money; and even for money-making it does not work very well. . . .[4]

But when it came to the consideration of an alternative, not only his
general idealist mode of thinking but some pretty crude class prejudices
prevented any sort of sympathy with any move in the direction of a
more democratic, let alone socialist, society. Though proclaiming
himself 'interested in political ideas, but not in politics', Eliot didn't
hesitate to express himself – in the *Criterion* or in critical work like *After
Strange Gods* – on political issues. In 1930 he was regretting that 'the
one most rational form of representation in the House of Commons, the
representation of the Universities, is, if the Labour Party has its way, to
be abolished'.[5] 'The *great* danger,' he wrote in April 1937, 'seems to me
to be the delusion of the Popular Front', and in October 1938 he was
still taking occasion (in the *Criterion*) to pour scorn on 'irresponsible
anti-fascists' and specifically on 'the heirs of liberalism who find an
emotional outlet in denouncing the iniquity of something called
"fascism" '.[6] Well, no one is going to claim that all the anti-fascists of
the thirties were always wise and responsible; but one doesn't have to
have very exalted standards of political judgment to question whether, a
month after Munich, six months before Franco's victory in Spain and a
year before Hitler's invasion of Poland, anti-fascism of any sort was
among the more irresponsible political attitudes of the day.

'I should think better of Communism', Eliot had written in 1932, 'if I
learned that there existed in Russia a decent leisure class.' He was
saddened by the idea of being able to afford only one 'very hardworking'
servant and felt it would be far more desirable 'to employ a large staff of
servants, each doing much lighter work but profiting by the benefits of
the cultured and devout atmosphere of the home in which they lived.'[7]
The use of the word 'home' in this last context seems an odd one for a
person not normally insensitive in his dealings with language.

One might dismiss such sentiments, perhaps, as mere unrealistic eccentricities, like Winston Churchill announcing in 1945 that he had not won the war in order to preside over the dismantling of the British Empire; but I don't think it is reasonable to let the right off as lightly as that. Churchill was not able to prevent the dismantling of the Empire; but he was able at Fulton to add his contribution to the Cold War, which is still with us. And in *After Strange Gods*, published in the year of Auden's 'Our hunting fathers' and *after* Hitler had come to power, Eliot could write, of the society he desired,

The population should be homogeneous . . . What is still more important is unity of religious background; and reasons of race and religion combine to make any large numbers of free-thinking Jews undesirable. There must be a proper balance between urban and rural, industrial and agricultural development. And a spirit of excessive tolerance is to be deprecated.[8]

I bring in Eliot partly to make the point in passing that those who have subsequently felt that the left-wingers of the thirties should show adequate remorse for their political gullibility in those days don't generally seem to have felt that *his* political stance required much remorse; but, more importantly, to try to get the role of the left poets in the thirties into historical perspective. For Eliot, one of their masters, had now become one of the influences they reacted against.

The first thing nowadays everyone says about Auden and Spender and MacNeice and the others is how very middle-class they all were. And of course it's true. They came from comfortable, cultivated professional middle-class families and the cultivation was of the Oxbridge kind with all that implies in elitism, intellectual snobbery and privilege. Also language. Auden's 'Our hunting fathers' is an example. It is a politically radical poem saying more in a few lines about the slogan 'Forward from Liberalism' than Stephen Spender could manage in a whole book or T. S. Eliot could bring himself to face at all. But the *mode*, the language, is pure Oxbridge. Take the adjective 'southern' in the middle of the second stanza. I think it is a brilliantly effective word, managing to combine a whole number of references and suggestions including Keats' beaker full of the warm south, Eliot's line from *The Waste Land* ('I read, much of the night, and go south in the winter'), and the whole tropical way of life of the white colonialists (from topees and tiffin to 'mopping-up operations' on the frontier, and the stiff upper-lip when Rhodes meets Livingstone). But no one could pretend that the culture behind that word 'southern' had anything 'popular' about it. This raises a problem. One of the recurring obsessions of many of the left poets was their unresolved doubt as to whether they ought really to be poets or politicians. Their books and letters are full of self-doubt. Spender writes a letter to Day Lewis (November 1938): 'You seem to assume that, given the present situation, the only thing a poet can do is to merge himself in the working-class movement, completely.'[9] Edward Upward's autobiographical novels hinge almost entirely on the *choice* he felt he must make between being a poet and being politically responsible.

It is a rather strange situation. Here were poets who wanted to be radical, felt deeply that capitalist society was rotten, but could only reach a certain point in their sense of political commitment, partly at least because they couldn't quite resolve the problem of writing poetry which they could feel was really poetry, yet progressive. Because taking part in the 'struggle' seemed to involve abjuring the only sort of poetry they could conceive of, they often felt themselves trapped by a false choice. It is rather as though they had taken aboard Wilfred Owen's statement: 'All a poet can do today is warn,' and added, 'but not by writing poetry.'

Some of the responsibility for the difficulties the poets found in reconciling their vocation with their politics must no doubt rest with the Marxist left, including its most serious and effective organization, the Communist Party. Philistinism is a persistent and difficult problem in the British labour movement. And there was also undoubtedly a tendency (not discouraged by Soviet example) to oversimplify the relation between literature and politics and to want poetry to be 'political' in a rather narrow 'tactical' or propagandist way, which was not much help to artists who needed to develop their *art* as well as (indeed as part and parcel of) their political understanding.

But it won't do to blame the whole business on sectarian attitudes within the Communist Party or the weaknesses of the Marxist literary criticism of the day. As a matter of fact most of the critical pages of *Left Review*, which it is now fashionable to dismiss as 'Stalinist', compare favourably with much of the left literary criticism of the seventies.

The problems of the Spenders and Upwards were at least partly due to their own extremely naïve view as to what 'poetry' or 'being a poet' involved, a naïveté which (one can see now as one looks back on it) fed about equally on neo-romantic and modernist views on literature, and emerged in their rather self-centred personal perspectives and their essentially purist conception of the poet's role.

The poets of the thirties whose work has stood up best seem to me to be those who plumped hard (at this stage of their careers) for an 'impure' poetry of a very open kind.

Louis MacNeice's essay on *Modern Poetry*, first published in 1938, is a case in point. It is a survey of contemporary poetry – his own and other people's – and is a plea for '*impure* poetry, that is, for poetry conditioned by the poet's life and the world around him'.[10] Starting from the point 'poets today are working back from luxury-writing and trying once more to be functional' MacNeice wrote:

I consider that the poet is a blend of the entertainer and the critic and the informer; he is not a legislator, however unacknowledged, nor yet, essentially, a prophet. . . .

The poet, he argues, is 'in a sense man at his most self-conscious, but this means consciousness of himself as man, not consciousness of himself as poet'. And he goes on to suggest that poets, for more than a hundred years, have been suffering from the wrong kind of self-consciousness;

They have felt that their expressed attitude to the world must be peculiarly the attitude of *poets*, that therefore much of the world was unfit subject for poetry because it was itself unpoetic.[11]

I am less concerned to discuss the 'correctness' of MacNeice's position than its significance as a breakthrough to a more 'open' view of poetry with democratic and progressive implications. Its implications in MacNeice's own work can best be seen in *Autumn Journal* but is also behind such a poem as 'The Sunlight on the Garden' (1938), a lyrical poem which I quote because it expresses so well – and so objectively – the *political* situation in which T. S. Eliot could think of nothing better to lament than the irresponsibility of anti-fascists.

> The sunlight on the garden
> Hardens and grows cold,
> We cannot cage the minute
> Within its nets of gold,
> When all is told
> We cannot beg for pardon.

Our freedom as free lances
Advances towards its end;
The earth compels, upon it
Sonnets and birds descend;
And soon, my friend,
We shall have no time for dances.

The sky was good for flying
Defying the church bells
And every evil iron
Siren and what it tells:
The earth compels,
We are dying, Egypt, dying

And not expecting pardon,
Hardened in heart anew,
But glad to have sat under
Thunder and rain with you,
And grateful too
For sunlight on the garden.

MacNeice's sense that poetry must work its way back from luxury-writing and become more 'functional' is a sort of echo of Hugh MacDiarmid's plea, in the *Second Hymn to Lenin* (1935),[13] that

Poetry like politics maun cut
The cackle and pursue real ends.

What MacDiarmid is saying is not that poetry can or ought to be replaced by sloganizing (he has already brought Burke and Joyce and Paul Morand into his argument). He takes his stand on behalf of 'a poetry of erudition, expertise, and ecstasy' and argues that what is involved is 'a many-sided active delight in the wholeness of things'. Auden – less directly politically committed than MacDiarmid – has his own version of the same need expressed, not inappropriately, in his 'Letter to Lord Byron':

I want a form that's large enough to swim in,
     And talk on any subject that I choose,
From natural scenery to men and women,
     Myself, the arts, the European news . . .

What Auden did supremely well in his early poetry was to explore and speculate on the condition of Britain in the period between the wars. One of the characteristics of this poetry is that it has at the same time a very individual, idiosyncratic sometimes private flavour (which at its least successful depends on a certain cliquishness and on 'in' jokes) and is yet preoccupied with general, public, impersonal yet central factors and ideas. His lyrics are as intellectually subtle and sometimes as intellectually challenging as his more obviously argumentative poetry. It has been well pointed out that what allows him to be 'unselfconsciously personal' is 'his awareness of being the spokesman for, or representative of, many people'.[15] His almost constant use of a 'persona' is a device which allows him to dramatize situations without depersonalizing them or adopting the rather heavy, hectoring tone which poetry concerned with public issues can easily fall into.

He had an extremely sharp instinct for significant trends and for contemporary atmosphere and he was interested in everything. If psychology was his major preoccupation, to emphasize this can easily give a false impression, partly because it wasn't just Freud but a wider selection of 'healers' (Lawrence, Blake, and Homer Lane) whom he drew on, partly because there was so much else that interested him: many aspects of science and scientific theory, history and anthropology, music, religion and philosophy and of course – supremely – literature. What he had to say was not always true but it was always intelligent and stimulating and very seldom sentimental. So that his poetry at its best had the effect of opening up the modern world rather than leading the reader inwards into his personal obsessions and limitations. Although clearly a very unusual and quirky man, he managed on the whole, as a poet, to see himself objectively and humorously.

Auden's involvement in political struggle during the thirties, though it never brought him to a theoretical position which Marxists would be likely to consider very satisfactory, seems to me to have been an altogether positive factor in his development as a poet for several reasons. In the first place, it led him to explore continuously the connections between his private or purely personal experience and the public, historical developments of the time. In the second, it encouraged him to find out what he had in common with other people and to see himself as a part of a social situation, not merely as one lonely man, uncertain and afraid. In the third place it helped him, at least for a time, towards a view of language and indeed of poetry itself which was fruitful precisely because it was outward-turning and socially orientated.

Now it is true that by the end of the thirties Auden was denying the active, social role of poetry:

> Art is not life and cannot be
> A midwife of society (1939)[16]

and

> For poetry makes nothing happen; it survives
> In the valley of its saying where executives
> would never want to tamper;
> . . . it survives
> A way of happening, a mouth (1940)[17]

But a few years earlier he had written

> No artist, however 'pure', is disinterested[18]

and

> You cannot tell people what to do, you can only tell them parables; and that is
> what art really is, particular stories of particular people and experience, from
> which each according to his own immediate and peculiar needs may draw his
> own conclusions.[19]

This last statement is a rejection of poetry as propaganda; but it is an acceptance of the political role of the poet and of the fact that poetry can and does make something happen. And it was during the period in which he held this view that his strongest and most political poetry was written.

For a poet to think of himself as a 'mouth' or 'voice' is fair enough. Saying things is what he is good at. It is when the voice becomes abstracted from changing reality that the trouble starts. It is then that it is likely to begin talking, as Auden in his later years did more and more, about the poet's duty or responsibility being to 'the language', rather than to something impure like human need. This is what purism involves: the treatment of 'language' or 'poetry' or 'art' as though they had some unchanging purity of their own, some autonomy like that of the celestial voice which crops up at critical moments in Italian opera, though always in practice in a specific human context. Celestial voices are all right as long as everyone agrees (even if they don't quite say so) that they are just another convention to help get past difficult moments. But when the poet *really* thinks his duty is to the Language or to Poetry, what actually happens is that he capitulates to conceptions of language and poetry that the ideologists of those with power have found suitable to their deeper purposes.

Auden had been enormously influenced by his experiences in

Germany in the late twenties and early thirties. On one level what attracted him to Berlin was no doubt the discovery of a homosexual underworld of working-class bars, unemployed young men, experimental psychiatrists and a variety of Wandervögel of several nationalities. But what he also learned in the Weimar Republic was the necessity of politics, the possibility of human solidarity, the nature of the Nazi movement, the corruption of bourgeois democracy and the potency of expressionist and radical art, particularly in the cinema and the political and satirical cabarets.

> Easily, my dear, you move, easily your head
> And easily as through the leaves of a photograph album I'm led
> Through the night's delights and the day's impressions,
> Past the tall tenements and the trees in the wood;
> Though sombre the sixteen skies of Europe
>   And the Danube flood.

The poem[20] which begins this way was written towards the end of 1934. It is in one sense a highly personal, even private, one, partly because the head is almost certainly a boy's head (although the poem was called 'A Bride in the Thirties' when published in *The Listener*) and seems to link with other love poems like 'Lay your sleeping head, my love'; but also in the sense that the trees in the wood are also symbols of 'false attitudes of love', linking, through other poems of the same period, with the wood in which the babes are lost in the fairy story, the dangerous forest of the Freudian unconscious, the wood of the peat-bog soldiers in the Nazi concentration camps and the crosses in the war cemeteries spread out beneath the skies of Europe. Purists may object to such cross-references between different poems (they are nearly as common in Auden as in Yeats), but I do not see why it should be felt to be essential that each poem should stand entirely on its own − something which doesn't in practice ever happen anyway.

This poem of Auden's (and it is typical of a whole number of his poems of the period) goes on, using the resources we often associate with film techniques:

> Ten thousand of the desperate marching by
> Five feet, six feet, seven feet high;
> Hitler and Mussolini in their wooing poses
> Churchill acknowledging the voters' greeting
> Roosevelt at the microphone, Van der Lubbe laughing
>   And our first meeting.

> But love, except at our proposal,
> Will do no trick at his disposal;
> Without opinions of his own, performs
> The programme that we think of merit,
> And through our private stuff must work
>   His public spirit.

I don't know whether such quotations can quite convey the energy or originality of Auden's verse. What he is saying – that the private is entwined with the public life, that our conceptions of love and its possibilities are themselves determined by the sort of society we live in and our attitudes to it – is not of course in itself profoundly original; but I do not think any previous English poet had made so vigorous an attempt to write poetry that absorbed and coped with the relation of the mass media to the nature and quality of our perceptions and assumptions.

'Spain 1937'[21] was one of the poems Auden himself was to mutilate most drastically. It is also – partly for this very reason – a poem one has to return to in any attempt to define or assess the nature of Auden's political poetry. Why did he come to dislike it quite so much? It is not in any crude sense a propaganda poem exhorting the already converted to support a clearly-defined cause. It centres around the importance of choice, and Spain becomes the moment of choice for reasons which, embodied as they are in a series of disparate images, are – purposely one feels – not easy to disentangle or fix priorities to.

> On that arid square, that fragment nipped off from hot
> Africa, soldered so crudely to inventive Europe;
>   On that tableland scored by rivers,
> Our thoughts have bodies; the menacing shapes of our fever
>
> Are precise and alive. For the fears which made us respond
> To the medicine ad, and the brochure of winter cruises
>   Have become invading battalions;
> And our faces, the institute-face, the chain-store, the ruin
>
> Are projecting their greed as the firing squad and the bomb.
> Madrid is the heart. Our moments of tenderness blossom
>   As the ambulance and the sandbag;
> Our hours of friendship into a people's army.

In an interesting and sympathetic discussion of this poem Samuel Hynes has said

The striking thing about these lines is that they treat the Spanish war in psychological, not political terms, as an eruption of the sickness of modern society: In Spain, the enemy is *us* – our fears and greeds (as usual Auden involves himself in the class he condemns), and the people's army is psychological, too, a sort of metaphor for loving feelings. It is more than a metaphor, though; in Spain 'our thoughts have bodies', what was mental has become physical, and therefore mortal.[22]

I am not sure that this is the right way to put it (and I quote Hynes because the way he reads the poems seems to be a usual one). It is true, of course, that the passage, and indeed the whole poem, keeps associating or linking psychological attitudes with a political situation, private neuroses with public events, and that the public events – the war – are never analysed in an overtly political way. But when the speaker of the poem says that in Spain 'the menacing shapes of our fever are precise and alive' is he really interpreting the Spanish war in psychological terms, that is to say treating the mental as more basic than the real? I would have said that the precise relationship between the private and the public in 'Spain' is left open and that the general view of that relationship emerging from the poem is similar to that implied by MacNeice when in *Autumn Journal* (written in 1939) he looks back at his pre-war visit to Spain and writes that he could not then know that

> . . . Spain would soon denote
>   Our grief, our aspirations;
> Not knowing that our blunt
>   Ideals would find their whetstones, that our spirit
> Would find its frontier on the Spanish front,
>   Its body in a rag-tag army.[23]

Auden in 'Spain 1937' seems to be saying that the political decisions or choices which have to be made about Spain today are essential because history (a keyword in the poem) is not a force outside men and their dilemmas and neither are men and their dilemmas outside history. I would suppose that the reason he took so violently against the poem, particularly the final statement, later on was indeed because he recognized that in it the balance between materialism and idealism was so fine. He was to assert, intemperately, that the final lines of the poem,

> History to the defeated
> May say alas but cannot help or pardon

expressed the 'wicked doctrine' which equated goodness with success.

Since this is patently *not* what the lines do express, the explanation of his treatment of them can only be, I think, that at some level he remained conscious of their authenticity and feared it. 'Spain 1937' is in a number of respects a vulnerable poem, but not in those that its author in his revisions chose to fix on.

'Spain' is certainly an unusual sort of political poem, schematic in its structure (past – 'struggle' – future), and somewhat abstract in much of its effect because the 'struggle' tends to be oddly isolated from the historical processes within which it is evoked. The images, though themselves specific and 'concrete' and sometimes rich and vivid (such as the lines describing the coming of the volunteers to the International Brigades), are related to one another mainly through their place in the structure of the argument, which is about history and necessity and choice. Yet, though it is in this sense 'about' theoretical and philosophical questions, it doesn't come up with any very satisfying or conclusive theoretical insight. There is also the problem that one may suspect, without being quite sure, that homosexual tensions get deeper into the poem than the words quite admit. It is indeed a very 'impure' poem, and Marxists of a predominantly theoretical cast of mind have always tended to find it unsatisfactory.

Its strength, as it seems to me, lies in the way, for example, Auden succeeds in giving the words 'Madrid is the heart' a remarkable sense of the way political action can become central, involving choices whose implications and consequences reverberate through every area of life and consciousness. He isn't saying, 'We must forget our personal obsessions for a bit and take part in the struggle, which is the "real" thing', or 'The Spanish War is "really" a kind of reflection of our personal problems.' Rather, he is asserting a close and complex connection between personal fears and political possibilities and leaving the precise nature of the connection open.

This is what, from the first, gave 'Spain' its particular power and no doubt explains Auden's strong subsequent revulsion against it. I remember the first time I heard the poem read aloud (by Ian Watt) at a lunch-time meeting in Cambridge which ended with a collection for Spanish medical relief. It was certainly an example of poetry helping to make something happen: but I don't think any of us in the audience thought we were being hectored or got at.

And I remember, nearly forty years later, while Franco was still there, being taken by a young Spanish colleague who could not remember the war, to see the vast appalling monument of victory which the Nationalists had built in the hills outside Madrid, near the Escurial. After we had walked round in silence I said to my Spanish friend: 'What were you thinking about?' 'About the Republican prisoners who had to build the thing,' he said. 'What were you thinking about?' 'About my friends,' I said, and there was a line of poetry I couldn't get out of my head:

> History to the defeated
> May say alas but cannot help or pardon.

Political poetry, I would suggest, is poetry in which the question of power gets recognition and expression. Experience is presented not in a cocoon (the poem's form tending all the time to separate it from everything outside itself), not in some sort of purity and isolation as an autonomous whole, but in a way that gives a sense of the power-forces present in the situation evoked. Too strong an emphasis on the autonomy of any human experience or activity always tends to remove it from the pressures, the power-forces, which go towards making it what it is. Poetry that makes us conscious of power opens up the world rather than attempting to enclose a part of it in some sort of mystic purity. One of the virtues of the best poetry of the thirties was that it arose out of and helped define the power struggles of the time.

The impact of Auden's poetry on young intellectuals in the thirties was so great, I think, not because he was offering them the theoretical truth or the confirmation of their existing prejudices but, rather, because with great intellectual and verbal energy his poetry probed and explored many areas of consciousness – scientific, psychological, sociological, political, aesthetic – and came up with striking and stimulating connections embodied in phrases and images of vivid contemporary resonance. It is rather as though H. G. Wells had had a poet's creative way with language, or Harold Pinter had actually got something interesting to say. And the 'poetic' quality is not of course a 'technical' linguistic knack or an abstract theoretical correctness but a quality of perception in which the verbal form and the 'content' (in so far as one can abstract either of them even for descriptive purposes) are one. The lines which begin

> Lay your sleeping head, my love,
> Human on my faithless arm[24]

will exemplify as well as any what I mean.

NOTES

1. Edward Mendelson (ed.) *The English Auden* (Faber and Faber, 1977), p. 245.
2. Christopher Isherwood, *Christopher and his Kind* (Eyre Methuen, 1977).
3. *The English Auden*, op. cit., p. 151.
4. *The Criterion*, vol. XI, p. 467.
5. ibid., vol. X, p. 482.
6. ibid., vol. XVII, p. 59.
7. ibid., vol. XI, p. 275.
8. T. S. Eliot, *After Strange Gods* (Faber and Faber, 1934), pp. 19–20.
9. 'Young Writers of the Thirties' Exhibition, National Portrait Gallery, 1976.
10. Louis MacNeice, *Modern Poetry* (OUP, 1938), Preface.
11. ibid.
12. Louis MacNeice, *Collected Poems* (Faber and Faber, 1966), p. 84.
13. Michael Grieve and Alexander Scott (eds.), *The Hugh MacDiarmid Anthology* (Routledge and Kegan Paul, 1972), pp. 191ff.
14. *The English Auden*, op. cit., p. 172.
15. Monroe Spears, *The Poetry of W. H. Auden* (OUP, 1963), p. 89. ·
16. W. H. Auden, *The Double Man* (Random House, 1941), p. 17.
17. *The English Auden*, op. cit., p. 242.
18. ibid., p. 334.
19. 'Psychology and Art To-day', in *The Arts To-day*, edited by Geoffrey Grigson (Bodley Head, 1935), pp. 18–19 (quoted in Samuel Hynes, *The Auden Generation* (Bodley Head, 1976), p. 168; reprinted in *The English Auden*, op. cit., p. 341.
20. *The English Auden*, op. cit., p. 152.
21. Robin Skelton (ed.), *Poetry of the Thirties* (Penguin, 1964), p. 133–6.
22. Samuel Hynes, op. cit., pp. 253–4.
23. Louis MacNeice, *Collected Poems*, op. cit., p. 112.
24. *The English Auden*, op. cit., p. 207.

W. H. Auden

Louis MacNeice, John Cornford and Clive Branson: Three Left-Wing Poets

more realistic rep – see 93.

MARGOT HEINEMANN

1. INTRODUCTION: THE THIRTIES NOW AND THEN

After having been largely dismissed by the critics for a generation as too ideological, the left-wing poetry of the thirties is getting much more attention today.[1] Universities and colleges run courses on it, critical books keep coming out, and exhibitions and lectures by survivors are crowded. As Roy Fuller noted after speaking at one such occasion, it's the positive commitment that rouses interest now. In the thirties, he says, no one would have queued up to listen to surviving writers of the 1890s.

> The Thirties were a time when the brotherhood of man was not only believed in but seemed capable of practical achievement. The labour movement, despite its weaknesses, couldn't be regarded as other than international in scope. The crises of the times were such as to seem to require a social revolution to cure. . . . Poets envisaged a growing audience whose ideals were social justice, and they tried to bring into their verse a subject-matter of real concern to such an audience (*Professors and Gods*, André Deutsch, 1973, p. 137).

However, the myth of the thirties too often presented to students is a selective and devaluing one. Its components vary, but learned at school or university or through critical monographs, are roughly as follows.

1. The left-wing poets who mattered were Auden, Spender and Day Lewis. Other young intellectuals were led into Communism by their work (with some help from prose writers like Isherwood and Upward), and left it disillusioned when they did at the end of the thirties.

2. The Marxism and leftism of the period was romantic, ill-informed and often intellectually dishonest. Writers advocated revolution and violence but were remote from understanding or experience of what the words meant (see, for example, Orwell's well-known essay 'Inside the Whale'). Some were starry-eyed innocents, others cynics or cowards.

3. Both the politics and the poetry were utterly discredited by later events.

4. Hence the thirties were for left-wing writers 'a low dishonest decade', from which nothing can now be learned except that the British people, unlike the intellectuals, were instinctively wise to keep out of phoney ideological conflicts until it was almost too late, when the word was finally given by the proper authorities.

There are alternative versions of the myth. But all lead to the conclusion that the poets were mistaken in trying to mix writing and politics, art and life. The epitaph on the thirties was supposedly written by Auden in 'In Memory of W. B. Yeats' in 1939:

> For poetry makes nothing happen; it survives
> In the valley of its saying where executives
> Would never want to tamper.

It's time for Marxists to provide a better account of the period – though not by idealizing it or turning tragic defeats into victories. The harsh fact is that the working-class and anti-fascist movements, heroic though they were, were just not strong enough. Moreover, they had illusions and were sometimes mistaken. Yet this does not mean their efforts were wasted: without them the disaster would have been far worse. The commitment of the thirties generation helped to ensure that in the end it was not the fascists who won, and it has been part of whatever advance the movement has made since:[2] and that goes too for the writers.

For it is just not true that poetry 'makes nothing happen'. Yeats himself knew that when he brooded:

> Did those words of mine send out
> Certain men the English shot?

Obviously no one would argue that all poetry is, or should be, concerned with or directly committed to political struggle (Auden's *Spain*, a poem sold as a pamphlet to help Spanish Medical Aid, was exceptional even in the thirties). But in the longer term the poets do help to form the way we see our world and the possible alternatives to it, not only by their explicit statements but by the way they shape the very language in which we think. In that sense poetry does help to make things happen or prevent them from happening – however distressing that responsibility may sometimes be. And in times of exceptional tension, like the thirties, poetry may work a good deal more directly than that.

Under the pressure of great and menacing events, many writers in the early thirties felt the need to 'make action urgent and its nature clear'. Yet the inherited language of poetry had seldom been so difficult and remote from most people. 'There is a gap between what is commonly called "highbrow" and "lowbrow" taste, wider perhaps than it has ever been:'[3] a barrier which seemed to frustrate the wish for commitment. Auden wrote regretfully in 1936: 'Personally the kind of poetry I should like to write but can't is "the thoughts of a wise man in the speech of the common people".'[4]

However, 'the speech of the common people' as a medium for poetry, as Brecht or MacDiarmid were to some extent able to use it, is not easily come by in a society where idiom and imagery, like experience and education, are deeply divided by class. More than style is involved. When Auden tried to write a manifesto in an assumed 'popular' voice, in 'A Communist to Others' (1933), the result, though intelligible certainly, was not a good poem: he just didn't know enough, either about workers or about politics. The speech is neither theirs nor his.

In practice, one line of thirties poetry by left-wing writers was philosophical, allusive and esoteric in imagery, the poets writing frankly for their own group as intellectuals speaking to intellectuals. This is as true of Christopher Caudwell (his poems unpublished in his lifetime) as it is of William Empson, whose barbed political wit flashes out of the riddling complexity of his thirties verse, some of it still impenetrable for scholars despite the courteous notes.

There's nothing very obscure, though, about 'Just a Smack at Auden' ('Waiting for the end, boys, waiting for the end'), or the searching humility of 'Autumn on Nan-Yueh', which explains why Empson is *not* writing didactic anti-fascist verse for English readers.

> Politics are what verse should
> Not fly from, or it goes all wrong.
> I feel the force of that all right,
> And had I speeches they were song.
> But really, does it do much good
> To put in verse however strong
> The welter of a doubt at night
> At home, in which I too belong? . . .
> England I think an eagle-flight
> May come too late, would take too long.
> What would I teach it? Where it could
> The place has answered like a gong.

Another line was surrealist, with David Gascoyne, George Barker, much of the early work of Roy Fuller. Certainly at that time in Britain the notion of one single acceptable style was very far from being formulated, let alone imposed on leftward-moving writers.[5]

Nevertheless there were many who urgently wanted to be involved *as writers* in movements against fascism and war, and to find forms and language corresponding to the terrible simplicity of the issues as they saw them. This trend was expressed by Montagu Slater,[6] one of its editors, in the second number of *Left Review* (November 1934):

A writer's usefulness depends on his influence: that is, on the size and enthusiasm of his public: or, in the case of writers' writers, on his ability to set scores of other pens writing. In either case any lasting influence depends on his power to express the inarticulate feelings and forces that make for change. Here is a world threatened with the mad destructiveness of Fascism and imperialist war. The opposing force is in fact the mass of mankind, more or less articulate, more or less organised, more or less awake. And the writer's job becomes, as I believe, that of gaining a first-hand knowledge of such opposition in terms of people; learning to talk 'as a living man to living men'.[7]

A more accessible style seemed necessary if one was aiming at a much wider audience for poetry. It was not, however, only a matter of audience, still less of literary fashion. For the poet's dialogue with himself or those closest to him, the language in which he thinks, is transformed too by such a change in stance. As Edgell Rickword put it:

The theory of contemplation as the essence of poetic vision is the reflection of the squeezing-out of the poet from social-political life which has been going on now for a century. But it has no universal historical validity and the creations of the major poets refute it (*Left Review*, April 1936).

For the writers this meant a break with the self-image of the poet as necessarily solitary and alienated. 'On the whole,' wrote MacNeice in *Modern Poetry* in 1938, perhaps too confidently, 'modern poetry is becoming more lucid, and that is because its subject is becoming less esoteric.'

The search for a different poetic language led to a renewed interest by the left in popular verse, traditional ballads, broadsides and protest songs. *The Poet's Tongue*, an anthology compiled by Auden and John Garrett (and hailed on the left as a breakthrough), deliberately arranged its contents in alphabetical order so as to mix up folk, music-hall and popular items with high culture. Auden experimented in his own verse with ballads and blues, MacNeice with the sound of jazz and bagpipes,

Day Lewis with carol and folksong. Some poets wrote directly for political drama, pageants, declamation or singing. Montagu Slater included choruses and songs in his documentary plays *Easter 1916* and *Stay Down Miner* and in historical pageants organized by the Co-operative movement. Randall Swingler wrote song lyrics for Alan Bush, Benjamin Britten, Bernard Stevens and others, and translated versions of international revolutionary songs which found their way through performance or song-books[8] into the rhythms and images of other poets.

However, the lack of outlets on the left meant that the more personal kinds of 'committed' poetry remained largely unpublished.[9] And any hope of uncovering good working-class poets ready-made remained stillborn.[10]

It was the civil war in Spain, felt as their own cause by anti-fascists all over the world, which focused the whole thing and gave rise to the most memorable and poignant poetry of the thirties. Legend tells students that English poets idealized the war in the manner of Rupert Brooke (at least in its early stages), even that they felt a mingled repulsion and fascination with its violence. It is hard to find much of this in the actual poetry, however. Indeed an alternative objection by some critics is that these poems contain contradictory and jarring feelings – disgust at the obscene destruction in any war, alongside a conviction that *this* war has to be fought and won because freedom and justice depend on it.[11] Such poetry is felt to lack the harmony and consistency of Brooke's one way or Wilfred Owen's the other (as if harmony were the most important virtue in war poetry)! And this is true enough: the International Brigade was an army of anti-militarists. There's nothing harmonious or whitewashing, no 'sunlight of belief',[12] in these stanzas from 'Barcelona Nerves' by Tom Wintringham, a Brigade officer who had served in the First World War:[13]

> Death means the girl's corpse warm-alive when buried:
> Death means the retching brothels where on black
> Death-tide, death-fear, an army of boys is carried
> To a pox-wreck.
>
> And life's a matter of beating this, of breaking
> By own hardness, and a held hand, out
> From fury, frustration, fear, the waiting, the shouting,
> The hate of fate.

> Neither fools nor children we who are joining
> (Twenty years ago I knew war's face)
> We make what can wreck others into our gaining,
> Into our choice.

Away from the danger and squalor, non-combatants were perhaps more likely to romanticize, but it's fair to say that not many did. More typical home-front poems were the sharp-edged satires of Edgell Rickword, Brian Howard or Rex Warner, hitting at the British Government's support of 'non-intervention' or at big business safeguarding its rights in Spain:

> From small beginnings mighty ends,
> From calling rebel generals friends,
> From being taught at public schools
> To think the common people fools,
> Spain bleeds, and England wildly gambles
> To bribe the butcher in the shambles.
>
> (Edgell Rickword, *To the Wife of a Non-Interventionist Statesman*)

> I ask your patience, half of them cannot read,
> Your forbearance if, for a while, they cannot pay,
> Forgive them, it is disgusting to watch them bleed,
> I beg you to excuse, they have no time to pray.
>
> (Brian Howard, *For those with Investments in Spain*)

> Lest the hand should be held at last more valuable than paper,
> lest man's body and mind should be counted more than gold,
> lest love should blossom, not shells, and break in the land,
> these machine-guns came from Christian Italy.
>
> (Rex Warner, *Arms in Spain*)

The left in Britain, passionately supporting the Republic, well knew it was doing too little to give effective help. Thinking of militiamen fighting in the icy mountains at Guadalajara, Jacob Bronowski felt like Napoleon driving his men to death in the Russian snows:

> What is my pity worth? I fret
> No frozen body, but my mind;
> And if I tremble, all my rage
> Weighs nothing in the bite of wind.
>
> Forgive me, men at posts, who stiffen
> For furies such as kings' and mine,
> And suffer me no more than speak
> the words your lips will never form,

The hope that hangs there like a breath
that fate shall break your frozen line,
Break kings and break tyrannic men,
that March shall break the world with storm.

(*Guadalajara*)

None of these satirical poems, as it happens, is included in Skelton's well-known Penguin anthology *Poetry of the Thirties* (thankful though one is that that collection appeared at all).[14] This has probably helped to form a one-sided and even sentimental idea of thirties poetry at its most intense moment, when in reality much of it was hard and bitter with frustration.

It ought to be noted, however — since critics often assume that after the first year of war the left lost its enthusiasm for the Spanish cause[15] — that factually support in Britain for the Republic was unshaken right up to the final defeat. This was shown practically by the great Aid Spain meetings, the record sums of money raised for medical aid, the growing trade union pressure, the food collections even in the poorest districts. It was shown also in the continued stream of poetry about the war. Day Lewis' heroic seafight narrative *The Nabara* was published in 1938; *Poems for Spain*, an anthology containing many new pieces, in 1939; Louis MacNeice's *Autumn Journal* in 1939, after the war itself had ended. And indeed poems about Spain continued to appear years after the fighting was over: from Hugh MacDiarmid, Sorley Maclean, and many others.[16] Witness this sardonic elegy by Martin Bell for David Guest, Marxist philosopher and lecturer killed on the Ebro in 1938, which encounters head-on the sceptical argument that because the war was lost and socialism has not yet come in the west, the lives of these men were thrown away for nothing.[17]

Well O.K., he was wrong
Getting killed in Spain
Like that. Wal Hannington
Sat and tried to argue him out of going.
He was wrong, he was wrong,
The angel has not descended, the state
Hasn't the faintest chance of withering away,
And nobody is sure which way Hegel is up any more,
He was the greatest hero I've met because he was brave,
And would argue with anybody,
And could interest people because he was interested.

> If he was so bloody interested he should have gone on talking,
>   gone on talking,
> Something might have been talked out.
> Near to a saint, he should not have got himself killed,
> Thereby making himself an ineffectual angel, a moth.
> The Professor of economics was right:
> He just couldn't keep still at a public meeting,
> He would keep turning round and standing up to see what was
>   happening and who was talking,
> And this was probably how the bullet got him in the trenches
>   at Jarama.

In the remainder of this article I want to concentrate on three left-wing poets who do not fit into the thirties myth as it is commonly presented – Louis MacNeice, whose writings give perhaps the most vivid and telling record of how the late thirties felt to English intellectuals, John Cornford and Clive Branson, Communists and revolutionary poets. To read their work – even the scraps of it I quote here – is to realize that much thirties poetry is alive now as literature *because* (not although) it's so deeply rooted in the extreme situation out of which it was written.

2. LOUIS MACNEICE

Is it stretching a definition to call Louis MacNeice a 'left-wing poet'? I do not think so, though he is usually presented in surveys of the period as a 'sceptical liberal' in contradistinction to the more radical and Marxist Auden, Spender and Day Lewis. In fact his work of the later thirties is if anything more 'political' than theirs. He was never a Communist (as Day Lewis and Spender were for a time), but he did come, however unwillingly, to a strongly felt anti-fascist and socialist commitment which – unlike Auden or Spender – he never seems to have felt much need to modify. As late as 1942, asked about his political views, he wrote:

Politics: distrust all parties but consider capitalism must go. Visited Barcelona, New Year's 1939, and hold that in the Spanish Civil War the balance of right was certainly on the side of the Republican Government; the situation, however, much more complicated than represented in the English press (quoted in S. J. Kunitz and H. Haycraft, *Twentieth-Century Authors*, New York, 1942, p. 889).

Son of a Protestant clergyman in Northern Ireland, educated at public school and Oxford, after his romantic early marriage MacNeice found himself in 1930 teaching classics at Birmingham University – in the great industrial city, yet cut off by elegance and comfort from being part of it. As he wrote in his witty autobiography *The Strings are False*:

For five years Mariette and I lived together in Birmingham and all that time we were living on an island. . . . The trouble is that you cannot write in a hothouse. Mariette would plug a leg of lamb full of rosemary and cloves, and that was the event of the day (Faber and Faber, 1965, p. 133).

Under the shadow of the crisis 'our intellectuals seemed to be living in a tank' – with the exception of the group of poets around *New Signatures* who had begun to be interested in Communism. MacNeice, though feeling that the Communists' programme was marred by wishful thinking and oversimplification, nevertheless 'joined them in their hatred of the status quo. I wanted to smash the aquarium'.

By far the most impressive of his poems to read now is *Autumn Journal* (published 1939), too long for the anthologies to give more than excerpts. In form it's an uncorrected diary of the months around Munich, with twenty-four entries or sections. In an introductory note MacNeice wrote:

In as much as it is half-way towards a didactic poem, I trust that it contains some 'criticism of life' or implies some standards which are not merely personal. I was writing it from August 1938 to the New Year and have not altered any passages relating to public events in the light of what happened after the time of writing.

This determination not to alter the record (in sharp contrast to Auden's thirties poems, so often corrected, rewritten or suppressed) makes for an unusual kind of dramatic effect. The honesty is itself impressive; but more than that, the growth and structure of the poem consists in the changing situation and the changing ideas and feelings of the poet about it. This is, after all, the order in which people live their history, moving forward untidily into the unknown rather than looking backwards with orderly hindsight and tidying away the mistakes.

The poem is descriptive rather than metaphorical: the tone deceptively relaxed and conversational, avoiding the definitive epigrammatic effect which stricter forms tend to give, yet in its power of sensuous imagery going far beyond the 'journalism' as which it's sometimes dismissed. The poet's lack of certainty, his tentativeness and probing, are suggested by the irregular rhythmic movement, almost at

times like the comic doggerel of Ogden Nash, yet capable at any
moment of becoming lyrical. Rhymes are often used to reinforce the
sense of discord and inconclusiveness, as when the eighth section ends:

> Glory to God for Munich,
> And stocks go up and wrecks
> Are salved and politicians' reputations
> Go up like Jack-on-the-Beanstalk: only the
>   Czechs
> Go down and without fighting.

The technical skills are clear in the beautiful ironic opening section,
with the poet returning from holiday in the old privileged country-house
world of shaven lawn and close-clipped yew, pure Betjeman England:

> Macrocarpa and cypress
> And roses on a rustic trellis and mulberry trees,
> And bacon and eggs on a silver dish for breakfast,
> And all the inherited assets of bodily ease,
> And all the inherited worries, rheumatism and taxes,
> And whether Stella will marry and what to do with Dick,
> And the branch of the family that lost their money in Hatry,
> And the passing of the *Morning Post* and of life's climacteric,
> And the growth of vulgarity, cars that pass the gate-lodge
> And crowds undressing on the beach . . .

Note the film-like selection of detail – the silver breakfast dish
epitomizing the old-fashioned gracious living that MacNeice with part
of his mind couldn't help enjoying; the absurd rhyme-words
(Dick/climacteric) delicately suggesting the absence of real dignity and
ease; and finally the ferocious snobbery against common people outside
the gates. As the poet returns to London, nostalgic for the beauty of the
older world and the wife who has left him, it's with the cheerful working-
class crowd back from holiday to its harder working year that he strives
to identify – not only the crowd as it is now, but what it may become in a
new order:

> Where skill will no longer languish nor energy be trammelled
> To competition and graft,
> Exploited in subservience but not allegiance
> To an utterly lost and daft

System that gives a few at fancy prices
Their fancy lives,
While ninety-nine in the hundred who never attend the banquet
Must wash the grease of ages off the knives.

'Sceptical liberalism' is certainly no way to describe this: even though the poet himself admits the personal temptation of the highbrow to 'sleep on a mattress of easy profits' and refuse to join any socialist movement for fear his motives may not be absolutely pure. Wit and self-mockery do not disguise his longing for solidarity and unity:

First no doubt to stumble, then to walk with the others,
And in the end – with time and luck – to dance.

This is still the relatively buoyant hopeful mood which filled so many intellectuals in 1938. What changed all that was Munich. The relevant sections of the poem (v–viii) are a vivid evocation of how it felt in those days:

Hitler yells on the wireless,
The night is damp and still,
And I hear dull blows on wood outside my window;
They are cutting down the trees on Primrose Hill.
The wood is white like the roast flesh of chicken,
Each tree falling like a closing fan;
No more looking at the view from seats beneath the branches,
Everything is going to plan;
They want the crest of this hill for anti-aircraft.

The vandalized trees prefigure the beginning of immense violence, smashing the peaceful world. Open-air meetings ('the national conscience') call on the Government to stand by the Czechs. The poet watches the territorials at work on half-hearted ARP, loses his dog, finds her at the police station:

and went for a cup
Of coffee to an all-night shelter and heard a taxi-driver
Say, 'It turns me up
When I see these soldiers in lorries.'

The taxi-driver and MacNeice share human reservations about war that a great many people felt, very different from the jingo mood in 1914 – war now seen as the squalid horror of Passchendaele, 'rivers in spate sprouting with drowning hands/ And men like dead frogs floating'. It was not only fear (though most people expected a war would *begin* with poison gas and obliteration bombing of London), but also a doubt, especially perhaps in the labour movement, whether *any* war under Chamberlain's Government could be a just one.

Nevertheless the poet steels himself to expect 'fireworks here by this day week', and feels a bitter sense of shame and let-down when instead the outcome is Munich and the betrayal of the Czechs ('Save my skin and damn my conscience'), which he realizes makes a worse war inevitable, defeat a real possibility. Visiting Birmingham where he lived through the depression, he recalls the sensuous anti-political *dolce vita* of his first marriage as an evasion, a guilty symbol of the indifference that has doomed England and Europe:

> We slept in linen, we cooked in wine,
> We paid in cash and took no notice
> Of how the train ran down the line
> Into the sun against the signal.

Nausea at his own cultural role in this set-up (the necessary starting-point for criticism of society in most radical intellectuals) is brilliantly given in the very funny 'back to normal' entries (ix to xiii) in which the teaching of classics, now at London University, is portrayed as the type of comic futility, persisted in because:

> If it were not for Lit. Hum. I might be climbing
> A ladder with a hod.

The only anodyne is some kind of political action, even though

> The nicest people in England have always been the least
> Apt to solidarity and alignment.

In a by-election at Oxford he works for the Popular Front candidate, who is duly defeated in a 'coward vote' by Municheer Quintin Hogg. Haunted by nightmare corpse-like figures from the concentration camps and battlefields, caught in a depression which neither drink nor love-affairs can lift, he travels via a fashionable Christmas in Paris to visit Barcelona, the heroic city now at breaking-point after two-and-a-half years of war, where

> Still they manage to laugh,
> Though they have no eggs, no milk, no fish, no fruit, no tobacco, no butter,
> Though they live upon lentils and sleep in the Metro

...The human values remain, purged in the fire,
And it appears that every man's desire
Is life rather than victuals.

And here at last he's able to find resolution to face the grim future, in his contact with the Spanish people:

> Whose matter-of-fact faith and courage shame
> Our niggling equivocations —
> We who play for safety,
> A safety only in name,
> Whereas these people contain truth, whatever
> Their nominal façade.
> Listen: a whirr, a challenge, an aubade —
> It is the cock crowing in Barcelona.

In its strength and its weakness, its waverings and its commitment, *Autumn Journal* marvellously evokes the period. At the same time it's very clear how MacNeice, a leftward-moving intellectual, respects and feels the need for a group less compromised, less attracted by the old society than himself to drive the way forward into the new. But the moment of unity passed with 1939. Kept out of the Navy by poor eyesight, he worked as radio producer and writer through the war, and wrote some of the few good poems about the London blitz; but he never did anything quite like *Autumn Journal* again.

3. JOHN CORNFORD

MacNeice and John Cornford met only once, in the spring of 1936. According to Macneice's own characteristically ironic anecdote (*The Strings are False*, p. 157) he had spent a weekend in Cambridge drowning his depression in drink and social life, and afterwards gave John and two other students a lift back to Birmingham. John he saw as sharply contrasted with the other two, who were 'one of those Birmingham students who wanted to be Oxford aesthetes of the 1920s vintage', and one Cambridge undergraduate, 'clever, careerist and bristling with statistics'. John was 'clever, communist and bristling with statistics', but

for him the conception of career was completely drowned in the Cause; he was going to Birmingham to stand trial for causing an obstruction while distributing communist pamphlets in the Bull Ring ... John Cornford was the first inspiring Communist I had met; he was the first who combined an unselfish devotion to his faith with a really first-class intelligence.[18]

On the way John sat in the back and talked about trade unions, and when the car got a puncture was 'cheerfully efficient', unlike the aesthetic character in the front:

This was the first and last I saw of John Cornford. Later that year the war broke out in Spain and being no careerist, he went out to fight there and was killed.

MacNeice was a sophisticated person who knew a good many Communists, or people who were regarded as such, including the Auden generation of poets. Nevertheless he notes Cornford as the first *inspiring* one; and this half-comic glimpse of a real Communist intellectual has some importance for his later writing (indeed there seem to be echoes of Cornford's *Full Moon at Tierz* in the last Spanish section of *Autumn Journal*).

John Cornford thought of himself as an active Communist and full-time revolutionary, rather than as a poet, though he had an intense interest in poetry and had written a good deal before he left school. While at University (1933–6) he wrote few poems and those not mainly for publication. His death in Spain, fighting for the Republic, made those he wrote there widely known; but it still seems odd to contemporaries to find him mentioned in so many histories of the period as 'the poet John Cornford'.[19]

Brought up in beautiful peaceful Cambridge, one of the most favoured environments in the world for intellectuals, he was conscious very early that this little world ignored the cruelty and violence outside it. Where Louis MacNeice even in Birmingham wrote of himself as 'living on an island', Cornford consciously cut his way out into a different life. At fifteen, as his letters show, he was already insisting that poetry should be able to include *any* kind of subject and feeling, not just the beautiful subjects and nice feelings found in his mother's poems (where he perceptively diagnosed real and darker emotions which were refused expression); and that it should be written in a language not too far removed from that of everyday life.

At that point he was excitedly imitating early Auden; at sixteen, still at school, studying his way into Marxism by way of the *Communist Manifesto* and *Capital* ('easier than I expected'). At the earliest possible moment, after winning a Trinity history scholarship at sixteen, he threw himself out of Stowe against his parents' advice, went briefly to the London School of Economics and joined the Young Communist League, just at the moment before Hitler came to power. In Cambridge, from 1933 onwards, he became a leading member of the University Branch of the Communist Party.

John himself wrote a good deal about the need for the poet to be consciously involved in the movement to change society. The role of detached observer he saw as a delusion, since everyone is inescapably involved in history and to do nothing is a form of support for the existing order. His expression of these views is sometimes over-simplified, but the instinct and argument surely right: a revolutionary poet does need to know and discover at first hand what he writes about, as material experience and emotional commitment, not merely as abstract idea. He was conscious of knowing too little about the reality of exploitation and struggle – much less, he felt, than most young workers – but he was already aware that Auden and Spender knew even less. 'Although politically they have rejected their class, they are still writing mainly for it.' He could learn only through participation and action.

However, 'action' for him was in no sense an escape from thinking or studying the reality under his nose. The work on the leading committee of the Cambridge Communist Party included demonstrations against war and reception of the Hunger Marchers, chalking walls and heckling Blackshirts. It also meant disciplined Marxist study and learning all he could about the labour movement. (As soon as he left school he had done some speaking to bus branches of the TGWU on London Transport finance, on behalf of the Labour Research Department.)

He read with the intense concentration and method he brought to his political work, whether he was studying history, or the Elizabethan/Jacobean dramatists (whose release of intellectual energy at the birth of a new social system he felt in some ways analogous to his own), or the speeches at the Seventh World Congress of the Communist International, or criticizing the teaching of history at Cambridge from a Marxist angle. Given the life he was living, the question that looms so large for Stephen Spender at this time – should I write about my own feelings or about the revolution? – was a non-problem.

In modern poetry he was attracted especially by T. S. Eliot, Graves and Auden, all of whom he felt made poetry out of *any* subject and feeling. *The Waste Land* had been a great influence on him, evoking most powerfully the drabness and meaninglessness of the modern city and the disintegration of capitalist civilisation. But by this time he felt that Eliot had 'collapsed into subjectivity' in poetry, and that his social and critical attitudes (described by himself as Royalist, Tory, Anglo-Catholic) were leading him into anti-humanism, even a hesitant intellectual sympathy with a kind of clerical fascism.

Auden – sharper and more imaginative than the other *New Country* writers – had attracted Cornford ever since *Poems 1930*, which he read while still at school. Largely this was because of the imagery of Midland working-class towns and wrecked industrial landscapes (at the time these were John's 'ideal scenery' as well as Auden's), and the sense of a doomed society, about to come to a violent and tragic end. He preferred this to the more hopeful but vaguer and more romantic early verse of Spender and Day Lewis.

The short poem *'Org. Com. discussion on Literature'* (Galassi edn., p. 31) isn't deadly serious Marxist criticism, but it does make an authentic point about his own reactions. He did really feel that most modern poetry (including that of writers he greatly admired) was largely

> The important words that come between
> The unhappy eye and the difficult scene.

MacNeice in *Modern Poetry* (1938) argued that the new poets, while studying the issues, much as the man of action is forced to do, must nevertheless 'put in the shadows'. In fact, as Cornford's writings from Spain show – and the same could be said in a different way of his love-poetry – to go into action for one's belief is necessarily to confront complexity. It's much *easier* to simplify or distort if one is not involved at first hand. Wilfred Owen, the example and inspiration for so much thirties poetry, was certainly no model of clinical detachment. The poetry came out of the disgusting sights and smells of the trenches, out of his identification with the men among whom he fought, and when he came to think the war was being unnecessarily prolonged he still felt the need to return to the front where he was killed. If he had not been the kind of man to do that, he could never have written those poems where 'the poetry is in the pity'.

Cornford's war was a different one from Owen's, the feelings about it were necessarily quite different; but the total involvement is comparable. His poetry is not as it is because he was writing it as 'propaganda' in the sense in which MacNeice defines the term, 'consciously and solely concerned with converting people to a cause or creed'. His belief is 'felt belief' and is certainly, as MacNeice would have it, 'compromised with his own individual observation'. Simply, as he says later in *Full Moon at Tierz*, 'Communism was my waking time'.

The few personal poems John wrote while at university – available in Galassi's edition for the first time for many years – are sensitive and tender, yet at the same time sharply decisive. Their form is colloquial and simple compared with what he had written earlier and what most other poets were writing:

> All last night we lay so close
> All completeness of the heart
> The restless future will efface:
> Tomorrow night we sleep apart.

It is clear how far he was from the crude idea that every poem must directly serve a political purpose. To write revolutionary poetry, he believed, the writer must be committed and this would necessarily alter his perception of reality; but he never questioned the quality of, say, Graves's, love poetry.

'As Our Might Lessens' (1934–5),[20] the longest of the poems written during those years, is the personal statement of a serious mood among Communists. Here he confronts the bitterness of the defeat of the left in Germany and the shock of the first reports of Nazi brutality, realizing that for his generation the fight for socialism may well mean torture, shame and execution rather than the victorious barricades. Auschwitz and Belsen are foreshadowed here; the poem is a tensing of will and nerve for the ordeals ahead. The title and epigraph (taken from the Old English heroic poem of the Battle of Maldon) emphasize that this is a tragic historical moment of retreat, when desperate courage is needed and many will not live to see the revolution they fight for.

The poem opens with the victory of fascism in Europe, focusing on the perverted sexual-sadistic element in Nazism (linked with the ancient Roman imperial decadence), which crushes the natural sexual delight identified (as in Blake) with the forces of freedom and revolution:

> For those whose tortured torturing flesh
> Stirred at the body under the lash,
> The painted boy in the praetorian's bed.
> For those who were strong to live and love,
> Who claimed life had no need to starve,
> Camphor and pincers fouled urine and blood.

> For all but suicides and slaves
> This death is background to our lives,
> This is the risk our freedom has us take.
> Some may die bold as Schulze died,
> Many will live to avenge our dead,
> But this fear haunts us all. Flesh still is weak.

Just after Hitler seized power, John had written:

It would be interesting to see how long one would remain a Communist inside a Nazi barracks. That's the final test. I feel already I could stand any other. That one I don't know about (Galassi (ed.), p. 168).

The whole poem is in a sense a meditation on this theme; its centre the polemic against idleness and brooding at a time which above all demands passionate concern and cool organised political action. Dreams and fantasies, whether interpreted in romantic or Freudian terms, will change nothing:

> Not by any introspection
> Can we regain the name of action.
> Whatever dreams may mean to you, they mean sleep.
> Black over Europe falls the night,
> The darkness of our long retreat,
> And winter closes with a silent grip.

Individual heroism is not enough: the only hope lies with the revival of the revolutionary working-class movement.

> But moving in the masses' blood,
> Vienna, Amsterdam, Madrid,
> The ten years sleeping image of the storm
>
> Shows us what we stand to gain
> If through this senseless-seeming pain,
> If through this hell we keep our nerve and pride.
> Where the nightmare faces grinned
> We, or our sons, shall wake to find
> A naked girl, the future at our side.

There's no easy optimism, though; it may be that only 'our sons', a later generation, will win through. For the present, it's an iron time.

Metaphors and properties in this poem are physical, bodily, with words evoking muscular strain and effort – grub, wince, grip, shutting fist, strips, breaking up. Yet the argument is also intellectual, the references precise and historical. Before critics deduce a morbid and disturbed psychology in the pervading contrasted images of sex and torture, they should remember what was actually done then in Germany or in occupied France to anti-fascist leaders, or what has been done since in Spain or Vietnam, Brazil or Chile. It was reasonable to be afraid, and through poetry to come to terms with that fear.

Far from idealizing wars and armed struggle, Cornford fully expects them to be filthy and degrading; merely in face of fascism there's no other way but to meet force with force. And in counterposing sexual fulfilment to violence and repression ('all strength moves in the dance of a woman's body') he finds the most direct language for his passionate hopes – a language perhaps too simple and direct for many other writers of the thirties to use.

It was out of the black and near-desperate moment symbolized in 'As Our Might Lessens' that the international Communist movement came to realize the need for a change in its whole strategy and understanding of revolution. The Communist vanguard could not win on its own; the support of millions of workers' votes for Communism in Germany had not been enough. It was a matter of life and death for Communists to break out of their isolation (in part at least self-imposed) from other socialists and progressives, and to organize not just the industrial workers but the small middle class and intellectuals against fascism.

For Communist students this meant no longer seeing themselves as a small group of dedicated and exceptional revolutionaries crossing the battlelines of class to ally themselves with the workers, but rather as leaders of the great majority of students and youth, whether or not they accepted the need for revolution. Concretely, for John, it meant working to unite the Communist and Labour student movements, reaching out to find points of unity with Liberal and even some Conservative students.

The relatively short period from this change to the war – only four or five years in all – showed the vast potential of this kind of broad movement, the Socialist strategy that (as Eric Hobsbawm has pointed out) has most powerfully shaken the ruling class in Western Europe. In France and Spain it brought popular front governments to power; in Britain the great anti-Mosley demonstrations, the nation-wide solidarity with Spain, the rise of the Left Book Club to 60,000 members, the proliferation of left-wing theatre and writing. John Cornford didn't live to see much of this, and in retrospect it was all, of course, too little and too late to prevent world war. But it was to experience this vision in action that he went to Spain very soon after Franco's rebellion, because here at last the armed people were standing up to fascism. It was more than a 'liberal myth' (as Galassi calls it) that made him at the time of his death a symbol not just for Communists, but, as the dedication to the original memorial volume of his writing said, for 'all advanced and progressive mankind'.[21]

Lyric poetry is a labour-intensive kind of literature, and about the only kind physically possible to write in prison or the front line. Spain matured John's poetry through the intensity of experience and also because for some weeks he had, between skirmishes, little to do and nothing to read. To his isolation in these early days in Aragon we owe the poems by which he has been remembered. Later, on a more active front and with much more responsibility, he didn't so far as we know write any verse. Under shell-fire in the philosophy and letters building of the University City, where 'the fighting consisted of firing from behind barricades of philosophy books at the Fascists in a village below', he relieved boredom by reading Shakespeare and *Capital*. Two months later he was killed in action at Cordova.

Full Moon at Tierz,[22] his most ambitious poem, was written while serving with the militia on the Aragon front in August/September 1936. Composing it in his head a stanza at a time while on guard duty at night, he scribbled down and revised the sections in his notebook; it was first printed in *Left Review* after his death. Technically it's remarkable for its singing quality, the powerful rhythm which he associated with the working-class songs of Brecht and Eisler; and also for its strictness of form and the bareness and sharpness of imagery and language, behind which lie the lessons of Auden and Graves.[23] The regular stanza helped composition, and adds stress and precision to the tense speaking voice counterpointed against it.

A clear line of intellectual argument provides the structure, making it more like metaphysical poetry than like the Rupert Brooke 1914 sonnets with which Stansky and Abrahams rather ineptly compare it. Some critics, failing to grasp this central argument, have felt it ought to be a purely personal statement like his own 'Heart of the heartless world', and have seen the politics in it as intrusive propaganda rather than what it really is, 'belief compromised with his own individual observation'.

The opening sets the Spanish war in history as a crucial turning point (which indeed it proved to be). The forbidding mountains of Aragon all round fuse with the metaphor of historical process:

> The past, a glacier, gripped the mountain wall,
> And time was inches, dark was all,
> But here it scales the end of the range,
> The dialectic's point of change
> Crashes in light and minutes to its fall.

Elsewhere John had written: 'I don't think of Communism as inevitable, like measles, or the war, or the present crisis, but as *necessary* . . . It hasn't got to come; there's the alternative of gradually relapsing into an American anarchy as we are doing at present — also the prospect of another war.' The pattern of the future does not yet exist — only the line of fight now is clear. It is the opposite of the mechanical notion of Marxism as a kind of predestination:

> The intersecting lines that cross both ways,
> Time future, has no image in space.
> Crooked as the road that we must tread,
> Straight as our bullets fly ahead.
> We are the future. The last fight let us face.

On guard in the moonlit fields, he muses on the meaning of the coming battles and nerves himself to overcome his own loneliness and fear. In reading the mood here it may be helpful to know something of his own situation. Going to Spain on a presscard to see at first hand what looked like being a brief (because nation-wide) popular resistance to fascism, he had volunteered almost on impulse for the first militia willing to take him, and found himself fighting amongst anarchists and POUM supporters, many of them brave and sincere revolutionaries, but undisciplined, inefficient and led by a policy of 'second revolution' which seemed to him 'provocative and utterly dangerous'.[24]

Later at the front he had fallen in with a group of German ex-Communists, whom personally he liked and admired, and who 'genuinely believe the CI has deserted the revolution'. The struggle was a test not only of his own strength, but of the ideas he had made his own and which had brought him to Spain. As a single Communist, isolated by political differences as well as language, a raw soldier on the eve of battle:

> Now with my Party, I stand quite alone.

Out of this isolation he wills strength and courage sufficient to the need:

> Then let my private battle with my nerves
> The fear of pain whose pain survives,
> The love that tears me by the roots,
> The loneliness that claws my guts
> Fuse in the welded front our fight preserves.

Even some sympathetic critics, like Abrahams and Stansky, or Roy Fuller, have read the poem as 'sacrificing individuality and subtlety of language to slogans, quotations and snatches of song', suggesting that 'the whole reality is lost sight of in abstractions' because 'there was a political point to be made'. They miss the fact that the political differences on the left are part of his personal loneliness and pain. As he wrote in a letter around the same time:

I am beginning to find out how much the Party and the International have become flesh and blood of me. Even when I can put forward no rational argument, I feel that to cut adrift from the Party is the beginning of political suicide (Galassi, p. 180).

The fundamental unity of the movement – beyond particular argument or loneliness – is expressed emotionally in music, the *International*, the *Bandiera Rossa*, sung on demonstrations or at student parties or in fascist gaols. That's why they are quoted here.

In the final section the poet's homesickness links this battle with what is going on in the world outside. Spain is not just a romantic foreign adventure, it is life or death for Britain. The lyrical language here is loaded with deeper meanings. Oranienburg was one of the Nazis' first torture-camps: 'freedom's crooked scars' the swastika carved on the bodies of comrades. 'Clydeside and the gutted pits of Wales' are the old red working-class districts, now gutted by depression and silent in the face of the fascist threat; it's from there that the militant workers will have to come to fight (as indeed they did) alongside the Spanish militia.

> Now the same night falls over Germany,
> And the impartial beauty of the stars
> Lights from the unfeeling sky
> Oranienburg and freedom's crooked scars.
> We can do nothing to ease that pain
> But prove the agony was not in vain.
>
> England is silent under the same moon,
> From Clydeside to the gutted pits of Wales.
> The innocent mask conceals that soon

Here too our freedom's swaying in the scales.
Oh understand before too late
Freedom was never held without a fight.

Freedom is an easily spoken word,
But facts are stubborn things. Here too in Spain
Our fight's not won till the workers of all the world
Stand by our guard on Huesca's plain,
Swear that our dead fought not in vain,
Raise the red flag triumphantly
For Communism and for liberty.

The last lines proved not so much metaphorical as prophetic. Before many months were out, John had returned to Spain with a group of British volunteers he had recruited to join the first international units fighting round Madrid. In the 1938 songbook of the International Brigades (*Canciones de las Brigadas Internationales*), the 'Bandiera Rossa' (from which the final couplet is quoted) is bound up alongside the 'Red Flag' and the 'Himno de Riego'. Professor Tolley criticizes the use of the word 'freedom' in these last stanzas as 'vague'; but it wouldn't have seemed so to anyone involved at the time in the anti-fascist movement. It was the freedom of working-class organization that was threatened most of all.

In 'A Letter from Aragon', John's last poem, his belief is indeed 'compromised by his observation' of the ugliness of war – the stinking unheroic corpse, the bombing and panic, the wounded who are not too brave to moan and keep the sick poet awake. And the grim accuracy of this gives greater power to the affirmation at the end:

But when I shook hands to leave, an Anarchist worker
Said: 'Tell the workers of England
This was a war not of our own making,
We did not seek it.
But if ever the Fascists again rule Barcelona
It will be as a heap of ruins with us workers beneath it.'

Subsequent history, from the fall of Barcelona in 1939 through the long years of illegal resistance until now, gives these words even greater weight.

4. CLIVE BRANSON

Clive Branson's poems are still little known; he was primarily a painter and political worker. But his life and writings show how the revolutionary feeling continues long after the blows of the later thirties, after the Spanish defeat, after 1939.

Branson was the same age as MacNeice, came from an Army and public school background and studied painting at the Slade. By the time he was twenty-two he had read his way out of the attitudes and standards he had grown up with: he joined the Independent Labour Party and then, in 1932, the Communist Party. Like Cornford, he became engrossed in the practical activity of the movement – running a street paper, lecturing for the National Council of Labour Colleges (NCLC), speaking on Clapham Common, and especially building up Marxist classes and factory groups among industrial workers in Battersea where he lived. Later he fought in the International Brigade and was a prisoner of war.

The experience and imaginative energy of these years is felt in the pictures he painted when he got back from Spain, small townscapes of Battersea streets and workers and scenes from the blitz. Mainly realistic in outline, they are lit with an intensity of colour that is not at all naturalistic, suggesting liveliness and potential for splendour and change in the drabbest urban landscape. The drawings he sent home from India (where he was killed on the Burma front in 1944) were published with some of his letters and poems in *British Soldier in India*, and convey searing anger at the poverty he saw there. His talent was in its way as outstanding as Cornford's, and had longer to mature.

A few of Branson's poems were printed in magazines like *Poetry and the People*, but since none are in the current anthologies I include three here in full. The first was written in 1938 in the Spanish prison where brigaders from many countries were held, including some from the Thaelmann Battalion:

'To the German Anti-Fascists in San Pedro'

The evening went beyond the bars, passed by us,
His face at the window
His voice in a frame
He 'who ought to be shot' and will be
when the nazis get him home.
He was singing
this German prisoner, self-exiled workman,
common songs of the beer-garden in his home town.
Singing to memories of friends
who could not hear.

And others, some half dozen, sang too.
I have lain in my blanket at night
kept awake by lice and a dry itching skin
looked at the blue window panes broken
with a star up in one corner.
Outside a night-bird intensely sings
unseen and to no-one.
Only to memories of friends did he sing?
Only to the deaf ears of those ghosts?
Was there meaning in his song, or meaningless
Like that of the nightingale?
Mere repetition of a few notes through centuries
with no gain
Just a song of the beer-garden?
In the strains of music
In the discipline of song
this prisoner, the captive voice
sang of the freedom in trees, of cloud and wind
the movement of men on bicycles, hiking,
of animals not afraid of leaving their cages
who do not need the safety of their cell
the security of a gaol.

He sang the promise of a dream
sometime come true, of free men
whose homes are not prisons,
beds not graves, play not in murder,
work for creation.

This German sang to us of home
Our heritage in one another
Comrade, Brother – no foreigner.[25]

It's a striking poem and a very moving one, written as it is in the last
year of the war when he could have had no illusions about easy victory.
As well as any poem of the time, it suggests the solidarity and rational
confidence that sustained socialists through those otherwise bloody
years.

Second, a small piece from Palencia concentration camp. It's no
more than a couple of images, a painter's poem:

'In the Camp'

The storm has cleared the air
But not barbed wire.

> Here we can bask in the sun,
> should our eyes have forgotten,
> pointed at by the guard's bayonet.
>
> We're like young trees set
> on a wide landscape and mountain
> in a picture for ever certain.
> Clouds pass and fine weather
> and with them the liberty we long for.

I do not know the date of the last poem, *Foreword*, which is much more cheerful. Let it speak for itself:

> Because it's time for a revolution
> To end the beating-up of man by man
> To do away with the police nark, stool pigeon, assassin,
> Judge, gaol;
> Because in the common people
> We have found something much more beautiful
> Than king, God or individual;
> That is bad reason
> To blunt the nature of our fellow men,
> Their will
> To climb the steep hill, strip in the sun,
> Walk along the river bank, watch the water fowl, to fish
> Or sit lazily sucking the juicy end of rich grass,
> To take one's girl on a pillion ride
> Away from the town down to the sea side.
> The writer who says he has no time to care
> For the daffodil or cowslip shames
> The very revolution he proclaims.
> He is no better than the millionaire
> Who clears the ground of trees, shrubs, weeds
> To make his lawns monotonously green,
> Forbidden to all except the mowing machine.
> Don't insult the bugger on the dole.
> He loves the taste and smell of a good meal –
> Sure! – but he loves as well
> Fresh air, a salty breeze and brown earth still.
> It is for these, the joy of being in a man,
> That the factory hand is ready to risk all,
> Can take what's coming to him, and rebel.

It is impossible to separate poetry of this kind from the experience out of which it comes. 'The overtly political poetry of the period is too often theoretical,' says Professor Tolley on the 385th and last page of his monumental commentary *Poetry of the Thirties*, 'and the overpowering feeling that a writer should be political or concerned with the issues of the day may often have diverted the true impulses of poetry.' But Clive Branson wrote this way because he lived and thought and saw the world this way, not because he thought it was correct to 'divert his true impulses' to write political poetry.

For some critics, the left-wing writer can't win. Either he is writing about what he doesn't know, and is therefore too theoretical and 'ideological': or about what he does, in which case he is merely reflecting reality without transforming it into art. For the reader, living like the poet in difficult times, the commitment seems necessary and appropriate: less would have been less truthful. We may agree with MacNeice that it's difficult for poets to write well from beliefs they haven't quite grown into, as he thought Auden, Spender and Day Lewis were sometimes doing in the thirties. But that, as he rightly saw, is not an argument against revolutionary poetry: only an argument for growth.

Both Cornford and Branson died young, killed in the wars they foresaw and failed to prevent, and it's difficult to read their poetry now with detachment, remembering that loss. But the directness of language in which they define and clarify feeling is something they share with other revolutionary poets of the time. Note for example how simply, yet how profoundly the origins in early childhood feelings of a personal socialist commitment are given by A. L. Morton in these lines (from the December 1934 number of *Left Review*):[26]

'So I Became . . .'

I remember first
the day long drive in the high trap
to buy a calf in a village dizzy with windmills.
Numbness of fingers
dividing apples and cake
and my father's voice:
'Travellers must share and share.'

The word endured
was overlaid with notions of other kinds
making one's way   and privilege of class
with self esteem   and rights . . .
but endured.

The word grew strong and mated with other words
Justice   fair dealing
grew tall in innocence
over the world's wall.

The mills spun sunlight
out of a fleecy sky.
I dreamed no other.

Till I awoke   And a cold dry
wind and a smoke black
World filled with bent backs
and upright chimneys   A world
where words meant
nothing   And justice did not run
outside four walls.

Words failed to serve save
to curse in Hamlet's word or Job's
the day.

Talk of justice in a new tongue
caught the low flame.   A Traveller's
Justice.   Justice dividing.   True
warfaring talk.   My father's voice
dividing the whole world like the last apple
on the Dalham road.

So I became
What ever I now am.

What the author became was the first popular English Marxist historian, as well as a poet and literary critic. For him, as for others, the thirties began a line of socialist intellectual work that has been sustained for another forty years.

NOTES

1. One difficulty in understanding the period is that many of the finest poems of the thirties have been out of print for a generation or more. The best easily available anthology, Robin Skelton's Penguin *Poetry of the Thirties* (1964), rescued some of them and restored the original text of some others (notably Auden's); but it is short and somewhat one-sided (nothing for instance from *Left Review* or *Poetry and the People*). It is frustrating that while thick academic critical volumes keep appearing

– the latest being Samuel Hynes's well-researched *The Auden Generation* (Bodley Head, 1976) – you can only read *New Country* or *New Signatures* in specialist libraries.

Two recent publications have, however, greatly improved the situation. *The English Auden* edited by Edward Mendelson (Faber and Faber, 1977) provides most of the original texts of thirties poems which had either disappeared or been drastically rewritten in Auden's later collections; while the 1976 volume of John Cornford's poems and papers (*Understand the Weapon, Understand the Wound*, edited with an introduction by Jonathan Galassi, Carcanet Press, Manchester) was the first since 1938 to make these available.

2. This point is argued more fully than I have space to do here in the last two chapters of *Britain in the Nineteen Thirties* by Noreen Branson and Margot Heinemann (Weidenfeld, 1971; Panther paperback, 1973).

3. Introduction to *The Poet's Tongue* (London, 1935) reprinted in *The English Auden*, op. cit., p. 330.

4. In *The Highway* (journal of the Workers' Educational Association), December 1936; reprinted in *The English Auden*, op. cit., p. 360.

5. This becomes evident if one actually reads, say, *Left Review*, instead of taking the word of later commentators like Julian Symons for how narrow it was.

6. Writing here under the pseudonym 'Ajax'.

7. The first sentence of this extract is quoted by itself in Julian Symons, *The Thirties* (Cresset Press, 1960), p. 71. The longer quotation makes clear Slater's real meaning, which has been widely misinterpreted and misunderstood.

8. For example, *The Left Song Book* (edited by Alan Bush and Randall Swingler, Gollancz, 1938), and sheet music published by the Workers' Music Association.

9. Slater and Swingler both left a mass of poetry still unpublished at their deaths. Some of it is printed in the valuable short study of their work by Arnold Rattenbury (in *Renaissance and Modern Studies*, vol. XX, 1976), where a book on Swingler's writings is promised (see also, John Lucas (ed.), *The 1930s: A Challenge to Orthodoxy* (Harvester Press, 1978), which contains this material).

10. See the interview with Edgell Rickword in *Renaissance and Modern Studies*, op. cit., p. 8 (in Lucas, op. cit., p. 3).

11. e.g. Samuel Hynes, *The Auden Generation*, op. cit., p. 247.

12. The phrase is Julian Symons's: 'Those who died in this sunlight of belief were in a sense the lucky ones' (*The Thirties*, op. cit., p. 123).

13. He was incidentally one of the editors of *Left Review*. The poem is in Stephen Spender and John Lehmann (eds.), *Poems for Spain* (Hogarth Press, 1939), p. 29.

14. They, and many others, were included in *Poems for Spain*, op. cit., which has never been reprinted as a whole.

15. The view originally comes from Orwell, who was certainly disillusioned himself, but in this not I think representative (his reasons are on record in 'Inside the Whale' and *Homage to Catalonia*). He was followed by Julian Symons, op. cit., p. 126. Robin Skelton (*Poetry of the Thirties*, p. 19) and Samuel Hynes (*The Auden Generation*, p. 243) repeat the statement without offering any factual evidence.

16. See T. S. Law and Thurso Berwick (eds.), *Socialist Poems of Hugh MacDiarmid* (Routledge, 1978), pp. 27, 84, 87, and Sorley Maclean, *Spring tide and Neap tide, Selected Poems*, 1932–72 (Canongate, 1977), pp. 18, 24, 80.

17. Martin Bell, *Collected Poems* (Macmillan, 1967), p. 67.
18. MacNeice got the story slightly wrong. What John had actually been arrested for was distributing trade union recruiting leaflets on behalf of the trades council outside the factory, and the trial was a test case to establish the right of the trades council to do this without police harassment.
19. See *Understand the Weapon, Understand the Wound*, op. cit., pp. 44–62.
20. ibid., p. 32.
21. *John Cornford, a Memoir*, edited by Pat Sloan (Jonathan Cape, 1938).
22. See Galassi (edn.), p. 38; or Skelton, *Poetry of the Thirties*, p. 137.
23. As a boy Auden had advised him: 'You might do more with stricter forms . . . as the very nature of the form forces the mind to think rather than to recollect' (Peter Stansky and William Abrahams, *Journey to the Frontier*, Constable, 1966, p. 173).
24. The political comments are quoted from the impressive analysis, *The Situation in Catalonia*, which he wrote for the British CP on his brief return to England (Galassi, op. cit., pp. 108–24).
25. Published in *Poetry and the People*, no. 11. A wider selection of Clive Branson's poems will be found in the *Penguin Book of Spanish Civil War Verse*, edited by Valentine Cunningham (1979).
26. Reprinted in A. L. Morton's *Collected Poems* (Lawrence and Wishart, 1976), p. 50.

Between the Acts? English Fiction in the Thirties

PETER WIDDOWSON

1. FICTION AND THE 'LIBERAL CRISIS'

There is a tacit – and sometimes express – judgement that the 1930s was a fallow decade so far as the novel in England is concerned. The rich harvest of modernism had been gathered in, and had, by dint of its own richness, left the ground impoverished. The most significant achievements of Lawrence, Joyce and Virginia Woolf – so the argument runs – had been received, and the important work of other novelists writing in the thirties, with a few exceptions, really belongs to other decades, before or after. Waugh, Huxley and Wyndham Lewis somehow 'belong' to the twenties (the absurdity of the argument is instantly revealed if one looks at the publication dates of some of their major productions), while Anthony Powell and Henry Green 'belong' to the post-Second World War period; Graham Greene – even for a while in his own eyes – really belongs to the period of his Catholic novels, i.e. from about 1940 onwards; Orwell is, of course, a thirties writer, but the books which are regarded as constituting his fictional 'achievement' are the post-war fables, *Animal Farm* and *1984*. Only Isherwood, by way of his two Berlin novels, is rated as a significant *thirties* novelist. The work of other 'indigenous' novelists like Rex Warner, Ralph Bates and Grassic Gibbon is caught up momentarily by the sweeping beam of literary history, and is again released as of solely 'period' interest.

It is an interesting instance of what we might call the ideology of literary study. The impact of modernist formal experimentation is so profound – regardless, or perhaps because, of the worldview it endorses[1] – that other, possibly dissenting, modes of fiction pale into insignificance or appear retrogressive. I do not intend to expatiate here on that ideology, either within its own academic terms or in terms of its larger political implications. Nor can an essay of this length redress the balance by rescuing for the 1930s all the novelists I have indicated above. What it *will* suggest is that the thirties is a highly significant period for the novel, that what novelists were struggling to achieve is equally as complex and interesting as the work of the major modernist writers. It will also therefore imply that the established literary criticism of modernism, which detaches from their period 'supreme' exemplars of its own (unadmitted) preconceptions of 'culture' and 'value', is an instance of how the ideology of literary study distorts our perception of that period. It is with this in mind, and as a strategic example, that I have signalled Virginia Woolf in my title as one of the decade's novelists. *The Years* in particular, and to a lesser degree *Between the Acts*, are often only discussed in relation to her earlier ('better') works, and *not* as experimental novels *of the thirties*.

But my appropriation of the phrase 'Between the Acts' in the title of this essay was not simply to make that point. The real interest of fiction in England in the thirties (and this explains the literary judgement which disregards it) lies in the uncertainty of direction, the tense irresolution, the novels so commonly reveal. At the formal level this uncertainty expresses itself in the diverse modes of fiction employed and their operation in practice: the structural and textural discoveries of modernism, formal realism, documentary reportage, fable, allegory, satire and dystopia,[2] emerge, and often merge, in the novels of the period. But this formal problematic belies another more complex dilemma which is at once literary and ideological. Faced with what Christopher Isherwood once called[3] the 'fantastic realities' of the 'everyday world', the novelist's problem, acutely in the thirties, was how to address them. The novel form had, traditionally, concerned itself primarily with the individual's negotiations with society; however much emphasis was given to the nature of the society which bore on the individual, the individual remained the pivotal focus. Indeed, the major examples of modernist fiction themselves are arguably 'major' precisely because they express, with different degrees of self-awareness, the *ne plus ultra* of that worldview. The explicit concern with 'consciousness', the turning-inward to the displaced perception of the world in the register of individual minds is, both in literary and ideological terms, a kind of recognition of the embattlement of liberal-bourgeois individualism.

What happens in novels in the thirties, I suggest, is an attempt, in many different guises, to break out of that impasse. Novelists, from the liberal modernist Virginia Woolf to Marxists like Edward Upward and Rex Warner, sought to engage with the social reality of their times.[4] The crisis of capitalism, the rise of fascist dictatorships or, more generally, of totalitarian regimes, the fear of impending war, the rapid development of science and technology – particularly in relation to armaments – the sense of depersonalized control by way of monopoly capitalism and mass communications systems, all constitute the 'fantastic realities' of the decade, which, by threatening the individual so massively, precisely displaced him from the centre of the field of vision. An individualist ideology nevertheless survived, and the pressure delivered by such a situation forced the novel to expand in an attempt to find a strategy for engaging directly with the large processes of society which form and control the individuals within it.

I am claiming, then, that the fictional dilemma of how to come to terms with the 'fantastic realities' of the present is a manifestation of the ideological crisis of liberal-humanism in the 1930s,[5] the crisis, as Caudwell puts it in the Foreword to *Studies in a Dying Culture*, [6] of bourgeois culture in which the myth of the 'naturally free' individual, on which bourgeois ideology is based, is in direct opposition to his actual experience – 'enslaved . . . to forces whose control is now beyond him, because he does not acknowledge their existence. . . .' 'So far from being free, he is whirled like a leaf on the gales of social change.' Nevertheless, the deluded belief in the 'free' individual persisted. And Virginia Woolf's title, *Between the Acts*, draws attention precisely to the informing uncertainty which is the prime characteristic of this 'crisis'. It is not merely the problem of how to act against the forces which threaten (the question of 'forward from liberalism'); it is the bewilderment of discovering that the present is a kind of no-man's land, that it is, as it were, *in between* cultures, that its dimly perceived forms are those of a world one does not recognize, has no equipment to comprehend. The problem for the novelist who wishes to take stock of it, to analyse and re-present it, is obviously acute. Each of the novelists I have elected to deal with – Virginia Woolf, Aldous Huxley, Edward Upward, Rex Warner, George Orwell, Graham Greene, and Christopher Isherwood – is a product of high bourgeois culture, and each is in some way alienated from it and particularly from its contemporary forms and tendencies. This alienation may lead to cultural despair or a commitment to socialism, but it has in common a profound antipathy to present society. And this produced a common problem for them as novelists: how to realize this antipathy as more than subjective hatred, how to give mateial form to the 'abstract' social pressures which engender it?

This uncertainty, the sense of being at the end of a cultural phase, also accounts for a particular paradox which informs much of the fiction of the period. In novels which seek to engage with the 'fantastic realities' of the present, the present itself is curiously displaced. For the most part the focus is either on the moribund and 'responsible' past, or on speculative fabular worlds which are sometimes satires on the present and sometimes projections of the future; or on seedy and insignificant-seeming lives at the fringe of society. The 'fantasy' of present realities seems to resist fictional treatment: the attempts to address the enormity of the forces which are sensed to be at work in the present lead to a focus – on what? The crushing weight of the corrupt past in its death-throes, an unknown but threatening future, a present without value or definition – a present 'between the acts'.

In fictional terms this means, I suggest, three broad categories. First, there are modes of narrative realism which purport to describe, analyse and reconstitute, in the 'world' of the book, 'things as they really are', and which therefore, by definition, are concerned with the past, with – at the most – a bringing of the action up to date by the time of their ending. Second, there are modes of fabulation which create fictitious worlds of their own, subject therefore to the laws of their own logic.[7] Third, there is a form of synthetic realism – part naturalist, part 'gothic' – which offers 'images' of the present, albeit obliquely, and which, in its self-conscious, sharply-focused reference to 'real' historical events and cultural signs, at once invokes the present social reality and betrays the distress of an ideological position which (paradoxically) recognizes that it can do nothing to alter it.

What I want to argue, then, is that fiction in the thirties is only dismissed as 'impoverished' by a literary ideology which endorses the closures of modernism, and that novelists of many different persuasions attempted to make the novel transcend the inherent individualism of the form and to address history rather than individual case-histories. Edward Upward, in 1937, expressed the problem very clearly:

> . . . speculation about future literary forms is idle unless it is accompanied by the realisation that already now the old forms can no longer adequately reflect the fundamental forces of the modern world. The writer's job is to create new forms now, to arrive by hard work at the emotional truth about present-day reality.[8]

2. VIRGINIA WOOLF: THE LIMITS OF A PRIVATE HISTORY

In 'The Leaning Tower', a paper given to the Workers' Educational Association in May 1940, Virginia Woolf made some interesting comments on the work of the younger thirties writers in relation to the English literature of previous generations, which – in spite of the gross over-simplification of her model – identifies something of the problematic I have been outlining above, and suggests the frame of mind in which she herself was writing fiction in the period. She holds that writers until roughly the First World War wrote from a 'steady tower', built on money and education, looking down on the peaceful and 'stationary' class structures of society. Most importantly, the nineteenth-century writer 'accepted them. He accepted them so completely that he became unconscious of them'.[9] 'Unconsciousness' is Virginia Woolf's key term, and she offers a perceptive (albeit unintended) analysis of liberal ideology in its dominant phase, in relation to it: 'the classes are still [in 1914] so settled that [the writer] has almost forgotten that there are classes; and he is still so secure himself that he is almost unconscious of his own position and of its security. He believes that he is looking at the whole of life; and will always so look at it' (17). The war – 'like a chasm in a smooth road' (ibid.) – changed all that. For Virginia Woolf, the change appears in the generation educated after the war who were writing in the thirties. Not only from their 'tower' could they see 'everywhere change; everywhere revolution' (21), but the tower (still based on an expensive education) was now a 'leaning tower'. They were, therefore, conscious of being on it, conscious of their own privilege, conscious of class structures and class-injustice and resentful of being party to them. Their principal characteristic, then, is 'consciousness': 'they were stung into consciousness – into self-consciousness; into class-consciousness, into the consciousness of things changing, of things falling, of death perhaps about to come' (28). The result, Virginia Woolf astutely points out, is that they largely 'wrote about themselves' (ibid.). The problems incident on extreme self-consciousness are indeed a frequent motif in the fiction of the period, as is the absence of a secure, stable world-view. But what is equally noteworthy in Virginia Woolf's remarks is the absolute silence about her own situation – in the light of her penetrating comprehension of the younger generation's. The assumption is that she is of that secure generation who grew up before the Great War shattered civilization. But the very obsession with that event in her work, her own class- and self-consciousness, the fact that she formulated the conceptions of 'The Leaning Tower' in the way she did, her own fiction in the thirties, all question that assumption. Whether the silence is ideological 'unconsciousness', or conscious suppression, is a matter for debate.

Nevertheless, the two novels she wrote in the thirties – *The Years* (1937) and *Between the Acts* (1941) – suggest both her intention to confront the life of her time and the resistance her own cultural and aesthetic predispositions set up against it. Both novels attempt to face the present by understanding the past – *The Years* by a chronological series of stopped moments of time from 1880 to the 'present day' – 1936; *Between the Acts* by the large interpolation of a 'pageant' of English history from earliest times to the present – 'a June day in 1939'. Both clearly pick up themes and techniques from earlier fiction: the concern with time and change, the focus on families and groups of friends, the suppression of plot and narrative, the use of mental impressionism. The difference, however, is that in neither case is the emphasis now on the nature of the registering consciousness; time is now seen less metaphysically as 'decay' and more historically as *process*; family groups are symptomatic, rather than the subject of interest in and for themselves; 'Art' as a bulwark against dissolution is less secure (compare Miss La Trobe's pageant in *Between the Acts*, with Lily Briscoe's painting in *To the Lighthouse*); references outwards to historical events – more especially in *Between the Acts* – are less for their effect on individual characters, and more as a context for the whole action. In other words I would claim that Virginia Woolf was here attempting to break open her own achieved fictional form, which had by way of its closures allowed the exploration of individual consciousness, and was attempting to write historically.

The Years, which she significantly regarded as an 'essay novel', part of one composite work with her 'history' of women's struggle, *Three Guineas* (1938),[10] was certainly a difficult book to write, taking her from 1932 to 1937 to complete. The novel is a chronicle of one family, the Pargiters, through two generations and – by implication – of the crushing weight of middle-class culture down into the present. The larger part of the book covers the period up to the Armistice in 1918. Then there is a time gap of roughly eighteen years to the last section, 'Present Day', which is a regathering of the family for a party at Delia's house. By now, of course, most of the family are old, and the 'present day' section is predominantly constituted by the fragmentary malcommunication of aged people who know each other too well to listen, of memories of the past, and of the disenchanted musings of Peggy and North, the younger relations bound to the past yet excluded from it.

In one sense, then, Virginia Woolf's structure is consciously ironic: the 'present' is in fact the past. But it is also significant that the novel, despite its 'historical' structure, breaks off at the end of the First World War – as though history stops there – and presents the present solely as an isolated moment in 1936. The novel, in other words, introduces a closure on its own historical sense; and in so doing reveals the limitation of a *family* history as a measure of wider historical change. The Pargiters' present may be accounted for by a history which stops in 1918, and Virginia Woolf's point may indeed be that the present of the mid thirties is the responsibility of that pre-war past, but the weight of this cannot be fully felt if the emphasis remains exclusively on the family and its past. History is privatised.

The same might be said more generally – despite the fuller realisation of the Pargiter culture – of the relation between private history and social history in the earlier parts of the book. The crippling effects of bourgeois domestic ideology are firmly felt, but the results in the wider culture – the responsibility, say, of the Pargiter culture for the First World War and the subsequent civilization – are not realised, although they are implicit. It is here, I think, that the novel reveals its problematic. Virginia Woolf remained in the tradition of nineteenth-century liberal individualism; *The Years* itself closes strangely with an affirmation of Eleanor – at seventy, and the victim most directly of Pargiter ideology – greeting the new day:

'And now?', she cried, looking at Morris, who was drinking the last drops of a glass of wine, 'And now?' she asked, holding out her hands to him. The sun had risen, and the sky above the houses wore an air of extraordinary beauty, simplicity and peace.[11]

And North, seemingly with Virginia Woolf behind him, has earlier mused:

What do they mean by Justice and Liberty? he asked, all these nice young men with two or three hundred a year. Something's wrong, he thought; there's a gap, a dislocation, between the word and the reality. If they want to reform the world, he thought, why not begin there, at the centre, with themselves? (437)

Stillness and solitude, he thought to himself; silence and solitude . . . that's the only element in which the mind is free now (457).

The Pargiter culture has been seen to trammel or cripple such 'Bloomsbury' liberal -humanist values. But in fact, Pargiter culture is only the public manifestation of the same individualist ideology which centrally informs those 'values'. A full analysis of the present society would reveal Virginia Woolf's own values *as party* to the inimical culture of the present, their unperceived responsibility for, and

inadequacy in the face of it. (Her Introductory Letter to the Co-
operative Guild's *Life as We Have Known It* in 1930 (reprinted,
London 1977) obliquely reveals her sense of this.) To focus on the past
of the Pargiter family alone, suppresses that connection.

Between the Acts is a more uncompromising work. Written with the
Second World War underway, and set on its eve, the novel takes
history out of the individual situation and holds it up (as Miss La Trobe
does in her pageant) to the audience. And contemporary history drums
insistently at the edge of the action (Giles's reflections continuously
invoke the coming war: 'Europe, bristling with guns, poised with
planes'; 'sixteen men had been shot, others imprisoned, just over there,
across the gulf, in the flat land which divided them from the
continent').[12] The riven insecurity of the family — which owns the
country house and land where the pageant is performed (in other words,
the pageant is the 'history' of that culture); the failure of love between
Isa and Giles, and the garish substitution of Mrs Manresa as 'Love'; the
absence of communication between characters; the incomprehension of
the audience (shown by the mirrors at the end of the pageant to be
themselves the 'orts, scraps and fragments' which constitute civilization
[219]): all signify a recognition that civilization is breaking up. Miss La
Trobe, the writer and producer of the pageant, 'the artist', is towards the
end made to focus this whole movement:

'After Vic.', she had written, 'try ten mins. of present time. . . .' She wanted to
expose them, as it were, to douche them, with present time reality. But
something was going wrong with the experiment. 'Reality too strong', she
muttered, 'Curse 'em!' . . . Panic seized her. Blood seemed to pour from her
shoes. This is death, death, death, she noted in the margin of her mind; when
illusion fails. Unable to lift her hand, she stood facing the audience (209–10).

Nevertheless, there is again a final affirmation — albeit by way of the
'heart of darkness' (Conrad's primitive and ultimate reality) — that
another 'act' will begin. It is the 'act' which Miss La Trobe, eight pages
earlier, has envisaged as the opening of a new 'pageant':

Before they slept, they must fight; after they had fought, they would embrace.
From that embrace another life might be born. But first they must fight, as the
dog fox fights with the vixen, in the heart of darkness, in the fields of night.

. . . The window was all sky without colour. The house had lost its shelter. It
was night before roads were made, or houses. It was the night that dwellers in
caves had watched from some high place among rocks.

Then the curtain rose. They spoke (248).

Between the Acts is a valediction to the nineteenth-century liberal-humanist cultural tradition of which Virginia Woolf as a novelist was a late efflorescence. What makes it particularly revealing, however, is the uncompromising artificiality of the pageant as a device for accommodating history, and the self-commentary Miss La Trobe's 'art' makes on the art of the novel itself. The 'failure of illusion' implies a demystification of the rhetoric of fiction as well as of a civilization. The pageant, crude and expressionist in itself – as it also is as a constituent of the novel – does nevertheless contain history and a more than individual experience and consciousness (which in Isa's inconsequent, private 'poetry'-making is now seen to be a self-indulgence). The inference is that Virginia Woolf recognised that to encompass the large processes of social and cultural change, an art less private than her own was required, that her own art was indeed a part of the 'illusion' which was 'failing'.

3. ALDOUS HUXLEY: FABLES OF DESPAIR

Between the Acts was Virginia Woolf's last novel before her suicide, and it seems to reveal a profound uncertainty about the genre's ability to transcend its own ideology – which is the observation and synthetic recreation of felt individual experience. Aldous Huxley, another already established liberal novelist, raises the same question from the other pole. In 1932 he produced *Brave New World*, a satiric dystopia which by way of exaggeration and fantasy suggests the mutually-supporting destructive tendencies of science, monopoly capitalism, mass communications and totalitarian government. At the same time he proposes the folly and stupidity of humanist individualism: at its most degraded in the Reservation, at its most noble in John the Savage – who is nevertheless destroyed by his own idealism. (In fact, and despite Huxley's statement in a later preface[13] that the book's failing was that it only offered two alternatives – 'insanity' and 'lunacy', the residual sympathy is with John's individualism; indeed the satire would not operate without an assumption that the 'brave new world' is evil because it is anti-individual.) By dint of the infralogic of a fabulated world to express his loathing for contemporary culture, Huxley's subjective views receive, as it were, 'objective' status. But such a strategy contains two connected problematics: first, it addresses 'fantastic realities' by reconstituting them as 'realist fantasies', and second, in so doing, it *parades* its partiality – the fact that the 'brave new world' is overtly 'made up' permits disregard as a primary right. To put it another way, *Brave New World* is only *satire* if the reader agrees to accept Huxley's reading of the world as true; otherwise it is fantasy. Realism, on the other hand, at its most persuasive, establishes a dialectical referentiality between its own 'world' and the real world it invokes and inhabits, so that even if its partiality is apparent it can nevertheless claim some status other than that of pure subjectivity. But 'fantasy', once we have perceived how exclusively locked within its own terms of reference it is, can be no more than a self-fulfilling prophecy – unless the form is consciously and expressively used as itself a 'sign' of dissociation from social reality. The dystopic mode of *Brave New World*, then, enables Huxley to express a vision of the present, but it is not *about* the present. And if we choose to regard the 'fantasy' as, in this case, unwittingly a 'sign', then it can only signify Huxley's cultural pessimism, his rejection of history and desire to disengage.

This becomes clearer, in a significant way, in the later, more complex *Eyeless in Gaza* (1936). Here Huxley, like many novelists in the period, returns to the past in order to explain the present. Despite the dislocated chronology, this is the 'history' of Anthony Beavis, an embittered and dehumanized intellectual, up to the point (1933/4) when the hard shell of his life is fractured. His conversion to mysticism and pacifism by Dr Miller, and his attempts in the present (1934) to act according to the new precepts are no more than the bringing-up-to-date of his history. The novel is in fact a sort of spiritual autobiography of Huxley himself up to about 1932, an 'explanation' of the misanthropic state of mind which produced *Brave New World*.

The significance of the novel for my argument is that while much of it has been at pains to reveal the influence of the past as a conditioning *process* on the characters – which leads in the case of Anthony to the recognition that 'Love' is the solution to the world's problems – the Anthony of 1934 seems to suggest that the moment of recognition is, in itself, of prime importance. But the question arises: could Anthony have reached the 'solution' *without* undergoing the process? If not, then the patterns of behaviour he (and the other characters) represent will always be dominant until the moment of recognition is achieved by the individual – if indeed it can be achieved without the *fortuitous* intervention of a Dr Miller. That is to say: the novel *as history* suggests that experience through time equals knowledge or truth (which Beavis/Huxley, later in the book, seems to endorse: 'imaginative literature' should be 'a complete expression . . . leading to complete knowledge (with the whole mind) of the complete truth: indispensable preliminary condition of any remedial action, any serious attempt at the construction of a genuinely human being'[14]).

But the novel *as polemical assertion* (i.e. the 1934, 'present', sections) seems to suggest that such history is irrelevant if 'the truth' is grasped instantaneously and unequivocally. *Eyeless in Gaza* in fact contains both 'realist' and 'fictive' elements: Anthony's history, *what has happened*, is realist (and is indeed a resonant account of the sterile bourgeois culture of the pre- and inter-war years), whereas the speculative or 'ideal' sections – 'the present' – are either overtly fictive (the contingency of the meeting with Dr Miller in the South American Jungle – Chapter 49) or dogmatic (bald statements of the new philosophy, e.g. Chapter 17). The effect is that the convincing depiction of what *has* happened rebuts the statements of what *should* happen. The problem – as the paradoxes of the final, proselytizing, chapter suggest – is fundamentally ideological, which the modality of the novel may be said to approve. Beavis/Huxley recognizes that the 'condition of life' is separation and evil, but wishes to affirm the 'ideal' which is unity and good. The 'ideal', however, can only be attained by individual conversion: that is, *in spite of* the material condition of life, rather than by changing it. But if *what happens* through time to individuals (like Anthony Beavis) is the material condition of life – which is what the novel so convincingly confirms – then the ideal can only ever be an abstraction, a repudiation of those material conditions. This too is confirmed by the fictive 'present' of the novel: statements of hope, as the last lines of the book explicitly signify, are the sole means of transcendence – 'Dispassionately, and with a serene lucidity, he thought of *what was in store for him. Whatever it might be, he knew now that all would be well*' (400, my italics). Beavis's self-confidence here is, paradoxically, the quintessence of individualist cultural despair. So too is Huxley's last novel in the thirties, *After Many a Summer* (1939), in which he combines the Millerian theorizing of *Eyeless in Gaza* with a Brave New World-like California to produce a fable so imprisoned in its own worldview, and hence so self-fulfilling, as to become the ultimate 'fantasy' of that despair.

4. EDWARD UPWARD: JOURNEY TO THE BORDER OF FICTION

The intractability of social reality for fiction in the thirties was not, however, solely a problem for 'liberal' novelists. Edward Upward, Rex

Warner and George Orwell also faced the problem in their different
ways, and also evince a similar ambivalence to 'history' and 'prophecy'.
Upward, who produced very little fiction in the thirties, but who,
according to Isherwood in *Lions and Shadows*, was a forceful influence
on himself and the 'Auden group' in general, exemplifies the problem
for fiction very exactly. His 'Sketch for a Marxist Interpretation of
Literature' (1937)[15] is, for example, clearly informed – beneath its self-
confident tone – by a recognition of it. Upward here dismisses both
descriptive realism, even if it is written 'with complete faithfulness (to)
the surface of life in England today' (46), and 'literary allegories and
fantasies, sophisticated fables' (48), because neither is 'true to life':
realism, because it ignores 'the real forces at work beneath the surface
of life', and is thus 'pessimistic'; fantasy, because it 'implies in practice a
retreat from the real world into the world of imagination'. (Upward,
nevertheless, returns in a later paragraph to the possibility of a 'higher',
more 'scientific' species of 'fairy story' as the possible form for the
future (54) – with his own practice, doubtless, in mind). The essay is
thereafter marked by a series of telling silences and tensions. For
example: having specified that such realities as economic crisis,
unemployment, fascism and the approach of war 'are beginning to be
reflected in the work of the *majority of serious writers today*' (49, my
italics), he omits to say who these writers are, and proceeds, for much of
the rest of the essay, to expose the inadequacies of the work of
Lawrence, Joyce and Proust. Even his basic point that a 'true writer'
must now be a socialist sinks into a private debate on how difficult it will
be to be both – a debate strikingly similar to the one 'the tutor' has with
himself towards the end of Upward's novella *Journey to the Border*
(1938). And the essay ends with no proposals for the writing of books
which are true to 'present-day reality' – only the statement, quoted
earlier, that the 'old forms' are inadequate, and the writer's job is to
'create new forms now'.

Upward's uncertainty also informs his own practice as a writer. His
loathing of the bourgeois culture in which he was brought up was
initially expressed in the Mortmere fantasies he and Isherwood
developed at Cambridge.[16] 'The Railway Accident' (1928) was the only
one to be published. The story is the kind of fantasy I referred to briefly
earlier in which the mode of expression is less a method of getting one's
own way on behalf of a particular world-view, and more a version of
'gothic' in which the form itself becomes a 'sign' for neurosis, fear,
uncertainty. The details of experiential life are so selected, highlighted

and juxtaposed that, although identifiable as real in themselves they take on a sinister significance which their own substance cannot justify; and the bland narration of *outré* events as though they were ordinary anecdotes, combined with a deliberate uncertainty as to the sanity – or even the identity – of the narrator, evoke, as it were, the underside of a seemingly innocuous stone.

If my train did not go to Mortmere I could get another the next day, or Welken might guess what had happened and send his car. The first gasometers, restful, solemn like stumps of semi-amputated breasts, curved past the window in frost-bright air. Wireless poles and drying pants in soot-black gardens with mustard and cress sprouting from window boxes would soon follow. Now for many months of complete summer I should idle in gardens warm with croquet and the tinkling of spoons, shadowed by yews. Naked bathing would be usual and the rector would fish for pike off log-rafts.[17]

Upward, like Isherwood and Graham Greene, as we shall see later, re-invests the trivial with suppressed meanings. 'The Railway Accident' both invokes, in Harold Pinter's phrase, 'the weasel under the cocktail cabinet', and Upward's own neurosis at perceiving it. *Journey to the Border*, Upward's longest fiction in the thirties, is also, for the most part, an expression of neurosis, but here it is more structured. This novella, like so many other *rites de passage* novels by the young left intelligentsia in the thirties, is a tale of conversion: a journey to the border of insanity, beyond which lies the sanity of commitment to Marxism. The series of temptations and fantastic experiences which 'the tutor' undergoes during his – in actuality, perfectly normal – day at the races with his *nouveau riche* employer are, of course, 'fabulated', but they have an experiential referent, a 'real' explanation, in the neurotic sensibility of the tutor who hates his work and the bourgeois culture he is forced to accept and service. 'Fantasy' becomes a form of realism when it is used to express the fantasies of neurosis:

The pest would spread far beyond the racecourse, had without doubt begun to spread already. A desert of limitless ignorance surrounded the tutor. A desert of danger. He knew that the M.F.H.'s story of a plot was a lie, the story of an immediate external threat was a lie; but he knew too that violence was much nearer him now than it had been before the cheering. War had been distant from him before; now it was rapidly approaching. It might break out at any moment – visibly, tangibly, in one form or another. Audibly – a noise of reconnoitring aeroplanes, the bawling of sergeants. But not yet. The noise at present was nothing more than cheering.[18]

The actual crossing of the 'border', and the 'sanity' of the solution, however, are considerably more abstract and unrealised – presented in the form of statement and debate (part of which, in effect, is from Upward's 'Sketch' considered above). The analogy with Huxley's *Eyeless in Gaza* is inescapable: the *process* is experiential and individual, the *solution* is abstract and intellectual. Upward, like Huxley, expressed the decadence of bourgeois culture by way of a type of synthetic realism (the 'pessimistic', surface truthfulness of the 'Sketch'); but, as that essay implied, the discovery of a fictional myth which would transcend individual experience and be fully 'true to life' remained a problem. Upward wrote no more fiction – until the 1960s when he began to produce the flat autobiographical realism of his trilogy *In the Thirties*. Isherwood commented in 1938, in *Lions and Shadows*, that Upward ('Chalmers') spent years in the thirties, in 'desperate and bitter struggles', trying to 'relate Mortmere to the real world ... to find the formula which would transform our private fantasies and amusing freaks and bogies into valid symbols of the ills of society. . . .' He found it finally, Isherwood notes, 'in the pages of Lenin and Marx',[19] and thereafter in political, but not literary, practice. *Journey to the Border* prophesies that equivocal solution.

5. REX WARNER: FABLE AS DISCOVERY

Rex Warner seems to present the reverse of Upward's case. A Marxist in the thirties, his commitment was waning by the end of the decade, and he gradually turned to a self-conscious and sceptical liberal-humanism. His first novel, however, *The Wild Goose Chase* (1937), is a vigorous and self-confident fable of revolution. Warner uses fabulation to expose capitalism's use of education, religion, science, the intelligentsia, libertarian politicians, etc., to foster its illusions of totality, its myths of power, its tricks and deceptions (the giggling policemen who control by practical joking, the clergyman who claims he is 'just as much a revolutionary as any of you'[20]), and to induce a 'consensus' which 'justifies' exploitation. In this, it is satire of a devastating kind. Furthermore, its presentation of the revolution is highly realised in conception and action. But there are two 'dissenting' factors I wish to draw attention to.

First, *The Wild Goose Chase* is a highly schematic novel – it *is* a fable and is, therefore, as I suggested in relation to *Brave New World*, so manifestly fictive as to be self-fulfilling: things work out as they are intended to work out because there is nothing which is not proposed and designed by, or can resist, the determinism of this fictional history. Except – and this is the second point – the way in which the novel, in a sense against its own will, focuses on George as *hero* (in both the literary and the political senses). It is George, in a very significant way, who makes the revolution possible, and it is George who, even when the revolution is achieved, must continue to hunt the 'wild goose' (the 'adventure' of life, the 'future', 'imagination'). In other words, despite the materialist conception of history which the fable proposes, the book inclines to a form of romantic individualism. *The Wild Goose Chase*, then, at an intellectual level, brings about by fabulation the situation it intends; but it also contains a dissident tendency – carried perhaps by the predilections of the novel form itself – to focus on the individual. In this book, such a tendency is, in fact, largely controlled by the exclusive schema of the fable. But it is not surprising – given Warner's own gradual return to liberal-humanism – to find that his second novel, *The Professor* (1938), reveals this tendency much more explicitly.

This is also a political fable, a clear analytic enactment of the fatal contradictions of liberalism. And it is consistent to the end in proving that the Professor's liberal-humanism, his 'culture', is inadequate, that he should have gone forward from liberalism and joined the left to defeat the true barbarism of fascism. But the real focus of attention is the Professor himself *as character*: the first pages of the novel declare a pity for him, but again and again there is a psychological 'understanding' of him which is at odds with his fable-conceived absence of 'character'. What results is not just a generalised pity for the tragic flaw in well-intentioned liberalism, but a transferred attention to the tragedy of an *individual* liberal-humanist – which is exactly what the logic of the fable, both as fiction and as political analysis, demonstrates to be inadequate and dangerous. The 'flaw' in liberalism (and in the Professor's position) is shown to be the deification of the individual; the problem with 'realist' fiction has been its inability to focus other than on individual experience: and this is why Warner writes his *fable*, *The Professor*. But the individualism residual in the author, and implicit in the novel form, crosses and confuses this intention.

By *The Aerodrome* (1941), Warner's liberal-humanism is acknowledged, and the theme of the book is the affirmation of individual human lives, even at their most muddled and sordid, against the polished efficiency of the planned totalitarian future the 'Aerodrome' represents. It is a *Brave New World* (the two books have striking resemblances) in

which the life of the Reservation is unequivocally posited against the
megapolis of Ford. The novel is still conceived as a fable – in the
'Author's Note' Warner writes: 'I do not even aim at realism'[21] and the
structure of the book ('Village' *contra* 'Aerodrome'; the series of
artificial connections between characters, and especially between
fathers and sons), is highly schematic. The treatment of the 'future' – the
Aerodrome – is also, characteristically, the kind of satiric fabulation
Brave New World exemplifies. Nevertheless, the first-person narration
by Roy, the hero, automatically proposes the 'veracity' of realism, and
precludes the full-scale, 'omniscient', establishment of a fabular world
by making an individual experience the register of its existence.
Furthermore, Roy's narrative makes it more emphatically a novel with
an individual at its centre – an individual who is ultimately the cause of
the defeat of totalitarianism and the champion of 'Life' and 'Love'. It is
particularly significant, however, that much of the theme and action of
the book concerns the rediscovery and disclosure of the past, and of the
relationships of the characters which constitute it. The Air Vice-
Marshal's megalomania and thus the 'Aerodrome', it transpires, are
not the result of the logic of history, of the crisis of liberal-bourgeois
ideology, but the failure of 'Love', of personal relationships, in the past.
The older generation, *as individuals*, are responsible for the menacing
present and future. The echoes of Huxley, but this time in *Eyeless in
Gaza*, reverberate in this novel:[22] in particular, the nature of the
'responsible' past, and the emphasis on Love through the discovery of
the self (Roy 'finds himself' by recovering the past (334), just as
Anthony Beavis does). And the problems both novelists face are not
dissimilar. In Warner's case the 'reality' of his positive vision is the
Village (Life, Love); and one might have expected, given the
recrudescent liberal-humanism of the novel, a more affirmative realism
in defining it. Roy identifies the point for his author:

I, too, had regained what I had lost, a desire to see the world as it was and some
assurance of the ground on which my feet were treading. It was not for me, I
know now, to attempt either to reshape or to avoid what was too vast even to be
imagined as enfolding me, nor could I reject as negligible the least event in the
whole current of past time (335).

But the 'Village' is never solidly realized. It is, in fact, trapped by the
fabular structure and pattern: the Village must *mean* certain things,
because the schema demands them. But this modal ambivalence – the
unreal 'reality' – draws attention to a contradiction in the statement the

book wishes to make, just as, in an inverse way, it did in *The Professor*. The schematic unreality of the Village, the stated but unrealised values of Love and Life, the use of overt fictive contrivance (the disclosure of familial relationships, the death of the Air Vice-Marshal) to bring about its triumph and affirmation, certainly do not express the conviction by which uncompromising realism had positively affirmed its liberal-humanist ideology. The point is that 'the Village' is a fiction too – it is no more present reality than the Aerodrome (indeed less so in some ways), and Warner knew it. But what image of present reality could fiction present in the last years of the 1930s as an affirmation of the vitality of liberal-humanism? If it could not be convincingly enacted in fable, then its expression in fiction at all was problematic. Warner significantly wrote no more novels which attempted to engage directly with the realities of contemporary society.

6. GEORGE ORWELL: WHO TELLS THE TALE?

In the course of his writing career, George Orwell experimented with a wide range of fictional modes, from the conventional narrative realism of *Burmese Days* (1934) through the autobiographical 'documentary' reporting of *The Road to Wigan Pier* (1937) to the satiric fables of *Animal Farm* (1945) and *1984* (1949). But I want to concentrate here on two novels in the later thirties, *Keep the Aspidistra Flying* (1936) and *Coming Up for Air* (1939), which expose most pointedly the problem of making the 'fantastic realities' of the world in the 1930s the substance of fiction. (That the question, 'Why in fiction at all?' is never very clearly asked is, perhaps, an indication of the command exercised by the dominant cultural ideology.)

Keep the Aspidistra Flying is a puzzling novel because of its uncertainty of stance. There can be little doubt that Orwell uses Gordon Comstock, on whom the novel is entirely focused, to convey his own scorn and loathing for the 'money culture' of his time – as the tiny shifts in tense and person in any passage of 'Gordon's' reflections will reveal: 'At this moment is seemed to him that in a street like this, in a town like this, every life that is lived must be meaningless and intolerable. The sense of disintegration, of decay, that *is endemic in our* time, was strong upon him.'[23] But at the same time Comstock is 'judged', by the novel, for his pig-headed and self-destructive resistance to his culture. He is, finally, sucked back into his old job, into domestic life, his gesture of defiance a failure. But this reassimilation, in an odd sort of way, communicates itself as a positive affirmation. Love (Gordon and Rosemary) and new life (their baby) somehow counter the appalling cultural totalitarianism the book has been at such pains to identify. It doesn't take a logician to point out that there are confusions here. What happens to Comstock's judgements on society (and Orwell's surely) if his attitudes are wrong, as they must be if he really ought not to have cut himself off from society, however horrible? And if his return to the fold is not a total failure, has the 'money culture' triumphed or not? All Comstock/Orwell's judgements would imply that it had – as it must – and that his return to it is proof of its power. But not if he was wrong to be outside it? And if indeed the money culture is so powerful, how can individual factors (love and the new baby) constitute a real affirmation?

There are, I think, two related explanations for these contradictions. One lies in Orwell's own fundamental individualism, and the dilemma it gives rise to: a simultaneous hatred of vast inhuman systems and a recognition of the futility of individual action against them, which leads to the classic liberal anxiety: if you engage in communal action (i.e. socialism), are you, in effect, joining a version of the enemy (totalitarianism)? Orwell wants (and wants Comstock) to be both in, and against, society. The second explanation lies in Orwell's need, therefore, to express his loathing of modern capitalist culture in terms other than those of doctrinaire political polemic. Comstock, as an alienated 'character' in a novel, can respond directly to the 'realities' of his world; but because he is *a character*, Orwell becomes implicated in other dimensions of Comstock than his jeremiads on 'money culture'. And if Comstock, *as character*, is wrong or objectionable or stupid, or his judgements are 'explained' (and so explained away) by his character, then so too are *Orwell's* reflections on money culture. 'Reality' becomes no more than Comstock's jaundiced perception of it. The confusions reside here: Orwell needs a spokesman – Comstock; but in writing realistic fiction he creates a character he cannot defend – Comstock's self-immolating misanthropy is as futile and inhuman as the culture he is resisting. Orwell is forced to rescue him for humanity in order to rescue his own judgements. But by now it is by no means clear whether Orwell does (or indeed *can*) stand behind the character who has uttered so much of what he himself feels. Realism is more complex in its logic and operation than Orwell, in *Keep the Aspidistra Flying*, gives it credit for; and its focus on the individual makes social reality difficult to encompass – the more so, the more fully realised the individual character is.

In *Coming Up for Air*, a novel obsessed with the approaching war, Orwell solves the problem of the untrustworthy 'spokesman' by allowing George Bowling to tell his own story. Because Bowling is a 'trustworthy narrator', it remains, of course, one man's version of things. In fact, Orwell successfully exploits this, turning Bowling's obsessive iteration of his neurotic imagery (the bombs, the rubber truncheons, the boot in the face, the machine-guns squirting from bedroom windows) into a powerful metaphor for the fear of war. But, in being true to his character, Orwell is still stuck with this particular consciousness as the medium of the novel. For instance, because of Bowling's sudden desire to revisit Lower Binfield, the novel quickly retreats from the menacing present to a recovery of the past, and especially the Edwardian idyll of Bowling's childhood. However much Orwell intends to use the past as a measure of the present, and to point up Bowling's foolishness in expecting it to have remained the same, Bowling's memories shift the focus away from the present and indeed idealise the past. Orwell's problem, once again, was to make an individual experience transmit the terrifying social and political processes of his time – cultural decay, dehumanization, global war, totalitarianism. Unlike Isherwood, as we shall see, Orwell does not place Bowling, his narrator, fully within the frame of his novel, so that the way Bowling perceives things does not become part of the picture, his own world-view cannot be seen as itself responsible for the cultural shambles around him. Bowling remains an honest individual, an outsider without wishing it, threatened on all sides by forces he registers as frightful, and which the reader must take on trust because of his integrity. He is, in fact, both inside and outside the frame of the novel: George Bowling and George Orwell. Bowling is Orwell's ultimate 'realistic' representation of his own despairing individualism. There is, to me, a kind of inevitable logic, therefore, in terms both of Orwell's own development and of the fiction of the period more generally, that he should finally turn to fable and satiric dystopia. *Animal Farm* and *1984* are clear instances of the way an individual perception of the 'fantastic realities' of modern history can be given 'objective' status by the creation of total alternative 'worlds' fabricated to endorse it.

7. GRAHAM GREENE: THE REALISM OF NEUROSIS

The works of the last two novelists I shall deal with, Graham Greene and Christopher Isherwood, manage to relocate the 'fantastic realities' of the thirties in their period. And they do so, I would like to claim, by exploiting the novel form's characteristic strategies and materials. They attempt to present an analysis of a particular cultural moment in the material forms of that cultural moment. In so doing, of course, they remain trapped within the ideology of the genre – the novels only register the condition of the existing culture. For Upward, therefore, they would not be 'true to life'; because, while recognising 'the decadence of present-day society', they do not also recognise 'the inevitability of revolution'.[24] Or, to borrow Althusser's terms, they are still 'bathed' in the dominant ideology – although they also, I would argue, achieve a 'critical distance' from it.[25] And this 'critical distance' is won *precisely because* these novels continuously reconstitute the real relations between their own fictional 'worlds' and the material world they claim to reproduce.

Greene's fiction in the thirties is difficult to characterise. With the exception, perhaps, of *Brighton Rock* (1938), the novels ('entertainments', in Greene's term) do not openly parade his later concern with the Catholic conscience, although most have one of his fallen 'saints' as a focal character. They are diverse in location and subject, and they seem to resist thematic interpretation, both individually and as a group. The standard critical focus is on the 'seediness' of 'Greeneland' – which is, indeed, an important constituent. They are most easily designated *images*, and Greene's interest in film and film techniques makes this term particularly apposite. But images of what – of Greeneland? And what, then, is Greeneland? The answer is supplied, in the first instance, by the title of one of the early novels – *It's a Battlefield* (1934). *War* is the commonest device in Greeneland, not so much actual warfare – although this hangs at the edge of *The Confidential Agent* (1939) and *A Gun for Sale* (1936) – but the sense of a state of war between powerful and inimical social forces and puny human individuals. 'It was like war', D. thinks, in *The Confidential Agent*, as he walks through a depressed Midland mining village, 'but without the spirit of defiance war usually raised'.[26] What distinguishes this from what I earlier suggested was the traditional focus of fiction – the individual's negotiations with society – is firstly, that in Greene's fiction the individuals are degraded and insignificant-seeming, and are seldom the central focus for their own sake but for what they are subject to; and secondly, the form in which the relation is defined. In Greene's work, this is not a negotiation, it is war. Society is the predatory enemy, the individual the hunted; very occasionally he is a frightened and isolated guerrilla. The individual as hero has been truly displaced – a tiny figure scuttling across a vast battlefield. But this, as I shall suggest in a moment, does not make Greene's work any the less individualist – merely more 'realistic' than that which makes an affirmation by fabulated contrivance.

The force of Greene's fiction resides especially in the atmosphere of threat, of fear, of violence, and of neurosis. This is achieved in a number of ways which suggest how Greene turns realism into a kind of myth. The thirties novels are thrillers, in which pursuit and violent death are crucial aspects of the plot; the structure itself, in other words, is an expressive facet of the metaphor of menace and anxiety each novel as a whole becomes. Furthermore, as in the case of Upward's 'The Railway Accident', the normal and the trivial are invested with a significance they would not normally seem able to sustain, and thus become sinister.

He could hear the wireless playing in both houses. In the one house it switched and changed as a restless finger turned the screw and beat up the wavelengths, bringing a snatch of rhetoric from Berlin, of opera from Stockholm. On the National Programme from the other house an elderly critic was reading verse.[27]

The 'restless finger' and the 'snatch of rhetoric from Berlin' are the characteristic details which imbue the whole of Greene's world with unease. And the physical world, too, is imbued with – or rather made to reveal – a complicity with the corrupt and destructive forces which govern society:

The rain blew up along the River Weevil from the east; it turned to ice in the bitter night and stung the asphalt walks, pitted the paint on the wooden seats. A constable came quietly by in his heavy raincoat gleaming like wet macadam, moving his lantern here and there in the dark spaces between the lamps. . . . It was couples he expected to find, even in December under the hail, the signs of poor cooped provincial passion.[28]

This, together with the use of a montage technique, where small pieces of distinct actions are cut in with each other in counterpoint, Greene borrows from film. The point I wish to make is that Greene enriches his fictional texture to the point at which it becomes *almost* sur- or super-real, and the novels, rather than being directly about anything, operate as images or metaphors of a psychological condition, not of particular individuals, but a general social condition of being in a state of war: 'Although they loved each other, their minds were like two countries at war, with the telegraph wires down and the rails torn up.'[29]

The importance of Greene's work is that it never becomes totally 'gothic', never merely a correlative for a psychological condition expressing nameless fears and terrors. The warfare is material and socially located. The developing insanity of Conrad in *It's a Battlefield*, and his final pointless, and bungled, 'assassination' of the Assistant Commissioner, is effective at the mythic level *because* it is firmly 'explained' by the pressures of society's commercial and sexual morality; the menacing image of the hair-lipped gunman Raven, in *A Gun for Sale*, is given substance both by Greene's presentation of his history, and by the real power of the armaments manufacturer over the fate of Europe; it is the power of Krogh the Swedish capitalist in *England Made Me* (1935) which destroys everything it touches; and the Kafka-like bewilderment of D. in *The Confidential Agent* is made telling by placing it in the context of a real war, the Spanish Civil War, and the irresponsible influence of the Midlands' coal-owners. The point is that Greene's war is between individual human beings and a society dominated by a rapacious capitalism. The psychological terror evoked by his novels has its 'real relations' there. But both the mythic force of Greene's fiction, and its invocation of real contexts, depend on the establishment of a coherent and convincing 'world' within the book which is experiential and specific. The precise and detailed reference to the material world of Europe in the thirties, however synthetic Greene's use of it, is the constituent which gives substance to his metaphors of neurosis and their social causes.

Greene's registering, then, of the evils of capitalism and their effect on individual lives, in the thirties, is a form of contemporary humanist 'realism'. Indeed, although his individuals are obscure and abject, and are not themselves the central focus, it is exactly in this that both his liberal-humanism and his realism are revealed: the *real* crime of monopoly capitalism and its 'warfare' is the displacement of the individual.

For the most part, Greene's stance is tacit in the novels, and he follows the 'real' logic of events in his world, leaving his commitment to the individual implicit in his evisceration of capitalist culture, showing individuals as victims. But there is one occasion in particular when he 'rescues' an individual from the logic of his situation. In *The Confidential Agent*, D., against the odds, escapes from his pursuers, boards the rescue boat and finds Rose there too; their love is given a chance. And this is, significantly, one of the most contrived moments in Greene's fiction of the period; it is an affirmation, or at least a resolution, achieved by fiction alone. It is both unrealistic and unreal. What this means is, I think, that in the 1930s individualism was so beset that individuals in realist fiction could only be presented as victims, with the focus on the forces that destroy them. Greene's fiction, then, is indeed in the 'realist' tradition, but at an historical moment when liberal-humanism is at the point of breakdown. His metaphors of fear and neurosis, his exposure of the real relations which create such a psychological condition are, in themselves, an expression of that consciousness; they enact their own subject. Beyond this ultimate distillation of things as they really *are* (not will be), they cannot go. The force of Greene's fiction in the thirties resides, to no small degree, in the fact that he leaves his own conception of individual salvation outside the world of his books.

8. CHRISTOPHER ISHERWOOD: SNAPSHOTS OF THE LOST

The phrase 'fantastic realities' which I have used throughout this essay is Christopher Isherwood's from a Foreword he wrote in 1949 to Upward's 'The Railway Accident'.[30] Upward and Isherwood together created the 'Mortmere' myth, and spent a considerable time trying to make it 'have *some* relation to everyday reality'.[31] Through Upward, too – and by way of E. M. Forster's fiction – Isherwood discovered what he calls 'tea-tabling'. Chalmers' letter to Isherwood explains:

The whole of Forster's technique is based on the tea-table. . . . In fact, there's actually *less* emphasis laid on the big scenes than on the unimportant ones: that's what's so utterly terrific. It's the completely new kind of accentuation – like a person talking a different language. . . .[32]

This technique (which also helps to define the method of Patrick Hamilton's much underrated novel *Hangover Square* (1941)[33]) focuses ostensibly on the 'tea-table', on the seemingly trivial and peripheral, leaving large and important issues and events outside the tea-room. Occasionally, however, their presence is glimpsed or felt; and this qualifies and gives a context to what is going on at the tea-table. Indeed the events at the tea-table are themselves given a new significance, or rather, their *meaning* is thrown into relief, and they become implicated in the larger context beyond the tea-room. 'Isherwood', for example, describes returning from a wealthy Jewish party at a country house outside Berlin:

As we came down the Tauentzienstrasse, they were selling papers with the news of the shooting on the Bülowplatz. I thought of our party lying out there on the lawn by the lake, drinking our claret-cup while the gramophone played; and of that police-officer, revolver in hand, stumbling mortally wounded up the cinema steps to fall dead at the feet of a cardboard figure advertising a comic film.[34]

By these means, Isherwood was able, in *Mr Norris Changes Trains* (1935) and *Goodbye to Berlin* (1939), to address the 'fantastic realities' of his period. Before this, in *The Memorial* (1932), he had, in common with many novelists in the thirties, explored the Edwardian past for some explanation of the post-war world, and had laid the responsibility for the crippled lives of his own generation – and the part the First World War had played in that – firmly at the feet of the older generation. Significantly, the influence of Virginia Woolf's fiction is appreciable in *The Memorial*. The emphasis in the Berlin stories, however, is unequivocally on the present.

Both books were to have been part of a larger work (unfinished) entitled *The Lost*. Both are attempts to account for, and give form to, the triumph of fascism in Germany in the early thirties and, more generally, the condition of Europe which brought this about. The incongruity of such grandiose themes and the apparent insouciance of the novels themselves is precisely the effect of Isherwood's 'new kind of accentuation', of 'tea-tabling'. But to what end? First, because such obliqueness was a way of addressing the 'fantastic realities' of the present; and second, more positively, because the rise of Hitler had a cultural and ideological explanation other than in the 'public' historical domain of post-First World War diplomacy, economics and politics, or in Hitler's own drive to power. And it is this that fiction may reveal in the symptomatic decadence of obscure and unimportant private lives. Isherwood establishes a complicity between Mr Norris's activities, or Fräulein Schroeder's menage, and the historical situation which is their context. Anni and her 'disciplinary' talents – 'her whole costume [had] the effect of a kind of uniform'[35] – and the sinister calm of Olga's ersatz presence – 'her feet were jammed into absurdly small high-heeled shoes, out of which bulged pads of silk-stockinged flesh. Her cheeks were pink and her hair dyed tinsel-golden, so that it matched the glitter of the half-dozen bracelets on her powdered arms' (30) – are forced into contiguity with a world in which

Hate exploded suddenly, without warning, out of nowhere; at street corners, in restaurants, cinemas, dance halls, swimming-baths; at midnight, after breakfast, in the middle of the afternoon. Knives were whipped out, blows were dealt with spiked rings, beer-mugs, chair-legs, or leaded clubs; bullets slashed the advertisements on the poster-columns, rebounded from the iron roofs of latrines (89).

The decayed bourgeois gentility and political irresponsibility of Fräulein Schroeder are not the harmless foibles of an elderly 'character', they are part of the matrix of Hitler's rise to power; and Mr Norris's 'ingenuous' double-dealing (in which Bayer and the Communists are betrayed for financial gain), is more profoundly culpable than it may seem. Indeed, Mr Norris as emblem is capitalist corruption in its late phase; it is not without point that Isherwood makes him a product of the Edwardian past, seemingly out of place in the present:

'My generation was brought up to regard luxury from an aesthetic standpoint. Since the War, people don't seem to feel that any more. Too often they are merely gross. They take their pleasures coarsely, don't you find? At times, one feels guilty, oneself, with so much unemployment and distress everywhere' (15).

But, *in fact*, Norris is the present's informing evil genius – charming, perverted, false, merciless, avaricious, unprincipled and reckless. And he is English. In neither book is it solely Germany which is responsible for the state of affairs. The main characters in both novels are as much English (or American) as German; and Mr Norris, Helen Pratt, Peter Wilkinson, Clive and Sally Bowles, for instance, are as much symptoms of decadence and indifference as Kuno and the Nowaks. So too, we should be clear, are the narrators of each novel – 'William Bradshaw' (Isherwood's middle Christian names) and 'Christopher Isherwood'.

Much has been made of Isherwood's supposed 'objectivity', his straight 'reporting' of the situation in Germany, based especially on the famous claim at the beginning of *Goodbye to Berlin*: 'I am a camera with its shutter open, quite passive, recording, not thinking . . . Some day, all this will have to be developed, carefully printed, fixed' (7). It is easy to conflate Isherwood the novelist with his namesake in the novels, and it is a mistake. Two points need to be understood immediately: first, given the fact that Isherwood left Berlin early in 1933 and the two novels were published in 1935 and 1939, the real author is looking *back* at their supposed authors; second, that they are *fictions* (Isherwood even claims that *Lions and Shadows*, his 'autobiography' should be read as a novel),[36] and it should be assumed, as a matter of course, that first-person narrators are 'characters'. Who, then, holds the 'camera'? A younger and fictionalized (possibly 'untrustworthy') 'Isherwood'. These novels are portraits of the artist as a younger man – in which it is as imperative to take account of the nature of the registering consciousness as it is in Joyce's novel. Both narrators are, in fact, placed and judged in the books – as much by their claim to 'detachment', 'objectivity' and their camera-like status as by anything else. Indeed, Isherwood presents his own earlier passivity and detachment as just as culpable for the rise of Hitler in Germany, and the situation in Europe generally, as Mr Norris's deviousness or the fatal ingenuousness of the Germans he meets. This is very obvious in *Mr Norris Changes Trains*, where William Bradshaw's 'detachment', and his sense of superiority of understanding, is heavily emphasized as a way of exposing his basic ignorance and naïvety. As he leaves a meeting with Bayer, in which his political innocence has been displayed, he thinks:

None of them trusted Arthur. Bayer didn't trust him but he was prepared to make use of him, with all due precautions. And to make use of me, too, as a convenient spy on Arthur's movements. It wasn't necessary to let me into the secret. I could so easily be pumped. I felt angry, and at the same time rather amused.

After all, one couldn't blame them (70).

It is, of course, William's trust in Norris which involves him in aiding and abetting Norris's activities and thus jeopardising Bayer. The irony is that all the while William thinks he is the worldly-wise protector of Mr Norris – 'I began to look round for excuses for his conduct, and, like an indulgent parent, easily found them' (83) – Norris is, in fact, exploiting exactly that gullibility and 'superiority'. The same is true of *Goodbye to Berlin*, although by the last parts of the final 'Berlin Diary' section, 'Christopher's' grasp of the reality of the situation is greater, although still bewildered. The narrator's very assumption here of his camera-like objectivity is an immediate sign that the 'character' of the narrator must be taken into the frame; and indeed the novel is, at one level, a register of 'Christopher's' self-satisfied and self-indulgent exploitation of the situation in Germany on behalf of his 'camera' (the ghoulish habit of taking snapshots of disasters), modulating, on the last page, to a horrified, wondering, recognition of the reality of the situation and his own ambivalent position in it:

The sun shines, and Hitler is master of this city. The sun shines, and dozens of my friends . . . are in prison, possibly dead. . . . Rudi's make-believe, story-book game has become earnest; the Nazis will play it with him. The Nazis won't laugh at him; they'll take him on trust for what he pretended to be. Perhaps at this very moment Rudi is being tortured to death.

   I catch sight of my face in the mirror of a shop, and am horrified to see that I am smiling. You can't help smiling, in such beautiful weather. The trams are going up and down the Kleiststrasse, just as usual. They, and the people on the pavement, and the tea-cosy dome of the Nollendorfplatz station have an air of curious familiarity, of striking resemblance to something one remembers as normal and pleasant in the past – like a very good photograph.

   No. Even now I can't altogether believe that any of this has really happened. . . . (204)

Isherwood's own sense of the 'fantastic realities' of his time is signalled in the dream-like uncertainty which envelops the knowledge of the reality. A crucial instance of Isherwood's placing of 'Christopher' in this novel, and the responsibility that other nationalities share for the German situation by their passivity and detachment, occurs when Sally, Christopher and Clive, the American who lets even them down, watch the funeral of Hermann Müller – 'the whole drab weary pageant of Prussian Social Democracy'. Clive asks who 'this guy' was: '"God knows", Sally answered, yawning' –

She was quite right. We had nothing to do with those Germans down there, marching, or with the dead man in the coffin, or with the words on the banners. In a few days, I thought, we shall have forfeited all kinship with ninety-nine per cent of the population of the world, with the men and women who earn their living, who insure their lives, who are anxious about the future of their children . . . It was a curious, exhilarating, not unpleasant sensation: but, at the same time, I felt slightly scared. Yes, I said to myself, I've done it, now. I am lost (52).

'Christopher' is not the photographer of 'the lost', he is one of them – although it takes most of the book for him to have any inkling of what that means. The exposure of 'Christopher's' ideological naïvety is continued more expressly in the later novel *Prater Violet* (1946).

   Isherwood is, of course, playing a complex trick. The 'records' made by his untrustworthy narrators are, after all, still presented as records of the situation in Germany in the early thirties: that is what the novels, by the 'real' Christopher Isherwood, consist of. In effect, he exploits the assumed 'objectivity' of his ingenuous Herr Ishyvoo to express his 'tea-tabled' version of Berlin and the incidence of fascism, and simultaneously makes that false and dangerous 'objectivity' a constituent of the ideological matrix. The displacement of focusing on the 'tea-table' is characteristic of the young novelist's distorted vision (as *Lions and Shadows*, the 1938 'autobiography', itself confirms), *but it is also* a way of addressing the 'fantastic realities' of the situation for Isherwood the actual novelist. Isherwood's supreme act of 'tea-tabling', then, is to place a transmitter in the consciousness of his younger self. In that way – and the last sentence of *Goodbye to Berlin*, as I noted above, highlights it – a reality so bewildering as to be a nightmare finds a myth of expression.

But Isherwood's extreme self-consciousness about 'the novelist' points more generally to the issue I have been considering throughout this essay: the uncertainty of fiction's capacity to engage with social reality at a moment when the mystifications of liberal-humanism and realism (that is, their supposition that they are more than merely individualistic) were on the threshold of self-consciousness. Isherwood's obsession with the relation of novelist to novel – throughout the later parts of *Lions and Shadows*, in the ambiguous status of that book itself (autobiography or fiction?), and in the ambivalences incident on making 'himself' the narrator of the two novels I have been discussing – suggests his own consciousness of the problem. The inference that can be drawn, I think, is that Isherwood recognised that writing of any kind is, in a sense, always 'fiction', always *a view* of reality; that novels, of course, are most obviously fiction, while normally purporting, not to be; that, *therefore*, they convey *a* view most fundamentally and yet most deceptively; and that the logical answer is to place 'the novelist' within the novel. This of course does not solve the problem – there must always be a novelist outside the text – but at least his presence has been signalled. By this token, Isherwood's fiction in the thirties offers a 'record' of the 'fantastic realities' of the period by way of the self-admitted 'fantasy' of realism. His novels are, in effect, tacit confessions of liberal-humanist bewilderment about, and hence complicity in, the world they observe and fear. In *Goodbye to Berlin*, 'the novel' has become no more than an album of snapshots and diary-entries, dated 1930 to 1933, taken and written by 'Christopher Isherwood': fragmentary records – just as the two novels themselves are 'fragments' of the 'huge'[37], but significantly *unwritten*, novel, *The*

Lost – of an experience the author 'even now . . . can't altogether believe . . . has really happened'.

9. LIBERAL REALISM IN THE THIRTIES

I have been suggesting that in the nineteen-thirties a number of serious novelists, for the most part bourgeois humanists who were nevertheless sharply conscious of the crisis of their culture at that time, attempted to make that crisis the subject of their fiction. What this attempt reveals, I think, is the extent to which the novel form itself – the product, in England at least, of a bourgeois-individualist ideology – sustains an ideology of the genre. All novels declare a structure – that there is a 'world of the book', however fantastic it may be – which places it automatically in a comparative relationship to the world outside the book. At the most basic level, then, the novelist in writing a novel is the maker of 'a world' which is a configuration of an individual conception and perception of *the* world.

While the sustaining general ideology remained secure and self-confident, this basic strategy in fiction was profoundly mystified; and realism ('telling things as they really are') was assumed and consolidated as the dominant fictional mode. Realism, of course, was never a single characteristic way of writing, never solely 'naturalistic' (although its classic manifestations have assumed total conviction and 'truthfulness to life'); but it has invariably been closely referential, and has proposed a material experience of life. At its least self-consciously individualist, then, the novel engaged the real world most confidently. But as the sustaining ideology of individualism became subject to the revelation of its contradictions, by way of criticism from without and self-analysis within, its certainty began to crumble. Modernist fiction, in its focusing on consciousness as subject and its self-consciousness about its modes of presentation, is witness to this phase. Fiction turned inwards in part-recognition of its own basic individualism of perception; it became aware, as it were, of its own partiality, and justified itself by detailing the mental register as the primary focus. This, of course, has ideological implications; for it means a retreat from material history into itself, to a position where fiction can 'order' and make sense of a world whose social formations are inimical to it. Modernism, then, may be seen as the ultimate phase of liberal-humanist realism.

In the thirties, there is an attempt by novelists – themselves, of course, historically situated at a moment when liberal-humanist ideology is acutely jeopardized by both fascist barbarism and Marxist science – to make fiction re-confront the world of inimical social reality. But the individualist ideology of the genre, by now deprived of a sustaining general ideology, constrained the novelist. Virginia Woolf wrestled to free her modernist aesthetic of its introversion; Orwell discovered the limitations of narrative realism and, with others, its inherent tendency to deal with the past; others again experimented in their different ways with fantasy and fabulation, and hence with worlds located in a fictitious future; and others, by way of a synthetic realism, produced books which were in themselves metaphors of fear and shame of the present.[38] In this sense, the works of Greene and Isherwood convey most penetratingly a sense of 'things as they really are'; not, of course, as historically verifiable, nor as 'true', but as, in their own terms, *convincing* – albeit this is a case where, with Yeats, 'the best lack all conviction'. It was a Pyrrhic victory for the genre, perhaps; but not a victory the ordered retreat of modernism ought to obscure.

NOTES

1. Edgell Rickword in 'Culture, Progress, and the English Tradition', in C. Day Lewis (ed.), *The Mind in Chains*, 1937, p. 250, offers an interesting gloss on the 'ideology' of modernist technique.
2. Dystopias (*contra* Utopias) are usually set in the future, and show the present world gone wrong by way of exaggerated images of its own apparent logic of development.
3. In the Foreword to Edward Upward's 'The Railway Accident' in *New Directions in Prose and Poetry: Number Eleven*, New York, 1949. Reproduced in Edward Upward, *The Railway Accident and Other Stories* (1969), Penguin edition, 1972, p. 34.
4. This was, to John Lehmann in his Foreword to *New Writing in Europe*, Penguin, 1940, 'one of the most interesting developments in our literature for many years'.
5. By 'liberal-humanism', throughout this essay, I mean to identify a worldview and cultural force most confidently articulated in England in the nineteenth century by such writers as John Stuart Mill, George Eliot and Matthew Arnold (although it has later, highly developed, expression in, for example, the 'philosophy' of the Bloomsbury group). It is by no means a precisely formulated system of ideas – indeed it is perhaps better regarded as the ideology of bourgeois liberalism in its dominant phase. It develops from eighteenth-century individualism, by way of the Romantic movement's deification of the individual, to a position in which the 'culture' of the individual being is the *sine qua non* of a truly civilized society. But it *begins* with the individual, and not the social and economic structures of society, in

its conception of change and reform (i.e. Progress). In this way, it 'forgets' or suppresses its reliance on certain particular forms of social and economic organisation which are similarly, but 'unacceptably', individualist in motive power. Arnold's conception of 'Culture' is the most obvious instance of what I mean by 'liberal-humanism'; but in relation to the novel form – itself the product in England of emergent bourgeois individualism – George Eliot's attempts to cultivate the individual by fostering an understanding of other individuals through the detailed presentation of their lives, is more apposite. 'Realism' and 'liberal-humanism' in her work are, to me, coterminous.

6. *Studies in a Dying Culture*, 1938, pp. xx–xxiii especially.

7. It is notable, in this context, that science fiction as a genre develops rapidly in the thirties, either as a form of escape from the realities of the present or as an attempt to find a distantiated position from which to consider them. It is witness, too, to the common perception of science and technology as one of the massive intangibles of the period.

8. 'Sketch for a Marxist Interpretation of Literature', in *The Mind in Chains*, op. cit., p. 54.

9. 'The Leaning Tower', in *Folios of New Writing*, Autumn, 1940 (Johnson reprint edition), p. 15 (all further page references appear in brackets in the text).

10. The phrase 'essay novel' occurs in *A Writer's Diary*, 1953, p. 189 (2 November 1932); the idea of *The Years* and *Three Guineas* being conceived by her as 'one book', ibid., p. 295 (3 June 1938). The *Diary* contains many comments on the 'difficulty' of writing this novel. Interestingly, Virginia Woolf certainly had in mind the 'family chronicle' novels of Walpole and Galsworthy, although she did not want to be crudely didactic or flatly realistic like them. Nor did she want to be propagandist – 'I have a horror of the Aldous novel', ibid., p. 239 (20 February 1935).

11. *The Years* (1937), 1951, p. 469 (all further page references appear in brackets in the text).

12. *Between the Acts*, 1941, pp. 66 and 58 (all further pages references appear in brackets in the text).

13. Foreword dated 1946, Penguin edition, 1962, pp. 7–8.

14. *Eyeless in Gaza* (1936), Penguin edition, 1962, p. 337 (all further page references appear in brackets in the text).

15. In *The Mind in Chains*, op. cit. (all page references appear in brackets in the text). Ralph Fox's *The Novel and the People* (1937) suggests the same difficulties.

16. For Isherwood's description of the 'Mortmere' days, see *Lions and Shadows* (1938), Four Square edition 1963, pp. 60–70 and 100–7.

17. *The Railway Accident and Other Stories*, Penguin, 1972, p. 40.

18. ibid., p. 184.

19. op. cit., pp. 168–9.

20. *The Wild Goose Chase* (1937), Penguin edition 1944, p. 130.

21. *The Aerodrome* (1941), 1944 (all page references are in brackets in the text).

22. It is surely not a coincidence that in both books there are two friends, one called Anthony; that one betrays the other by stealing his fiancée; that the injured friend is 'killed' on a mountain/cliff, hence symbolically killing 'love' and 'feeling' in the surviving friend?

23. *Keep the Aspidistra Flying* (1936), Penguin, 1973, p. 21 (my italics).

24. 'Sketch for a Marxist Interpretation . . .', op. cit., p. 49.
25. Louis Althusser, 'A Letter on Art', in *Lenin and Philosophy and Other Essays*, 1971, pp. 202–8. I am, of course, implying by this that these works are 'authentic', rather than 'average' or 'mediocre', art.
26. *The Confidential Agent* (1939), Penguin, 1973, p. 161.
27. *A Gun For Sale*, (1936), Penguin, 1970, p. 68.
28. ibid., pp. 66–7.
29. *It's A Battlefield* (1934), Uniform edition, 1952, p. 76.
30. See note 2 above for publication details.
31. *Lions and Shadows*, op. cit., p. 100.
32. ibid., p. 107.
33. Patrick Hamilton is one of the undeservedly forgotten novelists of the period. Like Orwell, he experimented with a range of different fictional modes to realize the decayed bourgeois culture he held responsible for the present state of affairs. From the limited specificity of flat narrative realism in his trilogy, *Twenty-Thousand Streets Under the Sky* (1936), he characteristically turned in his next novel, *Impromptu in Moribundia* (1939), to the uncompromisingly fabular. This deadly, satiric dystopia ought – given the prominence of *Brave New World* and *1984* – to be reprinted. His best novel of the period, *Hangover Square*, however, is a significant example of the synthetic realism I find in the work of Greene and Isherwood. Set on the eve of the Second World War, it is immediately comparable with Orwell's *Coming Up for Air* (is it a coincidence that the two protagonists are George Bowling and George Bone?), but it establishes – unlike Orwell's novel – a real reciprocity between the private and the public history. For a more extended consideration of Hamilton's work, see my essay, 'The Saloon-Bar Society: Patrick Hamilton's Fiction in the 1930s', *Renaissance and Modern Studies*, XX, 1976 (also published in John Lucas (ed.), *The 1930s: A Challenge to Orthodoxy*, Harvester Press, 1978).
34. *Goodbye to Berlin* (1939), Penguin, 1969. p. 175 (all further page references are in brackets in the text).
35. *Mr Norris Changes Trains* (1935), Penguin, 1965, p. 31 (all further page references are in brackets in the text).
36. op. cit., 'To The Reader', dated September, 1937.
37. In the author's note at the beginning of *Goodbye to Berlin*, op. cit.
38. Caudwell makes a very similar point about G. B. Shaw in *Studies in a Dying Culture*, op. cit., p. 18.

Working-Class Literature or Proletarian Writing?

CAROLE SNEE

Take away all that the working class has given to English Literature and that literature would scarcely suffer; take away all that the educated class has given, and English Literature would scarcely exist.

(Virginia Woolf, *The Leaning Tower*)

To write about the literary existence of a generation is to accept a necessary restriction of subject: you will be writing almost entirely about the middle class members of the generation . . . Virtually no writing of literary importance came out of the working class during the decade.

(Samuel Hynes, *The Auden Generation*)

These two statements separated by forty years represent the consensus of opinion amongst literary critics about the value of working-class writing. It is perhaps the one statement about our literary history which will gain almost unanimous support from critics, irrespective of their ideological position. The underlying, and frequently unquestioned, assumption is that there exists a hierarchy of texts with 'Literature' at the apex. Only certain works are then ascribed this status because of their 'beauty', their revelation of certain 'eternal truths' about social relationships, and their 'aesthetic' organization. Occasionally a radical critic will discover a 'great work of Art' written by a working-class writer, and then Robert Tressell or Grassic Gibbon are used as 'evidence' to prove that the working class are capable of producing fictional works which can take their place on the shelves along side Dickens or Scott. Thus certain working-class texts are appropriated as 'Literature', whilst working-class writing in general is ignored. Leavis's notion of 'Literature' may appear to be discredited at the level of theory, but the academic subject which he did so much to create lives on, extended, but essentially unchanged.

Although many Marxist critics have expanded the boundaries of literary studies by examining the relationship between creative practices and the social formation, there is still an implicit general agreement between Marxist and other critics as to which authors and works are 'great', and therefore worthy of study. Although many critics would now agree that literature is *not* a neutral body of imaginative writing, 'but an ideologically constructed canon or corpus of texts operating in specific and determinate ways in and around the apparatus of education',[1] this recognition is in itself in danger of being incorporated into the dominant cultural tradition rather than being used to challenge it. The current flowering of Marxist literary criticism in the universities and polytechnics is perhaps a testimony to the ability of the educational and cultural apparatus to accommodate, and finally absorb, potentially radical challenges to the cultural hegemony of the dominant class. For if the notion of a canon in itself is untouched, then new critical approaches by themselves cannot deconstruct the concept 'Literature'.

In all schools of literary criticism there is still a common and continuing concern with judgements of value, and varying theoretical models from Leavis to Althusser are used to justify and explain what we have *already* learnt to recognize as 'good art'. The canon is by self-definition good art, and therefore it has become the yardstick for all types of creative writing. Working-class writing is measured against it and because it does not operate from within the same problematic it is deemed deficient, and is thus dismissed from the category of literature. Current developments in Marxist aesthetic theory make *possible* a critical practice which is not simply the reaffirmation of received notions of culture, but as yet it has not begun to engage with forms of writing which are not an integral part of the dominant literary discourse. If critical practice is always concerned with the texts from the 'great tradition', then the idea of 'Literature' is created anew, albeit in different terms.

Because of the existing framework of literary criticism, any discussion of working-class writing poses immediate difficulties, not least of which is the problem of definition. I have deliberately used the term 'working-class writing' rather than the more commonly used 'proletarian writing', because the latter suggests an awareness of class as a primary determinant, which is not always present; it is a mistake to assume that a working-class writer will reveal automatically a class rather than a sectional consciousness. Thus I use the term simply to denote works written by a member of the working class about that class. Working-class writing attempts to bring into the centre of the arena the life experience of that class, and there is a recognition within the texts, sometimes implicit, sometimes explicit, that that experience is different from the traditional subject-matter of literature. However, whilst the very existence of published, working-class, creative writing may challenge 'commonsense' notions of culture and creativity, the texts themselves are not necessarily 'subversive', or indeed progressive.

In this essay the discussion is limited to working-class fiction in the thirties, although there was also a great deal of working-class poetry and writing from the theatre produced during the decade. However, many of the general theoretical points raised apply equally to all forms of working-class writing.

The three writers I examine, Walter Greenwood, Walter Brierley, and Lewis Jones, indicate in different ways some of the problems faced in attempting to evaluate working-class writing, and the problems faced by the writers themselves within their own projects. All three choose as their subject-matter working-class communities faced with mass unemployment, dole queues, and deprivation. However, although the themes are similar the treatment varies enormously, and in the different levels of consciousness embodied in the text these writers reveal the contradictions of the class about which they write, and from which they come. Given the limitations of space, this essay can give no real indication of the breadth, variety and volume of working-class writing during the thirties, and a detailed discussion of a limited number of texts seems preferable to a guided tour of working-class literary production from 1930 to 1939; a glance at the review sections and advertisements in any of the literary journals of the period will perform this latter task.

Members of the working class who attempted to use the written word in order to explore their own conditions of existence faced very specific problems of language, form, and publication. The written word is not a mode of discourse which has been developed by the working class, and there was no available working-class fictional practice on which these writers could draw. Their problems were further compounded by the fact that the working class was excluded from the dominant literary language by the educational apparatus, and its own cultural language was essentially oral. Even having surmounted these hurdles, the working-class writer was faced with the mystifying process of publication, and with a publishing industry which on the whole uncritically accepted the notion that all literary texts of value must emanate from the middle class.

The writers I deal with all use the realist novel form, a form which not only offers the reader the most direct access to the experiences embodied within the text, but is also the most readily available mode of expression for writers not schooled within a literary tradition. Essentially it is the form used for the magazine story, the popular novel

– in fact for most fictional writing aimed at a mass audience and thus excluded from 'literature'. However this is one of the great dangers of the form; for precisely because it is so familiar its ideology can remain silent and the text operate at the level of commonsense philosophy. The language and structure of the traditional realist novel is a mode of discourse developed and ascribed value by the dominant class; it reifies and codifies its experience and its perception of reality, and privileges certain feelings and experiences, whilst implicitly condemning others.

The traditional realist novel, with its emphasis on individual consciousness, subjectivity, and 'sensitivity', has been inextricably linked by critics with liberal bourgeois philosophy and the form and critical practice which has developed around it reifies individualism and individuality. Traditional novel criticism focuses on the intensely personal perspective of the writer as it is embodied within the text, whilst the texts themselves tend to operate through a series of individual characters, through whom the nature of social and personal relationships can be explored. Even in the great social novels of the nineteenth century, the shaping movement of the narrative begins with the individual, moves out into the social world, and finally back into the individual consciousness. It has become almost a critical platitude to see the realist novel, which reached its zenith in the last half of the nineteenth century, as the triumphant cultural affirmation of liberal hegemony, a celebration of the liberal-humanist world view, which perhaps finds its most complete expression in the works of George Eliot.

However, in order to explore the limits of the form, one also needs to examine some of the assumptions which underpin this particular critical practice, as well as the genre itself. The form cannot be divorced from the writer who is using that form, and allowed to occupy a critical space in which *it* controls the content; the writer's perception of reality is not necessarily modified by structural constraints, for it also constructs them. Is it simply the form which denies certain types of experience or 'solutions', or is it also the writer's own ideological stance? Clearly there is a relationship between the two, but it is important to remember that that relationship is not static; form is not 'neutral', but neither are its structural limits so rigid that they can only accommodate one particular perception of reality.

The dominant critical practice argues that because the realist novel has been concerned historically with the individual, and its narrative structures operate through one – or a series of – individual consciousnesses, its philosophy is always essentially 'liberal'.

Liberalism, so the argument runs, is the philosophy of individualism, and socialism the philosophy of collectivity, and therefore any works, even those which purport to be socialist, must, if they focus on individuals, be embedded within liberal philosophy. However Liberalism is not 'about' individuals, but is a particular way of perceiving individuality. The working class may have a different perception of the individual, and what constitutes individuality, but a concern for these issues does not *per se* reveal liberal ideology.

Terry Eagleton, perhaps the most rewarding and suggestive of the new English Marxist critics, has observed:

The languages and devices a writer finds to hand are already saturated with certain modes of perception, certain codified ways of interpreting reality; and the extent to which he can modify or remake those languages depends on more than his personal genius. It depends on whether, at that point in history, 'ideology' is such that they must and can be changed.[2]

If Eagleton is right we must conclude that all working-class writing is absorbed without trace by the dominant culture, until the specific historic moment which brings into being new forms and new languages. However, I would argue that it is possible to talk of 'working-class' writing outside that moment, precisely because 'ideology' is not homogeneous.

There is not one unified class ideology which exists without contradictions, nor is ideological hegemony imposed from above, but demands all kinds of negotiations and concessions between the dominant and subaltern groups. Thus working-class writing can exist within the dominant cultural formation, but in contradiction to it, in which case its very existence begins to challenge 'Literature' as an ideological construct. If the traditional realist novel form can be used to explore working-class experience, the form itself is not necessarily altered, but the conventional notion of realism as reflection and the critical practice associated with it, have to change. Thus I hope to show that the realist novel does not simply at best reveal and interrogate the dominant, unstated ideology, or exist uncritically within it, but can also incorporate a *conscious* ideological or class perspective, which in itself undercuts the ideological parameters of the genre, without necessarily transforming its structural boundaries.

1. THE CREATION OF WORKING-CLASS MYTHOLOGY: WALTER GREENWOOD'S *LOVE ON THE DOLE*

I want to examine first a novel which has come to occupy a very special place in the literary history of the thirties, Walter Greenwood's *Love on the Dole*. It was enormously successful when it first appeared in 1933, and before the end of the decade had been turned into a play, widely performed by left theatre groups, and a film for the commercial cinema. Even today it is still identified in the popular consciousness as a depiction of the worst aspects of life during the thirties, a reminder of what 'economic depression' means in terms of human suffering. It has been reprinted as a Penguin Modern Classic, thus acquiring the status of a 'classic novel', rather than a book reprinted in a paperback edition. The Penguin edition claims:

Walter Greenwood's *Love on the Dole* was the *Cathy Come Home* of the thirties, the first novel to be set against a backcloth of chronic unemployment. Raw, violent and powerful, it was a cry of outrage that did as much in its way as the Jarrow march to stir the national conscience.

It is a powerful claim indeed, and the novel's special impact both in the thirties and after is difficult to understand, for its retained power as a symbol far outweighs its impact as a text when read. Its status is partly due to the fact that it was the first novel of its kind by a working-class writer in the twentieth century, or at least the first to reach a wide audience and receive critical acclaim. The more difficult question to answer is, why did it become an immediate success? In trying to answer that question one is faced with the problem of the difference between a critical reading of the text, and the non-literary reading of the majority of readers.

Look at the bookshelves of most left political activists, certainly those whose political development was shaped by the socialist movement of the thirties, forties, and fifties, and certain texts appear again and again; *Love on the Dole* is there alongside Steinbeck's *The Grapes of Wrath*, Sinclair's *The Jungle*, and Tressell's *The Ragged Trousered Philanthropists*. Ask people who lived through the thirties about *Love on the Dole* and they will say that reading it made a deep impression on them and that it captured working-class life during the depression. Thus, part of its success can be ascribed to the fact that people felt they were reading a faithful and sympathetic recreation of their own experiences. But if this was the sole achievement of the text, then that in itself would not have been sufficient reason for its acceptance as Literature; indeed it would have militated against that acceptance. It has been able to receive both popular acclaim and literary recognition because it exists firmly within the tradition of 'Literature', despite its subject matter. Greenwood may have been a working-class novelist, writing about working-class life, but he never challenges the form of the bourgeois novel, nor its underlying ideology.

In *Love on the Dole* Greenwood writes of his own experience of growing up in Salford during the twenties and thirties. It is a deeply pessimistic novel, not because of its subject matter, but because within the novel Greenwood himself denies the possibility of change, or of any solution to the social problems he identifies. The novel is a cry of outrage, but the rage is impotent, for his own ideological position is essentially that of the liberal reformer. He reacts with horror at the injustices of society, but cannot really conceive of any alternative to that society. He writes within the naturalistic mode, and that technique reflects and reproduces his deep-rooted pessimism about the working class, for it enables him to depict the surface of working-class life in all its sordid squalor, but does not allow the reader to penetrate beneath that surface to see either its potential richness, or the possibility of the working class changing its own conditions of existence.

Although Greenwood locates the problems facing the inhabitants of Hanky Park at a specific historic moment, and shows they are the result of specific historic forces, the fictional world of Hanky Park and all it symbolises is presented as unchanging, and indeed incapable of change. This pessimism about working-class life is most clearly revealed in the formal structure of the novel, and in particular in its beginning and end. Chapter Two opens:

5.30 a.m.
A drizzle was falling.
The policeman on his beat paused awhile at the corner of North Street halting under a street lamp. Its staring beams lit the million globules of fine rain powdering his cape. A cat sitting on the doorstep of Mr Hulkington's, the grocer's shop, blinked sleepily.

At No. 17, Mrs Hardcastle, an old woman of forty, came downstairs 'Ah-ah-ing' sleepily, hair in disarray. She groped on the tiny kitchen's mantelpiece for the matches, struck one and lit the gas. The glare hurt her eyes: she blinked and stifled a yawn, stretched and shrugged her shoulders.

The last page of the novel begins thus:

5.30 a.m.

A drizzle was falling.

Ned Narkey, on his beat, paused under the street lamp at the corner of North Street. Its staring beams lit the million globules of fine rain powdering his cape. A cat sitting on the doorstep of Mr Hulkington's, the grocer's shop, blinked at Ned, rose, tail in air, pushed its body against Ned's legs.

In Mrs Dorbell's house, Helen came downstairs, 'Ah-ah-ing' sleepily. She groped on the tiny kitchen's mantelpiece for the matches, struck one and lit the gas. The glare hurt her eyes; she blinked, stifled a yawn, scratched her head with one hand whilst she stretched with the other.

Greenwood's message is explicit, the events, dramas, and tragedies, about which he has been writing, have had no effect on the material world of Hanky Park. Helen, the new Mrs Hardcastle, performs exactly the same tasks, in exactly the same way, as her mother-in-law does at the beginning of the novel. The ten years which have passed, the suffering which has been endured by all the central characters, mean nothing at all. The only two characters who manage to escape from the stifling, oppressive, and static world of Hanky Park are Larry through death, and Sally through prostitution.

Given the theme of *Love on the Dole*, it is a curiously unpolitical novel, with little reference to the political events which had contributed so directly to the misfortunes of all those who inhabit Hanky Park. The introduction of the Means Test in 1931 is the first overt reference, and there is no mention of the General Election which immediately preceded it, despite the fact that Larry as a socialist militant would presumably have been involved in the election campaign. Even more startling is the absence of any mention of the General Strike. The novel covers the years 1923–31, years of enormous importance to the labour movement, and to the working class, and one would have expected that the events of those years would have impinged more directly onto the fictional world of Hanky Park. That they do not is another indication of Greenwood's own unstated ideology; he perceives his subject in an intensely personal and individualistic manner, and the perspective is the same as that of the liberal social novel so common in the nineteenth century. He is saying to the reader, 'look, this is what working class life is really like, isn't it terrible?' as though to identify the problems is enough. However the liberal optimism of the nineteenth century, and the belief that conditions could be changed by simple reforms, is not available to a working-class writer of the 1930s, for that belief would have contradicted his own experience of his world. Thus all Greenwood is left with is his pessimism, and his anger, and because he himself has no clearly articulated alternative to the misery he identifies, he appears subconsciously to transfer the blame to the working class themselves, who are presented as being too stupid to bring about change, or to listen to Larry's message that socialism is the answer.

His own confusion prevents him from going beyond the reproduction of the surface reality of working-class life to penetrate its complexities and contradictions, and leads to the uneasy coexistence of two very different styles of writing. On the one hand there is the supreme realism which for the most part becomes naturalism, used in an attempt to 'show things as they really are', whilst on the other there is the constant strain of romantic fiction which confuses and mystifies the nature of personal relations. This is particularly evident in the treatment of Larry and Sally, two characters who for a substantial part of the book are held up as some sort of alternative to Hanky Park.

Larry is the classic romantic hero. Kind, gentle, and compassionate, he is plagued by ill health, with the associated undertones of being too good to live; he is set apart from his fellow workers by his greater insight into the human condition; 'his face attracted you ... lean, a gentle expression and a soft kindness, a frank steadfastness in his eyes invited confidence'. Take away his socialist beliefs and he could be the hero in any womens' magazine story. Greenwood presents him as a person whose 'essential self' is apparently untouched by the world in which he lives, and who has escaped the coarsening effects of working-class life so evident in the other occupants of Hanky Park. This romanticism affects Greenwood's portrayal of Larry, the socialist, and undercuts still further any suggestion that there could be an alternative to the degradation suffered by the working class. For Larry 'proves' that the working-class militant is exceptional, and above all is an isolated *individual*. Thus he in no way challenges the dominant ideology, but confirms that socialism is only a belief propounded by maverick individuals. He is so exceptional that the implicit suggestion is that no one could or should aspire to be like him. His socialism is rejected by all those around him, and he is constantly portrayed as a person whose 'natural' character distances him from the rest of his community. Harry, the other 'hero', who is destined to have all his adolescent dreams thwarted, and to remain trapped by Hanky Park, admires Larry but is unable to connect him to his own life in any meaningful way because 'his quality of quiet studiousness and reserve elevated him to a plane beyond that of ordinary folk'.

Sally is the only other character who can in any sense be said to rebel against life in Hanky Park, but although she is central to the plot, her character is sketchily drawn, and for the most part she operates as a pure romantic heroine. Like Larry she is different from those who surround her, and she is separated and segregated from other women by her beauty, she is

Eighteen, a gorgeous creature whose native beauty her shabbiness could not hide. Eyes dark, lustrous, haunting; abundant black hair tumbling in waves; a full, ripe, pouting mouth and a low round bosom. A face and form such as any society dame would have given three-quarters of her fortune to possess. Sally wore it carelessly as though youth's brief hour was eternal; as though there was no such thing as old age. She failed in her temper; but when roused, colour tinted her pallid cheeks such as the wind whipped up when it blew from the north or east.[3]

She stands in sharp contrast to the other women of Hanky Park who Greenwood describes as

Slatternly women, dirty shawls over their heads and shoulders, hair in wisps about their faces, stood in groups congregated on the pavements in the shafts of light thrown from the open doors of the public-house. Now and then they laughed raucously, heedless of the tugs at their skirts from their wailing, weary children.[4]

The romanticism and the naturalism both serve to mask the reality of being a woman, and both images belong in their own way to the same ideology of womanhood. Sally is the classic romantic heroine – woman on a pedestal. Her beauty is to be marvelled at. She tragically loses the one person she loves and who is worthy of her love and, overcome by grief and fear of poverty, she turns to prostitution. The other women represent 'woman as slut'. They are plain, unintelligent, and incapable of coping with life except through a drunken haze. The reader can make some sort of correlation between the description of the women and the social world which shapes them, but Greenwood's treatment militates against it.

His romanticism undercuts and finally negates the one hopeful note in the novel, the possibility of Larry's belief in socialism offering an alternative way of life for the people of Hanky Park. Sally's beauty and Larry's socialism are offered as two parts of an equation, as somehow explaining why they are different from the other characters. Thus a belief in socialism becomes as irrelevant, and accidental, as being born beautiful. The elements of romantic fiction also determine the way that Greenwood attempts to engage with the political events of 1931. The novel contains a very effective scene in which Larry explains the nature of surplus value to his workmates. It is a scene which is very suggestive of the money trick episode in *The Ragged Trousered Philanthropists*, and indicates more than an emotional commitment to socialism. However the effectiveness of the scene, and its political message, are marginalised by the mechanics of the plot. Larry is reported to the management for having made a subversive speech, and is promptly sacked. Yet it is difficult to believe that his political views would not already have been known to the management, or indeed that Larry would have still been in work in 1931 given his militancy. Greenwood needed Larry to be sacked as part of the dramatic climax of the novel; that is the real function of the incident, rather than to throw any light on the 'real world' outside the novel.

The only other overtly political event in the novel is also marred by the structure of the romance fiction which Greenwood superimposes on his naturalistic fiction. One of the climactic scenes in the novel is the march of the unemployed which is broken up by provocative police action. However, its precise meaning and function, both within the fictional world, and to the real world is difficult to locate. There has been no previous indication of any political organisation capable of planning such a march because up until this point in the novel Larry has been presented as an isolated socialist. Furthermore the political implications of the scene are undermined because of the personal romantic drama which becomes enmeshed with the wider political action, and the march of the unemployed begins to function simply as a setting for the personal drama which is about to reach its climax.

Ned is policing the march, and Larry is one of its organizers. Both are in love with Sally, and their personal rivalry becomes confused with the political struggle which generated the march. When the authority of the state is used to break up a legitimate march, the meaning of that action becomes lost in the romantic story-line which Greenwood has imposed. Larry is clubbed down by the police and taken to hospital, and from that moment the focus switches to the plight of one individual, and the reader never learns of the outcome of the march, or of its political effect. Greenwood refuses to follow through the implications of the demonstration scene, and indeed by this stage his chosen structure will not allow him to do so. Larry's death is attributed to his 'weak chest' which has been signalled throughout the novel, and not to the savage beating he received from the police. Thus the personal tragedy of Larry and Sally supersedes the tragedy of unemployment which is meant to be the theme of *Love on the Dole*.

Throughout the novel the romantic world in which Greenwood places Sally and Larry, and the world of Hanky Park which is depicted in supreme naturalistic detail, are in conflict. The coming together of these two worlds in the resolution of the plot reveals all the inadequacies and contradictory impulses of Greenwood's fictional world. Sally brings happiness in the form of work to her brother and father through prostituting herself to Sam the local bookmaker. Thus, the personal tragedies which constitute the plot are resolved not by political action, or social change, but by the chance good fortune that Sally's beauty was a commodity which Sam was prepared to buy. Greenwood himself seems aware of the inadequacy of his conclusion and draws attention to the fate of Jack, one of Harry's boyhood friends:

No influential friends to pull strings on his behalf; no wages for him tonight; no planning for the morrow. He was an anonymous unit of an army of three millions for whom there was no tomorrow.[5]

One of the central problems in *Love on the Dole* is that Jack and the others like him remain anonymous within the world of the novel, and this reminder of his fate only serves to emphasise the gap which exists between Greenwood's central characters and the world they inhabit. The Hardcastle family lead a self-enclosed existence. There are no uncles and aunts or grandparents close by – a strange phenomenon in an established working-class community. Consequently an important part of working-class culture, the supportive action of family and friends, is missing from the novel. Greenwood shows people living in close proximity to each other, but they exist in isolated pockets of space, as individual consciousnesses separated by their common experience, rather than united by it. He is a working-class novelist totally trapped by liberal ideology both as an explanation of the world, and as it shaped the novel form. Perhaps this offers at least a partial explanation as to why *Love on the Dole* has been excepted as 'Literature'.

2. WALTER BRIERLEY: FROM WORKING-CLASS WRITER TO AUTHOR

Walter Brierley is another working-class writer who took as the theme for his first novel the degradation and deprivation of life on the dole, yet he is one of the hundreds of writers whose work has been almost forgotten, a reminder of how ideologically partial the notion of literature is. *Love on the Dole* remains as the literary symbol of the hungry thirties, whilst *Means Test Man*,[6] Brierley's first novel, which is a more moving and pertinent comment on the decade, is now only available from specialist libraries. Brierley was a Derbyshire miner who wrote three novels during the thirties – novels which in their own way illustrate both the potential of working-class writing and the dangers which face a writer struggling to capture the experience of his own class, and also the ease with which he can uncritically assimilate the dominant ideology.

Brierley appears to have had no conscious ideological project, other than the traditional realist impulse to 'tell things as they really are'. However his ability to do that, in other words, to penetrate the dominant literary and political ideology and to reveal the 'real conditions of existence', varies enormously with each novel. It is his first novel, *Means Test Man*, which in this respect is the most successful, and Brierley's own empirical observations of life on the dole cause him to challenge and refute the then current misconceptions and commonsense notions about the unemployed.

The novel explores the degradation and humiliation experienced by Jack Cook, an unemployed miner, and the effect of his unemployment on himself and his family. When the novel opens he has been unemployed for three years. The length of his unemployment is in itself significant for it dates from 1931, the height of the depression, the year of the May Committee report which recommended cuts in unemployment pay and public spending, the year in which Ramsay MacDonald betrayed the labour movement and formed a National government to implement the proposed cuts, a government which introduced the Means Test.

A present-day reader may need reminding of these events, but the significance of Jack's three years unemployment would not have been lost on a contemporary readership. The novel is set in 1934, at a time when the unemployment figures were beginning to decline, and the National Government was confidently predicting economic recovery, yet for Jack Cook the chance of employment is as remote as it was in

178 CAROLE SNEE

1931. In this respect the novel is an important public reminder that in the depressed areas in these years unemployment remained almost as high as during the worst years of the depression.

The novel records a week in the lives of the Cook family – Jack, Jane, and their son. It is a week which has been repeated with minor variations each month for three years, for it is the week leading up to the visit of the Means Test man. The novel graphically charts the increasing tension within the household as Friday approaches, and the climax of the novel, the week, and their lives is this visit, which focuses for them and the reader the reality of their existence. Unlike Greenwood, Brierley does not simply record the poverty of life on the dole and its effects on people's material existence; he also explores its effect on their inner lives. The Cook family can cope with poverty and a reduced standard of living, but what they cannot cope with, and only dimly apprehend, is the effect of unemployment on the family and on their social relationships. By focusing on these aspects of unemployment, Brierley reproduces aspects of working-class life which had not traditionally found a place in fiction.

Roy Johnson has argued[7] that the sensitivity shown by Jack and Jane about the visit of the Means Test man, and Jack's own feelings about his unemployment and the importance of work, are an indication that Brierley himself was trapped within liberal bourgeois ideology and thus unable to reproduce a 'proletarian' consciousness. However, the importance of Brierley's focus is that he does not allow the middle class to appropriate sensitivity and feeling. Why should they be the prerogative of one particular class?

Brierley's conception of the importance of work goes far beyond the Protestant work ethic, and *Means Test Man* is a plea for the right to work, and a recognition of the complex function of work in a working-class community. Work is not just part of the reproduction of the capitalist means of production, neither is being out of work an escape from the capitalist profit motive. Brierley enables the reader to perceive the distinction between the actual work process which may be boring, repetitious, and badly paid, and the social relations which are also part of that process. In a job like mining the collective effort needed is considerable, and this collectivity is reflected in the nature and quality of social relationships in a mining community; to deprive men or women of the right to work is to deprive them of part of the communal support system which is an integral part of that work relationship.

Jack's unemployment affects his relationship with the rest of the community, and with his own family. Each day his psychological alienation is reinforced by the sound of the pit hooter, and the miners' boots on the cobbles everyday remind him that he is no longer part of that world, and thus no longer a 'useful member of the community'. His relationship with his former workmates has been fundamentally altered by his experience of being one of the long term unemployed, and even the casual act of being offered a cigarette is taken by Jack to be a recognition that he cannot afford to buy his own, rather than a gesture of friendship. Jack's sentiments are shared by another Derbyshire miner who was interviewed by Beales and Lambert for their study of unemployment:

The prolonged strain of living on the edge of domestic upheaval and the fact that our social urges have to be repressed, has ruined our lives and given us an inferiority complex. For myself, the dependence on the State for money without having honestly earned it, has made me creep within myself, losing faith in everything . . . closely examining, even suspecting, friendly gestures.[8]

The documentary evidence in that book, and indeed in most studies of unemployment containing interviews with the unemployed, suggests that Brierley captures very accurately the response of the working class to being out of work and on the dole. The fact that these responses do contain liberal values and judgements is an indication of how the dominant ideology is absorbed by all social groups as an explanation of the world, but it does not mean that in the expression of those values a member of the working class suddenly becomes middle class, or indeed that by recording that response Brierley himself is completely trapped within liberal ideology.

In *Means Test Man* Brierley offers a complex view of unemployment which in itself challenges certain commonsense notions of the problem, and which also brings into focus the way people as subjects are socially defined. Jack's unemployment means that he and his wife are forced by external factors to modify their relationship, and to break with the separation of conjugal roles which traditionally operates within their own community. Brierley has none of Greenwood's romanticism, and for Jack and Jane love on the dole becomes a very bitter experience. Both painfully come to recognize that Jane's love for Jack is partially determined by Jack's ability to fulfil his ascribed role and provide economically for Jane and the child; love does not conquer all but is shown instead to be the product of certain social relations which institutionalise sexual divisions, and then mystify them with a notion of love which is capable of transcending material forces. It is with insights like this that Brierley begins to break with the dominant ideology and its literary articulation.

The strength of *Means Test Man* lies in Brierley's recreation of his own empirical observations of life on the dole, and its effects, not simply as a 'slice of life', but as synthesised and artistically wrought experience which comments meaningfully upon the external world. In this respect it is very different from his other two novels, *Sandwich Man*[9] and *Dalby Green*,[10] which appear to have nothing to say of importance, no particular insight into working class existence, and in which Brierley assumes that naturalistic description is a substitute for experience and meaning. Although both novels are set in mining communities the central characters are in no sense typical of the working class.

Arthur, the principal character in *Sandwich Man*, is trying to educate himself out of the pits and indeed out of the working class, and Brierley records that attempt uncritically and indeed approvingly. In his single-minded dedication to study he selfishly exploits the love of his mother and of Nancy, the girl he is to marry, needing and feeding off their moral and physical support but prepared to give nothing in return. There is no suggestion from Brierley that Arthur's concept of education as material and intellectual *self* improvement is in any way reprehensible. His study of the traditional academic subjects of philosophy, history, and literature, distances him from his own class and leads him to view it almost with contempt. His education never becomes a way of understanding himself, his world, or his class, rather it becomes a process of alienation.

Brierley's style becomes self-consciously literary, and his prose lifeless and static. He is not only very obviously attempting to create 'literature', but literature also becomes a way of explaining the world. The work of Lawrence becomes for Arthur and Brierley a substitute for real understanding, and Brierley uses it instead of creating his own fictional world which is capable of exploring the problems facing Arthur, and making the reader understand them. He describes Arthur on the bus to Nottingham thus:

He glanced down the street where Lawrence was born; a shabby street with flat-faced houses and a grimy chapel. All the adult students in his group at Trentingham were crazy over Lawrence. Nancy was like some of the women in his books – well she had been lately – sex-driven out of all balance ... Lawrence undoubtably roamed around here, feeling penned in by his existence as a student and a teacher, driven or pulled to another expression, the real expression of himself. He felt the same about his pit life; it was an obstruction to his real self.[11]

Time and again references to Lawrence crop up, and Brierley uses him not as an illustration of something he himself is also writing about, but as a direct explanation. Any reader unfamiliar with Lawrence's work would find sections of *Sandwich Man* incomprehensible, and in the end one feels that as he obviously had nothing to say which Lawrence had not already said he should not have written the book, for Lawrence says it so much better.

Brierley's final novel, *Dalby Green*, is even further removed from working-class life in the thirties, for the central characters are a village shop keeper and his family. George Bestwick is an ex-miner thrown out of work by rationalisation, who turns to shopkeeping in order to support his family. Most of the novel seems an endless description of the minutest detail of a shopkeeper's life, with long conversations on half-penny profit margins and the catering arrangements for the chapel teas. Dalby Green is a world which had already ceased to exist in most parts of Britain, and by the end of the novel a new road, a new bus service, and a new housing estate on the edge of the village means that Dalby Green itself is about to be catapulted into the twentieth century. Again it is difficult to fathom why he felt impelled to write when apparently he had nothing to say.

These novels illustrate the very real difference between a working-class person who writes in order to explore his world, and a person from the working class who seeks to become an 'Author', with all that that implies in terms of the dominant literary culture. Once Brierley had made that transition, and sought to write about things which were more tangental to his own experience, his own weaknesses both in style and thought became apparent. He takes upon himself the mantle of creative writer, and stops really looking at his experience of the world and what that might mean. With no conscious ideological stance, and without the litmus paper of his own experience, his novels become an uncritical assimilation of liberal ideology, and his working-class origins of no relevance.

3. LEWIS JONES: TOWARDS A PROLETARIAN WRITING

Lewis Jones is very different from Greenwood and Brierley in that he brings to his writing a conscious political stance; his writing is part of his political activity and has a very specific political as well as literary purpose. It is this very intentionality which enables Jones to escape from the liberal ideology which is so closely linked to the realist novel and to introduce into its structures a proletarian and socialist consciousness. Jones was a miner, trade union leader, communist, and political activist, who lived most of his life in the Rhondda, and in writing *Cwmardy* and *We Live*[12] he attempted to recreate the life experience of his own mining community, and the Welsh working class. Although both novels are heavily autobiographical, it is the shared experience of the collective life which he tries to capture and not his own individual history. The first novel, *Cwmardy*, was inspired by the suggestion of Arthur Horner, President of the South Wales Miners' Federation, that

the full meaning of life in the Welsh mining areas could be expressed for the general reader more truthfully and vividly if treated imaginatively, than by any amount of statistical and historical research.[11]

In a period when the left placed great emphasis on factual accounts of working-class experience, and on direct political anlysis,[14] this is in itself an interesting observation, and a recognition of the power of the imaginative text. It also suggests a perception of the particular status of the fictional work and its potential ability to reveal the 'real conditions' existing at a particular historic moment. Statistical and historical research can reveal the forces which determine a specific moment, but they do not attempt to engage with the individual lives which shape, and are shaped by that moment; that is traditionally the terrain of the creative text.

In the Foreword Jones also states:

The work is really collective in the sense that my fellow workers had to fight the battles I try to picture. . . . We found many difficulties confronting us, not the least of which was the fact that, book or no book, the mass struggle must go on and all of us had to play our part. The jumpiness of certain portions of the book is evidence of this. It was written during odd moments stolen from mass meetings, committees, demonstrations, marches, and other activities. But I do not advance this as an excuse for the shortcomings, which no one better than ourselves knows it contains. Rather do I state it as a reason.

Jones's conception of creative work as outlined here is in itself a challenge to the ideology which surrounds the dominant literary culture, for writing is seen not as a private, essentially individual, practice, but as the product of collective, shared experience, and as an activity perfectly compatible with an active political life. However, although his intention may be radical, one must judge *Cwmardy* by the text which exists, and not Jones's conception of it.

One of the problems of the text stems from another observation in the Foreword when Jones states that all the events described, 'though not placed in chronological order, have occurred, and each of them marks a milestone in the lives and struggles of the South Wales miners'. Yet it is not enough for a reader to be told that a novel is 'true' because all the incidents contained within it happened in 'real life', for the reader also needs to be convinced of the veracity of the fictional world. A novel needs to create an internal 'real' world of the text, which has its own coherence and 'explanations'; it is this world which interrogates the 'external' world, and reacts with it and upon it to reveal its 'real conditions of existence'. If the internal world of the novel appears at times to be unreal, or to exist in disjunction with the outside world, the ability of the text to comment upon that world is marred.

Cwmardy contains scenes and incidents of great power and strength, like the death of Jane in child-birth, and her funeral, and the horror of the pit explosion, or the solidarity of the strike, and there is tremendous vitality in the prose when Jones focuses on Big Jim and Shane, characters who represent all the finest attributes of the working class, but who still live within the pages of the novel as people rather than cyphers. However these separate successes never become part of a unified whole, and *Cwmardy* is finally a collection of cameo portraits and vignettes, unable to recreate the 'full meaning of life in the Welsh mining areas', because too much of that life is missing from the novel.

The central incident in the novel is the major strike at Cwmardy pit which ends with the troops being sent into the valley. The strike takes place in 1910, and is obviously based upon the Cambrian Combine dispute when Churchill sent troops to the Rhondda in a similar fashion. It is a long, bitter, and bloody strike, and Jones records how the miners and their families become increasingly aware of their collective strength as a result of their struggles against Lord Cwmardy, the pit owner. Before the strike Jones makes no mention of trade union organisation in the pit, although Ezra is referred to as the miners' leader, a title which presumably denotes some official position. By the end of the strike, the men – convinced by their experience of the efficacy of collective, united action – decide to join the Federation. Jones's political message is clear, but is only achieved by reinterpreting the history of the Welsh people during the Cambrian Dispute.

The Welsh have a great sense of the importance of their own working-class history, their struggles and their organisations, and it is significant that Jones, who as a trade union activist, communist, and councillor, contributed a great deal to that history, should ignore so much of it in writing *Cwmardy*. By 1910, the year of the strike, the miners throughout South Wales were organised in the Federation, and thus it is difficult to see why there is no mention of it until after the conclusion of the strike, although there are two possible explanations, one political, the other structural.

Jones's political intention in writing *Cwmardy* was to show the strength and potential power of a united working class at the moment when it becomes aware of itself and its own abilities. In that sense the strike becomes more than a description of one particular strike: it is a symbol of working class power, and the fact that the strike and the final victory come initially from the activity of an unorganised section of the working class has great ideological significance for the theme of the book.

Cwmardy was written in 1936–7, at a time when the political situation in Europe seemed to make another war inevitable, and when the labour movement, which one would have expected to mobilise against war and fascism was disorganised and dispirited. All the key political initiatives by the left in the thirties – the unemployed marches, activity against the Means Test, anti-fascist demonstrations, and support for Republican Spain – were the result of rank and file activity and took place outside the traditional structures of the labour movement, indeed often in opposition to it. It is hardly surprising that Jones, an active communist, should choose to portray a successful strike which arises from rank-and-file action. The message is clear: we can win, we can form our own organisations, but we can only do it together in struggle. It is an attractive message, and an important one for the thirties, but Jones is only able to make it by sacrificing an important part of the history of his own class and its trade union organization.

It would also be possible to argue, and indeed traditional novel criticism would suggest, that it is the realist novel form itself which forces upon Jones certain explanations, and that it is the formal demands of plot, character, and narrative, which do not allow him to deal with the complexities of the South Wales miners' trade union, and the conflict between its Lib/Lab leadership, and its pit-face militants (in other words, the real background to 1910) – that that is a subject which cannot be accommodated within the realist form. But that cannot be the answer, for Jones does successfully capture the subtleties and complexities of the political situation in the coalfield in his second novel, *We Live*. Their absence in *Cwmardy* cannot simply be attributed to the restrictions which the form itself imposes. The real explanation lies partly within the politics of the thirties, and partly with Jones's inexperience as a writer.

One senses throughout *Cwmardy* that the author has certain preconceived notions about the novel inevitably derived from his own reading, and that he feels that it needs to operate through individual characters and dramatic incidents and engage emotionally with individual lives, and that these apparent demands of the form conflict with its own clearly-stated interest in communal life, the activity which binds people together rather than marks them off as individual presences. A lack of confidence in his own technical skill leads him to use familiar fictional devices and traditional structures. For instance, the early sections of the novel focus almost exclusively on the Roberts family, with the community as background, and his attempt to relate their lives to that community often fails because the fictional world does not cohere.

The real strength of the novel lies in the descriptions of collective action, and in particular in the scenes which surround the strike. It is almost as if at this point Jones becomes 'recorder', rather than writer of fiction, and he allows his perception of the significance of those events to override his conception of 'the novel'. It is the strike which galvanises the collective will of the community and reveals to individuals, not their own power, but the power of the class to which they belong. Up to this point the novel works through individual protaganists, but then the focus switches and those protagonists become part of a historical process. Jones describes the meeting which calls the strike thus:

Down on the rubbish dump thousands of miners and their womenfolk were waiting for the meeting to begin. . . . A lorry in the centre of the huge mass of people held Ezra and some other men. Presently a glorious baritone lifted itself from the throng in the lilting melody of an old Welsh hymn. Its strains floated over the crowd like a shawl encircling a child. The people lost their individual identities in the vibrating rhythm of the tune which impelled their emotions into expression through bonds of vocal unity. In a matter of seconds every voice had taken up the refrain. . . .

The men on the platform stood with bared heads and took part in the singing until it finished, when they all, with the exception of Ezra, sat down. . . . Each of the thousands of eyes was fixed upon him when his cold voice split the air as he reported all that had happened since the previous meeting. With steady calculation he built his case against the company and eventually concluded with the words:

'That is the position, fellow workmen, either we fight or starve. You will yourselves decide which.'

For a minute after his voice ceased the whole world seemed to slumber, then it awoke to a terrific shout that rattled and throbbed in the blood of the people present. It ascended in increasing crescendos, pushing itself up the mountain with brazen resonance until it banged itself against the windows of the Big House.

'Strike! Strike!'[15]

The whole emphasis in this description, and indeed in all the descriptions of mass activity, is on the common experience of the group, and on its shared culture, language, and heritage. The loss of 'individual identitites' within the crowd is not to be mourned, for what is gained is a far richer sense of communal identity.

It is with descriptions like this that Jones begins to break with the liberal ideology which surrounds the novel form, for in both his novels the crowd is seen as a group of individuals asserting its collective will, and ironically (given the equation liberal = individual), it is precisely this recognition of the importance of the relationship between the individual and the mass which breaks with liberalism. Not for Jones the notion that people in a crowd become a mob, liable to be swayed by fervent oratory to act against its own interest, but rather a recognition that through the experience of the mass an individual finds his fullest means of self expression. One of Jones most moving descriptions is that of the mass march of the unemployed against the Means Test, in *We Live*.

'Can you hear anything?' he asked.

They both looked simultaneously past Len, and he, seeing their amazement, turned his head to look in the same direction. He drew his breath sharply and his perspiring face went a shade whiter. The mountain which separated Cwmardy from the other valleys looked like a gigantic ant-hill, covered with a mass of black, waving bodies.

'Good God,' the man next to Mary whispered, 'the whole world is on the move.' . . .

The people seemed overwhelmed with the mighty demonstration of their own power, which they could now see so clearly. . . .

Len momentarily felt himself like a weak straw drifting in and out with the surge of bodies. Then something powerful swept through his being as the mass soaked its strength into him, and he realised that the strength of them all was a measure of his own, that his existence and power as an individual was buried in that of the mass now preganant with motion behind him.[16]

Jones identifies the balance between the individual consciousness of events and the collective will. He does not negate the individual, but shows there are forms of individual expression which do not operate within the liberal bourgeois concept of individualism. It is the beginning of an introduction of a new form of consciousness into the realist novel.

In *We Live* Jones overcomes the problems faced in *Cwmardy* because of the conflict between his intention as stated in the latter's Foreword, and the notional demands of the form. It centres upon the same group of characters as *Cwmardy* but he handles his theme with far more confidence, and creates an internally consistent and coherent world. The plot does not revolve around the developments in individual lives, but around collective political action in which his central characters participate. It begins with the struggles of 1921, moves on through the General Strike, to the unemployed marches of the thirties, and culminates with Len being killed in Spain. The lives of the main characters become important not as individual human drama, but because of their relationship with, and sense of responsibility to, the wider community, and to their class. In Jones community becomes far more than a collection of individuals who live in the same physical location; it is a group whose shared experience stems from their common relationship to the means of production, and it is that relationship which gives them a common perception of reality.

Although it is a realist novel and works through the formal structures of concatenated plot, central characters, dramatic incident, and points of climax, *We Live* breaks with the liberalism of the form by not reproducing an individualistic philosophy. It is the community, and more crucially the class which becomes the central 'character', and the Roberts's and Jones's are not at the centre of the novel because they are in any way special, or because of a heightened sensitivity which gives them special insights into their world, but rather as representatives of their class, and its special qualities. Jones takes events of enormous significance in British politics – the miners' lockout, the General Strike, the Depression – and explores the significance of living through those events, and contributing to the history of one's class. The reader is aware of Jones the man, the novelist, and the narrator, as a participant able to give a special insight which comes from his own class

background, and *We Live* is more than the imaginative recreation of
specific historical moments in a fictional world, for that world explains,
comments upon, and informs the reader of the significance of those
moments in the 'real' world.

It is a fiercely political book, but Jones is aware at all times of the
relationship between the personal and the political, the individual and
the mass, and it is this insight which enables him to capture the
complexities of individual lives and of political life as they interwine and
inform each other. The resulting subtlety of character and refusal to
simplify and produce caricatures can be seen in his creation of Ezra,
the miners' leader.

Ezra had come to Cwmardy because he was blacklisted and thrown
out of his home in his own valley as a result of his union activity. He is
left to raise his daughter alone when his wife dies because of the poverty
and strain which his victimisation imposes on the family. He carries on
his trade union activities in Cwmardy, and although passionately
committed to the bettering of pay and conditions for the miners, his
belief in their ability to win any prolonged struggle with the pit owners
has been weakened by his own experience. His own empirical
observations, and his political philosophy of gradualism and reformism,
derived from the Welsh Lib/Lab tradition, leads him to compromise,
and finally to betrayal of the miners after an eight month lockout, a
betrayal which stems from his belief that the miners have suffered
enough and cannot win. As he becomes more pessimistic about his
class, Mary his daughter becomes more radical, and finally joins the
Communist Party, knowing that her father will see it as a betrayal of his
principles. At all times Jones treats Ezra with sympathy and
understanding. He does not function within the novel as a political
cypher, one minute great union leader and militant, the next class
collaborationist, but is shown to be a person torn by conflicting loyalties
and emotions, who finally has not sufficient personal strength, or faith in
his class to carry on fighting. His story is potentially human drama in
the traditional fictional sense, but Jones never offers an individualistic
account of his dilemma. His problems are not simply seen as personal
problems, or his tragedy as a personal tragedy; but through Ezra Jones
reveals both the potential strength of the class to which he belongs, and
its weaknesses. His 'failure' is not located within his own character, or
seen as moral weakness, but is shown to be a failure of the labour
movement and of his own class which could not sustain him.

Jones's insight into the conditions of his class is not limited to the obviously political areas of trade unions, political parties, etc.; he is also very conscious of the problem faced by women in a capitalist society, and the way that society defines them. Traditionally labour history has been seen essentially as the history of men's struggles for better wages and working conditions, and until recently even when labour historians did examine women it was as workers, trade unionists, or strikers, rather than locating the problems they faced as women. Jones foregrounds those women who have been 'hidden from history', because they exist outside the traditional structures of the labour movement. In *Cwmardy* he explicitly attacks the view of women held by many working-class men,

'The boys in work talk of girls as the owners talk of us. The owners make us slaves in the pit and our men make our women slaves in the house. I've seen my father come home after a week's work and chuck his small pay on the kitchen table, chucking his worries with it at the same time. My mother had the job of running the home and rearing him and me on money that wasn't half enough to pay the bills. Yes. A man's worries finish in the pit. Once he comes home it is the woman who has to carry the burden. . . .'

'I have heard my butties talk about women exactly as if they were cattle – to be taken up the mountain and then laughed at in the pit. If that is love, I don't want it. . . .' 'Look at our women today. They are on the picket lines with us, they are in the riots. It is they who give our men guts to carry on.'[17]

In both novels Jones seeks implicitly to expose the ideological ways in which women are perceived. His women characters exist as equals with men, and are shown to be capable of the same political initiatives and understanding. Mary may join the Communist Party after Len but it is *her* decision, and the result of *her* reassessment of the politics which she learnt from her father; and although it strengthens her relationship with Len, her membership of the Party is not dependent upon that relationship. Women are always present at the mass meetings and demonstrations, and their presence is never seen as passive support for 'their men'; they understand the issues and their support is active and intelligent. Jones shows that the men's ability to win a strike is not simply determined by the amount of solidarity which can be achieved at the work place and with other workers, but is also dependent upon the solidarity of the women.

Women play a crucial role in the mass march against the Means Test in *We Live*, and it is the women who take the political initiative, and demand to see the chief unemployment officer:

'I'm very sorry, but Mr Parker can only see deputations by appointment.'

'That's not for him to decide,' said Mary.

She looked behind her and sighed before turning again to the inspector.

'There are women in this demonstration who have carried babies more than ten miles already,' she said, 'And I don't believe they are willing to do that for nothing. If you don't believe me ask them,' she invited, secure in her faith that the women would stand and the men would stand with them.

The inspector looked at the mass of people, who stretched beyond reach of sight, and very wisely did not accept the invitation. Instead he shook his head resignedly, then warned her: 'You will be held responsible for all that happens here to-day.'[18]

It is a very short scene which fundamentally challenges traditional notions of women's role in mass struggles, for they act whilst the men mutter apprehensively that 'the committee never decided it', and Mary's confidence that the men would stand firm behind the women is clearly not just based upon her experiences during one march, but upon the class politics of her own community. One only has to remember the portrait of working-class women painted by Greenwood to realise just how far these apparently obvious insights break against the dominant notions of women and their role. In his treatment of women, of the working class, and of personal relationships, Jones breaks with the liberal ideology which has for so long surrounded and helped define the realist novel form, and in *We Live* in particular he begins to explore ways of opening up the form to allow the introduction of a proletarian consciousness.

It is perhaps significant that of the three writers discussed here, only Greenwood remains as part of the literary 'map' of the period. Indeed apart from Tressell, and Grassic Gibbon, it is difficult to think of any working-class writer from any period who is seriously regarded on any literature course. Are we to conclude with Virginia Woolf, and Samuel Hynes, and indeed with most literary critics, that this is simply because the working class have never produced anything of literary merit? Or isn't it about time, perhaps, that we begun to question definitions of literature and culture which are only capable of encompassing such a partial view of literary production?

NOTES

1. Tony Davis, 'Education, Ideology and Literature', *Red Letters*, no. 7, 1978.
2. Terry Eagleton, *Criticism and Ideology* (New Left Books, 1976), p. 26.

3. Walter Greenwood, *Love on the Dole* (Jonathan Cape, 1933; quotations from Penguin Modern Classics, 1969), p. 15.
4. ibid., p. 143.
5. ibid., p. 255.
6. Walter Brierley, *Means Test Man* (Methuen, 1937).
7. cf. Roy Johnson, 'Walter Brierley: Proletarian Writing', *Red Letters*, no. 2, Summer 1976 (reply by Carole Snee, 'Walter Brierley: a test case', ibid., no. 3, Autumn 1976), and Roy Johnson, 'The Proletarian Novel, *Literature and History*, no. 2, Thames Polytechnic Publications, October 1975.
8. H. L. Beales and R. S. Lambert (eds), *Memoirs of the Unemployed* (Gollancz, 1934; reprinted, EP Publishing Limited, 1973), p. 91.
9. Walter Brierley, *Sandwich Man* (Methuen, 1937).
10. Walter Brierley, *Dalby Green* (Methuen, 1938).
11. *Sandwich Man*, p. 48.
12. Lewis Jones. *Cwmardy* (Lawrence and Wishart, 1937); *We Live* (Lawrence and Wishart, 1939) (both reprinted in paperback, 1978).
13. Preface to *Cwmardy*.
14. Cf. Left Book Club, journals like *Fact*, Mass Observation, and the widespread use of the documentary form.
15. *Cwmardy*, p. 154.
16. *We Live*, p. 243.
17. *Cwmardy*, p. 202.
18. *We Live*, pp. 246–7.

The Left Book Club in the Thirties

BETTY REID

The Left Book Club came into being in May 1936. It ended in 1948. The period of its main impact upon the British political scene was in the three or four years preceding the outbreak of the Second World War. Although this represents such a relatively short span in the lives of those associated with the birth and development of the Club, events moved at such speed, the days were so crowded, the involvement of thousands was so alive and intense, that today – some forty years on – the impression left is of a far longer period.

Nor is this solely the effect of ageing – the nostalgic recollection of old battles; it is a feeling common to all who participated in the anti-fascist movement of the time. Perhaps it was because of the tremendously strong conviction that there was within our grasp a genuine chance of influencing world affairs, of changing the course of history, of removing the shadow of war and poverty which had haunted our generation; and for those specifically involved in the work of the Left Book Club there was also the belief that, to these ends, it was capable of playing a significant part. No examination of the thirties would therefore be complete without some account of the Club and some estimate of its contribution to British politics.

Few of its books will survive, says Samuel Hynes in *The Auden Generation.*

To say this [he continues] is not to judge either the Club or its books – permanence is not necessarily a part of the value of topical writing – but simply to note that the Club *was* topical, that it belonged to its time, died with its time, and left virtually nothing behind.[1]

The reader must judge whether this is a valid observation or one that betrays no more than a superficial understanding of those years.

Before attempting to examine the political scene upon which the Left Book Club entered, it is necessary to give some account of the main facts about its own origins and progress.

(i) *The launching of the Club*

On 4 May 1936 Victor Gollancz wrote the editorial for a new

publication, *Left Book News*. Consisting of sixteen pages, this journal was given free to all who enrolled in the newly-formed Left Book Club.

The aim of the Club is a simple one; it is to help in the terribly urgent struggle for world peace and for a better social and economic order and against fascism, by giving all who are determined to play their part in this struggle such knowledge as will immensely increase their efficiency.

Members had to agree to take a book each month at a price of 2s 6d for a minimum of six months. Monthly 'choices' would be *new* books, to reach members on publication day, and simultaneously the ordinary edition would be available to the non-subscribing public at prices ranging from 5 to 18 shillings.

The selection committee was described as composed of Professor Harold Laski, 'a member of the Labour Party', John Strachey, 'in broad sympathy with the aims of the Communist Party', and Victor Gollancz who was concerned to spread 'all such knowledge and all such ideas as may safeguard peace, combat Fascism, and bring nearer the establishment of real Socialism'.

Writing this editorial on the day news came of the victory of the Popular Front in France, Gollancz said:

From a spectacle so magnificent the transition to our own Left Book Club must seem a trifle grotesque . . . but out of the small beginning that we are now making something big and important will come, if we have sufficient energy and sufficient faith. For what the Left Book Club is attempting to do is to provide the indispensable basis of *knowledge* without which a really effective United Front of all men and women of goodwill cannot be built.

After only a few weeks of advertising the Club was able to start its first month with a membership of 7,000. The occasion was marked by the publication of two books: *France Today and the People's Front* by Maurice Thorez and *Out of the Night*, a biologist's view of the future, by H. J. Muller. The combined price of the non-Club editions was 9s 6d.

In December 1936 the journal changed its name to *Left News*. By then it was available to the general public at sixpence a copy and its size varied from 32 to 56 pages, containing not only news about Club publications and activities but also political articles and book reviews which transformed it from a free house-journal into a valuable publication in its own right. (For researchers into this period a study of its pages, until it ceased in March 1947, is a highly rewarding one.)

By December 1936 it was also possible to announce the formation of over two hundred discussion groups of the Club and the appointment of John Lewis as a full-time organizer with the sole responsibility of working with these groups. The following month a Left Book Club Groups' Department was set up – entirely independent of the business side of the Left Book Club – which concentrated upon issuing comprehensive speakers' notes for opening discussion on the current month's 'choice', a monthly letter to group conveners, and the section in *Left News* devoted to information about the groups and their general needs. It also organized national and local rallies and, later, an increasing number of tours, summer schools, film shows, conferences and similar activities, while giving scrupulous attention to all correspondence, sending long and reasoned replies to readers' questions and opinions.

A year after its inception the Club had 44,800 members. Its first anniversary rally filled the Albert Hall and was followed by rallies in Birmingham, Glasgow, Cardiff and Manchester. The second anniversary rally required not only the Albert Hall but a simultaneous overflow meeting in the Queen's Hall (demolished by bombs in the war). The third anniversary was celebrated in the Empress Hall with an audience of 10,000. The speakers included the Liberal MP Richard Acland, Normal Angell, the pacifist, the Dean of Canterbury, Stafford Cripps, Lloyd George, Harry Pollitt, Wilfrid Roberts (also a Liberal MP), and John Strachey, with Victor Gollancz in the chair, and Paul Robeson as a special guest.

At this, the third anniversary rally in 1939, it was announced that the membership had grown to 58,000 and the groups to 1,200. Fifteen million leaflets had been distributed, two million bound books and half-a-million each of two pamphlets sold. This was to be the peak of the Club's achievements. September that year saw the outbreak of the Second World War and the Club faced a totally new political situation.

(ii) *How had it happened?*

Initially conceived as a means of distributing low-priced books on a mass scale, the Club had taken on an identity of its own and become something far more. This can be explained by the combination of a number of factors which resulted in a unique organization, perhaps impossible to repeat in any subsequent period.

First, the political situation in 1936 was the fundamental, all-important precondition for the development of the Club. Second, once it became evident that the Club was growing into something more than an educational scheme through the dissemination of cheap books, a clear view had to be taken of its relationship to the existing political parties and organisations. Third, there existed enormous obstacles in the publishing world of the time to reaching a vast potential serious readership. Fourth, there was an established, experienced and enterprising publishing house which acted as a launching-pad. Finally, there was the personality and ability of Victor Gollancz himself.

(iii) *The political background*

In the early years of the thirties, activists in the labour movement had concentrated on two main issues: on the one hand, on the exposure of intolerable social conditions and the acute poverty suffered by a large section of the working-class; on the other, still close to the experience of the First World War, they had sought to educate the movement about the origin and causes of that war, on the nature of capitalist crisis and imperialism, on the horrors of war itself and the consequences of an arms race and the private manufacture of armaments for profit and, by no means least, on the menacing time-bomb represented by the peace agreements of the post-war settlements. A substantial minority of these activists – far exceeding the membership of the Communist Party which in 1934 had fewer than 6,000 members – found inspiration in the Soviet Union, its fight to build socialism and its foreign policy, in the belief that this was the living demonstration that socialism provided a solution to the problems so starkly evident in the capitalist world. It was therefore internationalism, solidarity with the working class of other countries, and a deep hostility to the objectives of British imperialism that dominated the left in the labour movement.

Hitler's rise to power in Germany in 1933, the decision of the German Government to rearm and to withdraw from the League of Nations, the Soviet Union's entry into the League in 1934, and the Seventh World Congress of the Communist International in 1935 calling for Popular Front movements on a united working-class policy as a means to defeat fascism and prevent war – all combined to indicate a qualitative change in the political situation, though this was understood at the time by only a minority in the British labour movement.

Thus when the Left Book Club was inaugurated in spring 1936 – after the Franco-Soviet pact, just before the alliance of the French Socialists, Communists and Radicals had won the first victory for a Popular Front, and on what was to be the eve of the great struggle in

Spain (it broke out in July 1936) – the situation was ripe for a great anti-fascist movement. This the Club recognized and helped to develop. It provided it with powerful propaganda weapons, sent crusading speakers throughout the country to hold meetings where none had been held for years, and demonstrated in practice that people with widely differing views could work together, openly and in good faith, for immediate aims, building a barrier against fascism and halting the drive to world domination explicitly outlined in Hitler's *Mein Kampf*.

The selectors of the Left Book Club and all those involved in its development were nevertheless perfectly aware that the Club itself could never in any way be a substitute for the established political parties or the labour and trade union movement. Every effort was made to win the cooperation of these bodies on the widest possible basis, including the official Labour Party whose spokesmen were approached again and again to write for the Club. Lord Addison responded with a book on agriculture, and Attlee himself wrote *The Labour Party in Perspective* which became the August 1937 'choice'. Yet for the most part the attitude of the Labour Party was one of hostility. Whatever sectarian mistakes the Communists had made in earlier years, the deeply menacing world situation now required the Labour Party to make new efforts to give leadership to the widespread anti-fascist struggle. Of this it proved incapable.

To the question, frequently posed, 'Is the Left Book Club aiming at the organization of a Popular Front?', the reply was given and consistently repeated:

No, it is not. It is aiming at the creation of an educated public opinion . . . thus the Club is one of the most important factors in creating that mass basis without which a true popular front is impossible. . . .[2]

Club members were therefore constantly urged to join whatever political party corresponded most nearly with their views and aims and thus exercise their political rights to the full.

This was not received with any enthusiasm by the Labour Party. Ernest Bevin declared that the main object of the Club was 'to undermine and destroy the Trade Unions and the Labour Party as an effective force'.[3] Even as late as March 1939 – the week when Hitler occupied Prague, as Gollancz wrote in *Left News* – the Labour Party started a rival *Labour Book Service*. This move was accompanied by a letter from the National Agent, G. R. Shepherd, to all secretaries of borough, divisional and local Labour Parties, threatening those who persisted in buying Left Book Club books with expulsion and complaining of activities embarrassing to constituency parties. He gave as an example; 'One [Left Book Club] group has taken the initiative in holding public meetings on Spain, Czechoslovakia, etc., and in directing attention to the problem of the distressed areas. For some years there has been no activity of this kind in the district.'[4]

In the April 1939 issue of *Left News* Gollancz replied that to this charge the Club must plead guilty:

If this is an embarrassment to local Labour Parties, why then we must say roundly it is high time such parties should be embarrassed. It will not be until they cease, and Transport House ceases, to 'be embarrassed' by such activities that there is the slightest hope for the labour movement of this country.

There were of course many issues on which the Club membership was united. Whatever widely differing views were held on many fundamental beliefs, total agreement was reached on such matters as solidarity with Republican Spain, opposition to anti-semitism, or the British Government's policy on the rape of Czechoslovakia. On those questions it was possible for a group, as such, to carry out propaganda activity in its locality.

However, the major objective was never overlooked: in the last resort it was how the British labour movement as a whole, with its enormous potential strength and its capacity for swinging behind it additional millions of allies, would act. This alone would determine the future not only of Britain but of the world; and Club members, however new to political life, were never allowed to imagine that there were short-cuts offering alternative possibilities.

For the same reason, the occasional demands for a more structured organization of the groups with, perhaps, elected regional bodies, were always resisted. Each group had to be free to decide its own programme and beyond that the Club was based on nothing more than the initial commitment to purchase its books. Thus its groups and its platforms were able to unite men and women of all political parties and from all sections of society.

(iv) *The publishing scene*

It is important to recall the situation that then existed in publishing. Expensive books with a small circulation were the norm. Paperbacks were of the 'pulp' variety and most people did not buy books but borrowed them, either from the public library, or, later, from the chain of twopenny libraries which by the mid-thirties proliferated. Left-wing books received few reviews and were often not stocked. In 1935 Allen Lane launched his sixpenny Penguins. Though this was a major advance, there still existed considerable prejudice against paperbacks. The small minority who had travelled abroad were familiar with the Tauchnitz editions, but on the whole people who made up their minds to buy a book still wanted it in the conventional, long-lasting hardcover binding.

The firm of Victor Gollancz Ltd had acquired a very distinctive character and reputation in the publishing world. Although established only in 1928 it had built up a list of excellent novels and detective stories which booksellers were eager to handle; but in addition it had set out to produce a whole series of political, economic and educational works. Writing of this period Victor Gollancz said:

It was political publishing that I thought about night and day. . . . The passion to make people *see* . . . was again in my vitals; and now, I thought I would really do something about it.[5]

What he did about it was to publish such books as G. D. H. Cole's *The Intelligent Man's Guide to World Politics*, *The Outline of Modern Knowledge*, John Strachey's *Menace of Fascism* and *The Coming Struggle for Power*, G. R. Mitchison's *The First Workers' Government*, *What Marx Really Meant* by G. D. H. Cole, a biography of Lenin by Ralph Fox, Allen Hutt's *This Final Crisis*, *A Textbook of Marxist Philosophy* and *Christianity and the Social Revolution*, both edited by John Lewis, *The First Five-Year Plan of the Soviet Union*, and dozens of similar works.

All these were produced in the distinctive Gollancz style, with yellow dust jackets and startling typographic innovations. Gollancz himself was involved in everything, from initial editorial responsibility, production, publicity and sales, down to the supervision – and usually the writing – of every advertisement. No detail was too petty to engage his attention.

There was thus already in existence not only the apparatus of a well-organized publishing firm but a recognition by a wide range of public figures that the firm was a vehicle for important new political books. Gollancz himself was personally known and vigorously active in left politics. So the formation of the Club was a logical, though daring, step. Once taken, it became an integral part of the firm but with a new department to deal with the enormous technical business of the distribution of the Club books.

As already said, the Left Book Club Groups Department was set up some eight months later to foster the rapidly-growing discussion groups. At its peak it employed a dozen or more people and a very substantial outlay was needed to pay their wages and to promote the activities which became an essential part of the groups' needs. Without this, though probably the sale of books would not have been markedly reduced, the Club's influence and the degree of its political impact on the country would never have been achieved.   All this required central direction and it was here that Gollancz's own personality played an indispensable part, particularly from the start of the Club until the weeks immediately preceding the war. During the early stages, when he was absolutely convinced of the urgency and danger of the world situation, and as convinced that it was possible to do something about it, he devoted all his time and energies to the Club. A brilliant organizer, he had an uncanny sense for judging the right moment to launch new schemes. He was willing to stay up all night to draft a leaflet, driving himself and all those about him to the utmost limits, intervening personally with printers and editors, reading every letter that came into the office, as well as copies of the replies sent and – up to March 1937 – working out various fresh advantages for the members, such as additional, supplementary and educational books, making arrangements with other publishers, links with the newly-launched *Tribune*, introducing different categories of membership, organizing subscriptions to send a Left Book Club food-ship to Spain and a host of other enterprising ideas. The list is endless, and for each new item of interest to the members different coloured leaflets and cards were devised. It is true that the business department and booksellers were driven into a frenzy but, though some schemes were stillborn, Gollancz carried most of them through successfully, generating an atmosphere of excitement which, in its turn, accelerated support and interest, until it seemed that all barriers could be surmounted.

Gollancz was an eloquent and persuasive – if somewhat lengthy – speaker who built up an enormous personal following, especially among those who had been newly drawn into political life. His long editorials, which appeared regularly in *Left News* until August 1941, played an important part in this. A glance through its pages over that period demonstrates the number of meetings he personally addressed, representing constant travel and physical effort.

A large, vigorous man of swiftly changing moods, sometimes irascible and impatient, sometimes despondent but usually crashing through all obstacles to achieve some immediate aim, Gollancz naturally evoked not only loyalty and affection but also antagonism. The obvious accusation that he was a sharp businessman cashing in on the political movement was often made, both at the time and subsequently. The finances of the Club were inextricably – and perhaps wisely – mixed with the general finances of the firm, so that the total balance sheet of the Club was never available. Clearly it was impossible to confirm or deny the accusation and Gollancz was content to stand on the Club's own record and its contribution to the anti-fascist fight. Among those closely associated with him it is probable that none could be found who did not believe that, to him, the Club was truly a crusading mission of total commitment into which he was prepared to pour vast sums of money and his entire energy and waking thought.

(v) *The Monthly 'Choice' and other 'Choices'*

From May 1936 until October 1948 the Club published its monthly 'choice'. The list shows an extremely wide range of titles, covering such subjects as social conditions, economics, history, philosophy, the Soviet Union, China, India, France, Italy, colonialism, the smaller democracies, the law, and so on. Naturally there was a distinct variation in the quality of these books; but many people will remember Wilfred Macartney's *Walls have Mouths*, a searing indictment of the prison system, and such lasting works as A. L. Morton's *A People's History of England* (still in print). Many of the books, though written to be of purely topical interest, remain of immense value today. There was Ellen Wilkinson's story of Jarrow, *The Town that was Murdered*; Wal Hannington's *The Problem of the Distressed Areas* and *Ten Lean Years* (recently reissued); B. L. Coombes, a miner, produced his impressive autobiography *These Poor Hands*; John Strachey wrote, among his other books, *The Theory and Practice of Socialism*. *Man's Worldly Goods*, by Leo Huberman (also still available), Frank Jellinek's *The Paris Commune of 1871*, *Left Wing Democracy in the English Civil War* by David Petegorsky and *A People's History of Germany* by A. Ramos Oliveira, to mention only a few, are all still sought and read with undiminished interest by students.

The classic work on the growth of fascism, *Fallen Bastions*, by G. Gedye was the 'choice' for February 1939. Gedye had been *The Times* correspondent in Central Europe and gave the most graphic picture of the effects of the appeasement policy which opened the whole of Eastern Europe through Austria and Czechoslovakia to the Nazis, with the wholesale destruction of the powerful Czech army. This theme was also treated by Konni Zilliacus (writing under the pseudonym 'Vigilantes'), and by R. Palme Dutt in *World Politics*. All three books had a considerable effect in alerting public opinion to the suicidal course pursued by the British Government.

Had it been possible to force the leadership of the Labour Party to take strong action rather than tailing behind the Government's foreign policy, the course of world events might have been very different. For the most part, however, the Labour Party remained obsessed by its anti-Soviet and anti-Communist attitudes, blinding it to the consequences of this policy.

R. Palme Dutt's book was the 'choice' for July 1936 and his *India Today* that for May 1940. *Red Star over China* by Edgar Snow was the first and most remarkable of several books on the new China. G. D. H. Cole was the author of several 'choices', including the early *People's Front*, while Allen Hutt produced *A Post-War History of the British Working Class*, Hyman Levy *A Philosophy for a Modern Man* and Dr Hewlett Johnson *The Socialist Sixth of the World*. These all became extremely popular reading outside the Club membership, as did Simon Haxey's *Tory M.P.*, an analysis of the business and family connections of Conservative members of Parliament.

Over a hundred additional titles were made available cheaply to members, including books on Blanqui, Civil Liberties, the Labour Spy Racket, Greece, Ireland and Denmark, *Sigmund Freud* by Francis Bartlett, Reuben Osborn's *Freud and Marx*, *A Handbook of Marxism* (edited by Emile Burns), *Soviet Civilization* by the Webbs, *Poems of Freedom* (edited by John Mulgan, with an Introduction by W. H. Auden), Hymie Fagan's *Nine Days that Shook England* (about the General Strike), a marriage manual and the one and only children's book, *The Adventures of the Little Pig* by Frederick Le Gros and Ida Clark. The list could be extended, but this selection is enough to illustrate the scope and importance of the Club's output.

Every book had a closely-printed 4-page insertion: a 'Please leaflet' – '*Please* use this leaflet to get a new member' – with details of the Club, its origins and publications, with a coupon for the new member to return. This proved a valuable means of recruitment. Members were urged to use leaflets printed only on one side for mass distribution at meetings – one on every seat – while making more selective use of the

THE LEFT BOOK CLUB IN THE THIRTIES

expensive 4-page leaflet. It was this careful attention to detail that gave a feeling of direction and inspired confidence. (A similar feature was the insistence that in all publicity for meetings there should always be a streamer announcing 'Some free seats at the door', which ensured that on the night the hall would be filled.)

(vi) Pamphlets and leaflets

One of the most remarkable ventures of the Club was a mass distribution of pamphlets. John Strachey had written a small book of some 30,000 words called *Why You Should Be A Socialist* and Gollancz decided to try an experiment. If it were published for tuppence, would it be possible to get a large enough circulation through the Club membership to cover the cost? It was tried and the members responded enthusiastically. In the first year a quarter of a million copies were sold, often on a door-to-door basis. This was followed up by *The Truth About Spain*, *How to be Safe from Air Raids*, and *Act Now* by the Dean of Canterbury. The last of this series – 40 pages with two maps for a penny – was *Is Mr Chamberlain Saving Peace?* by Gollancz himself. This was written in three days – 23 to 26 March 1939 – and was designed to be the first topical 'crisis' pamphlet of the Club. There had already been topical *leaflets* produced, including one, *The Hitler Menace*, during the Munich crisis, two-and-a-half million of which had been printed and distributed in two or three days. But the new pamphlet was intended to provide a longer and more explanatory statement than a leaflet could.

It is the opinion of the selectors of the Left Book Club that the entire propagandist energies of the Club should be turned, for the next few weeks at least, on the maximum conceivable sale of this pamphlet.

While these leaflets and the pamphlet were being produced, the whole activity of the firm was subordinated to that work. Gollancz himself would write draft upon draft, weighing each word, altering, improving, correcting proofs as new information came in, writing postscripts, telephoning printers, organizing distribution and staying up all night if necessary to speed the process. No pressure was needed to mobilize helpers: the atmosphere was electric and the response overwhelming. It says much for the membership that this intensive effort was rewarded by complete success in terms of circulation.

(vii) *The Groups*

If today we were to take a map of Britain and pinpoint the areas where some 1,200 groups of the Club were formed – not forgetting the considerable number of groups abroad, to which a special section of *Left News* was devoted – marking the variety of specialist groups, theatre guilds, poetry circles, scientists, actors and many more, it would present a quite startling picture of the rich and abundant spread of Left Book Club influence in those years. Areas that had seen no public meetings since the General Strike; areas where no other political organizations of the labour movement existed: all were brought into this association which encouraged individual initiative and provided a basis for easy contact and discussion. If the growth of centres and premises and summer schools and conferences is also taken into account, quite apart from the estimated figure of nearly 46,000 meetings – excluding the big rallies in main cities – it will be seen that, however unequal the success and quality of the activities, the number of people for whom the Club formed some introduction to a new world of political ideas must have been immense. Moreover, the groups went on expanding and increasing until the outbreak of the war.

The war brought obvious practical difficulties in maintaining the organization of the groups. In addition, the sharp divisions over its character, and therefore over policy towards it – life and death questions on which passionate views were held – meant that there was no longer a continuing basis for the unity within which different viewpoints had hitherto been discussed. So, while for a few uneasy months attempts were made to stress the educational nature of the Club and to continue the groups as open discussion forums, it soon became clear that this was not possible. By the summer of 1940, the Groups' Department of the Club had been disbanded.

However, as an examination of the books published during and after the war shows, the role of the Club was by no means negligible, even without the groups. From a peak membership of 57,000 it dropped during the war to 15,000, and ultimately to 7,000 in October 1948 when the last book was published; even that, however, is a considerable circulation for a serious political book, and would be the envy of many authors today.[6]

(viii) *The composition of the Club*

People writing about the thirties often dismiss the Club membership as having been essentially professional and middle-class. This is no doubt often based upon the simple belief that workers cannot and do not want to read books. However, while it is certainly the case that the Club attracted large numbers of hitherto isolated intellectuals and professional people, there is also ample evidence that it claimed a substantial membership of manual workers, as well as those in minor clerical, distributive and similar 'white collar' occupations. These sections were often composed of men and women already staffing the labour, co-operative and trade union movement who had previously engaged in the WEA and other workers' educational organizations. They found in the Club a rich new source of books and ideas. It was precisely the meeting of people with widely differing backgrounds, socially and in working life, that contributed to the variety and attraction of the Club.

Another common fallacy is that the Club was dominated by Communists. Again, it is true that Communists played an active part in the Club and, indeed, it would have been strange had they not, for they were actively campaigning for the widest possible unity in the fight against fascism. Naturally, some critics take the view that anything advocated by the Communist Party must be opposed. That, however, was not the climate of the thirties – quite the contrary. When the question of the hour was the fight for collective security and for an agreement with the Soviet Union, when it was clear that Hitler's promise to move through Europe to attack 'Bolshevism' in the Soviet Union was regarded benevolently by the British ruling class, it is not surprising that far wider sections than the Communists concentrated upon a defence of the Soviet Union. The broad political composition of the membership of the Left Book Club reflected this most plainly.

(ix) The Influence of the Club

What, then, was the influence of the Club? Intelligent students of the period cannot, I think, fail to come to the conclusion that, far from being of a topical and ephemeral nature, the Club made a lasting impact upon the political life of Britain.

It brought into association with the labour movement new and hitherto unorganised sections of the population. It set a standard for the production of large editions of serious books and helped to create a demand which ultimately found expression in the great paperback sales of today. It sent into the armed forces thousands of men and women who had acquired a taste for the study and discussion of political affairs and wanted such facilities to continue within the forces. What is more, they obtained them. It thus beyond a shadow of doubt contributed to the victory of the Labour Party in 1945 and in the attitude to such questions as the independence of India and those social and constitutional issues that emerged so sharply in the immediate post-war years. Finally, it laid the basis for an understanding of the nature of fascism, of anti-semitism and of racism in a whole generation: lessons which will not decline in importance over the next decade in Britain.

The books themselves (with a few exceptions) were written with a desire to communicate with those whose actions to a large extent would determine the future. So successful was this that anyone active in the labour movement must have frequently had the experience of meeting people in positions of responsibility who are ready to say that their first introduction to socialist ideas was through the Left Book Club. It is indeed possible that there is a lesson for us today when there often seems a widening gap between writers on political theory and the activists in the labour movement, even though the latter are far better educated and informed than earlier generations. When we think, for example, of the impact of John Strachey's *Theory and Practice of Socialism* or Leo Huberman's *Man's Worldly Goods* we have to admit, even allowing for the more complex problems of today, that there is still an urgent need to provide comparable inspiration and information for those in the midst of struggle.

Left Book Club titles are eagerly sought today. Students and other young people scour second-hand bookstalls for them, collectors pounce on them, and dealers quote the current price for a nearly complete set at some £800. This is perhaps partly attributable to a fashionable preoccupation with the thirties; but it also occurs for precisely the reasons which gave the Left Book Club its unique quality: a timely response to a deep-seated desire for political education.

NOTES

1. Samuel Hynes, *The Auden Generation* (Bodley Head, 1976), p. 209.
2. Speech by Victor Gollancz at the first Albert Hall Left Book Club Rally (7 February 1937) (in *Left News*, March 1937).
3. Quoted in John Lewis, *The Left Book Club: An Historical Record* (Gollancz, 1970), p. 94.
4. ibid., p. 95.

5. In *More for Timothy* (Gollancz's second volume of autobiography) (Gollancz, 1953), p. 351.
6. See John Lewis, op. cit., pp. 139–56 for a complete list of books made available by the Club.

British Theatre in the Thirties:
An Autobiographical Record

ANDRÉ VAN GYSEGHEM

Editors' note: The following two articles on experiments in working-class and socialist theatre in Britain in the thirties were conceived as complementary. André van Gyseghem's article is largely autobiographical. Although he refers to his work with the Rebel Players and Unity Theatre, he concentrates mainly on his work in the progressive repertory theatre and Left Theatre and on the labour movement pageants. Jon Clark's article concentrates mainly on an examination of Unity Theatre (London), tracing its roots back to the Workers' Theatre Movement and examining its organizational, artistic and political development from 1936 to the outbreak of the War.

(i) *The state of British theatre in 1930*

It is important to relate our attitude in those days, our struggle to do something different, to the state of the British theatre as a whole. At the beginning of the thirties, it was predominantly a middle-class theatre. We were dominated by writers such as John van Druten, Noël Coward and Somerset Maugham, all of whom were writing fascinating plays, but for a very restricted audience. The working class seldom appeared, except as an excuse for comedy. There might be cockney comics, therefore, but the representation of the actual life of the working people was restricted to the early plays of Sean O'Casey and the work of Miss Horniman at the Gaiety Theatre, Manchester. She really encouraged the writing of plays dealing with a wider subject matter, with the aspirations of a whole different section of the community, and she was responsible for encouraging playwrights to write specifically on these subjects, like Stanley Houghton and Harold Brighouse. They were immensely important in their way, but they had little or no effect on the writers who were writing for the big, commercial theatre.

(ii) *The Embassy Theatre, Swiss Cottage*

This was the kind of theatre I was employed in when I came to the Embassy Theatre, Swiss Cottage, as artistic director at the beginning of the 1930s. We did a play for a fortnight, hoping that some West End management would buy it and put it on so that the Embassy would get some money from it! Fortunately, we had an extremely liberal-minded, unprejudiced manager in Ronald Adams, who had the nous to open new horizons a little and enabled me to look for plays of a slightly different nature. The first such play to impress me was Hans Chlumberg's *Miracle at Verdun*, which had been first performed in English by the New York Theatre Guild in 1931, and inspired Irwin Shaw to write *Bury the Dead*, which I later produced at Unity Theatre.

Miracle at Verdun concerned the dead of the First World War, who came back out of their graves and appealed to the League of Nations to prevent further war and suffering. It was a very complex play, and needed a form of presentation combining stylisation and realism. I found this intensely interesting. Apart from that play, the British theatre was hardly influenced at all by the Expressionist theatre of Germany, the plays of Kaiser and Toller, or the work of Erwin Piscator as director. What the Chlumberg production had taught me was that a play, which consists of both a form and a content, must have a unity, and that plays which were opening the gates to a wider theme demanded a different dramatic style than drawing-room comedy. You could not produce a play like the *Miracle at Verdun* in the style of a conventional proscenium, with full sets and every detail being exactly right. We had to stylise it to a certain degree, and without doubt this play, which was concerned with the aspirations of a whole generation of men, gave me a strong feeling for social theatre.

So I began to ask around. Was anyone else doing anything different at all? And then someone told me about the Workers' Theatre Movement, and I got myself invited down to a rehearsal in a tiny room in the East End of London, just off the Commercial Road. And there I saw a group, which eventually called itself the Rebel Players, rehearsing agitprop. I will say more of my work with the Rebel Players below.

By this time, the Embassy Theatre was gradually being influenced by my ideas. In 1933 I produced Eugene O'Neill's *All God's Chillun Got Wings* with Paul Robeson. Naturally, Robeson fascinated me by his talent, but he also showed that there was a whole section of life which was never shown in the theatre with any degree of seriousness. At that time the negro, like the working class, was always brought in for comic relief. O'Neill went much further than that, and Robeson put his own personal belief and strength behind his performances to make something very memorable.

After that, we were able to put on Claire and Paul Sifton's *1931* – which I adapted and renamed *Age of Plenty*. This was a play about the collapse of the US economy in 1931 and the tremendous social problems caused by mass unemployment. For us to get and show this play on the London stage was very remarkable at that time. It was entirely due to the bravery of Ronald Adams that we achieved it; and I, as the producer, was immediately labelled as a Communist, which of course I wasn't in those days.

We received a lot of publicity from the national press, mostly hostile and indignant, complaining about the left bursting into the theatre, disrupting it and using it as a weapon of propaganda. Thus the play had its effect, bringing the attention of a great many serious people to the problem of what was missing in the theatre. Here was something from the USA which was immediate, about the situation of ordinary people, speaking about their living conditions in very fine theatrical terms. In this play, which clearly needed a quite different theatrical form, the form and content were welded. This seemed to me to be the kind of theatre I was looking for, a play which expressed new ideas in a new form.

By 1934 I had been at the Embassy for a number of years, doing about a play a fortnight. I was exhausted and wanted to leave to do something different. So I left and, together with a young writer called Aubrey Menen, who was at London University and a great protégé of H. G. Wells, took an old house in the Finchley Road and started an experimental theatre. We pulled down the walls and built what we called a 'space stage' – a form of theatre which had not been seen in this country before. We had a stage which was apparently not fixed to the ground, with two platforms at different levels and a cantilever support underneath entirely in black so that the audience could not see what they were standing on. Our performances were based on events which had happened during the week or even during the day, so that the audience never knew what they were going to see that night unless they had read their daily paper! In addition, we had Margaret Barr and her dance group, who dramatized the events in dance and with their own music, mainly percussion. We were trying to perform immediately relevant material, welding together dance, drama and music, writing new plays for a new kind of stage.

We failed, of course. We got some splendid notices, but we made no money. We had very little seating accommodation, and it was really not a financially viable project. But it taught me a great deal about the theatre, and enabled me, for instance, to introduce dance as a dramatic form.

My last production at the Embassy Theatre came towards the end of 1935, when I got a cable from Ronald Adams (I was in Moscow at the time). The result of this was that I directed a production with Paul Robeson of *Stevedore*, by Paul Peters and George Sklar, a frankly revolutionary play with Robeson as the revolutionary hero, a Negro leader of a working-class group fighting against exploitation.

(iii) *Agitprop and the Rebel Players, 1933–6*

The background to the organization of the Workers' Theatre Movement (WTM) rested almost entirely on the success of the dramatization of Robert Tressell's novel, *The Ragged Trousered Philanthropists*. The play was still in the old form of writing, and by no means agitprop, but it was a step forward in the right direction, dealing with working-class problems and psychology. Through my visit to a rehearsal of the Rebel Players I had discovered agitprop, which was an absolute eye-opener to me. I had never seen anybody doing anything like it before. What impressed me most was that the whole group had an idea which they believed in with blazing sincerity. The plays were written to express this ideal and this sincerity, and the actors acted from their hearts and with their heads, but, unfortunately, without much technique.

It seemed to me that what was being done by the agitprop plays could be much more effective if it was more theatrically accomplished. By that I did not mean more sophisticated; but I felt more stress needed to be put on voice work, use of bodies, timing, well-spoken declamation, and a general feeling for the theatre. I put this to the Rebel Players, asked if I might work with them, and they agreed. We then found ourselves producing agitprop plays in the open air from the backs of lorries, taking them to the factory gates when there was a strike, or taking part in demonstrations. Here was a whole new audience, and a new kind of actor, expressing a new set of ideas in a new form. This made an enormous impression on me.

(iv) *Visits to Moscow and North America*

In 1933 around twenty members of the British Workers' Theatre Movement went to Moscow to take part in the International Workers' Theatre Olympiad, and I received a special invitation to attend and participate in the activities. Again, this was a fascinating experience, because we were able to compare the work the British groups were doing with groups from countries like Sweden, Norway, France and Belgium, all with similar ideas, and equal sincerity and conviction, but expressing them in different ways according to their training and background.

To a simple person from the professional theatre, this was a new language and a new world. Performances were mostly in the afternoons and evenings, and every morning there were endless conferences on the work that had been done the previous day. Thus I was learning, as well as sharing the excitement of the performances of the plays.

After my return to England and the failure of my experimental theatre with Aubrey Menen, I accepted an invitation from my new friends in Moscow to go and work and study in the Soviet Union. After some delay I arrived in Moscow, where I stayed for a year under the auspices of the International Union of Revolutionary Theatre. Erwin Piscator was at the head of it, and Friedrich Wolf and Gustav von Wangenheim, two of the leading producer/writer/actors in the socialist theatre of pre-1933 Germany, were on the staff. They were marvellous to me, gave me a salary as soon as I got there, and attached me as assistant director to Nikolai Oklopkhov at the Realistic Theatre. My book, *Theatre in Soviet Russia*, published in 1943, contains a detailed account of my experiences at this time, which had a very deep effect on me, both socially and theatrically.

After returning to England to produce *Stevedore* with Paul Robeson, I went back and finished my year in Russia, returned to London, and then went to the USA, where I was able to see a great deal of the work of the New York Group Theatre.

I also saw an entirely new form of professional theatre in the USA, the living newspaper, developed under the auspices of the Works' Progress Administration (WPA). The WPA was a social project of Roosevelt, aimed at preventing the arts from disappearing for lack of money and sustenance. For the first time in America you had state-subsidized and state-supported theatre. All the personnel, stars, walk-ons, painters, sweepers, designers, directors, musicians, were paid exactly the same wage, and you had a wonderful feeling of collective work, with very little differentiation of status. This again gave birth to a number of new playwrights. At that time, the American theatre was the chief source of English-language social theatre, which was virtually non-existent in Britain. There was a large group of writers in the USA, breaking down the barriers of the past and finding new things to write about. The most important plays were *Processional* (1924) by John Howard Lawson, *They Shall Not Die* (1934) by John Wexley, *Peace on*

Earth (1933) by Albert Maltz and George Sklar, *Stevedore* (1934) by Paul Peters and George Sklar, *Black Pit* (1935) by Albert Maltz, *Bury the Dead* (1936) by Irwin Shaw, *The Cradle Will Rock* (1937) by Marc Blitzstein, *Marching Song* (1937) by J. H. Lawson, and *Let Freedom Ring* (1935) by Albert Bein. Thus, if you wanted to perform a play with any kind of social conscience, you had to turn to America.

(v) *Left Theatre, 1934–7*

In 1934, with a group of people including Barbara Nixon, Lionel Brittain, Ina de la Hay and Miles Malleson, I started Left Theatre. I had become so interested in what was being done by the Rebel Players by totally untrained, non-professional actors, that I became convinced that there were people in the professional theatre who would also be glad to have something more important to say in their work than the plays which were being done at the time. And so we formed Left Theatre. It consisted entirely of professional actors, all of whom either gave their services free of charge or for a minimum remuneration, giving performances of plays with a social conscience and a wide appeal.

We opened with *Sailors of Cattaro* by Friedrich Wolf, a play about the mutiny in the German navy in 1918. Wolf was a very fine writer and a Communist, a doctor by profession who became well-known in Germany and on the continent for his play about abortion, *Cyankali*. We felt Wolf's strong, revolutionary play would give a good initial impression of the kind of things we wanted to say as a group. We then performed John Wexley's *They Shall Not Die*, a very fine Negro play of protest against the way Negroes were being treated at that time in the Deep South.

We followed that with a translation of Gorki's *Mother*, which Barbara Nixon produced, and then *Stay Down Miner*, by Montagu Slater. Slater was about the only British writer of stature who was consistently writing for the new realistic theatre of social conscience and working-class interests. He had originally written *Stay Down Miner* as a reportage novelette, describing the stay-down strikes of the Welsh miners in 1935. He then produced a version for theatre, which received its première in May 1936 by Left Theatre, with music by Benjamin Britten. Later that year, a second version for theatre, this time called *New Way Wins*, was performed by Left Theatre under the direction of Barbara Nixon, and taken out to the provinces.

These plays were usually just done for one, or perhaps two Sundays, and subsequently we would take them out to Shoreditch, Stepney,

Hackney, Woolwich, and elsewhere, for single performances. The aim was to take a new kind of play to a new kind of audience, very largely an audience which would perhaps go to the music-hall and certainly to the cinema, but not to the theatre. We felt our work could only be fully justified if we took it to the people it was being written for.

Another important step taken by Left Theatre was to try and get the support of the trade unions and the labour movement, so that whenever we went out into the provinces or to the suburbs, we could contact the local Co-op, Amalgamated Engineering Union (AEU), Left Book Club, Labour Party or Communist Party branch and get their members to buy seats for our performances. This attempt to establish close links with working-class organisations was something that was done very rarely in those days.

(vi) Unity Theatre, London, 1936–9

After the founding of Unity Theatre in 1936, largely on the initiative of the members of the Rebel Players group, we continued the agitprop side of our work, particularly in many of those plays with a small cast which could be played as a mobile theatre and taken to the audiences in the suburbs or in the provinces. I produced one of them, Newsboy, to begin with, and then helped later with similar productions. I also directed Ernst Toller's A Man and a Woman, a largely declamatory play, which called for agitprop treatment.

In 1937 I was elected President of Unity Theatre, and we turned, of course, to the American playwrights for much of our material. I particularly remember Irwin Shaw's Bury The Dead, a wonderful piece of drama, creating new forms of presentation with a very important and poignant message. Like Chlumberg's Miracle at Verdun, which inspired it, it depicted the 'return' of dead soldiers from the First World War. In fact, Shaw went much further than Chlumberg, showing the hostile reaction of the press and the Church to the event. He showed their emphasis on the 'personal angle' in going to the relatives of the dead men who were coming back to life, trying to get them to persuade the dead to go back to their graves and not to draw attention to the brutalities of war. There was a very emotional scene with a mother appealing to her son, who, when he turned towards her, revealed that half his head had been blown away. Then there was the working-class woman who almost bullied her husband to do something about the life they had been forced to live after the war. In the end, the soldiers rose and joined with the firing party, coming forward and facing the audience, as if marching into the future. A similar sort of event occurred in Chlumberg's play, but it finished on stage. However, in *Bury The Dead*, it was brought right into the audience. The soldiers rose, came forward, and nothing stopped them – they went right down the centre aisle of the theatre and out at the back.

I also directed James Hodson's *Harvest in the North*, not a great play, but a sincere effort to show the life of a Lancashire mill town. I was looking for a link between agitprop and the more philosophical kind of play. The actors at Unity became interested in the idea, and wrote reports on the background and personality of the characters they were playing. We attempted in this way to encourage the amateur actors to think creatively about their characters. We then decided to go one step further, and take the actors up to Rochdale for a weekend to see at first hand how the cotton workers lived. Most of our actors were themselves workers in London, but they had little or no knowledge of the atmosphere and way of life of the working class of Lancashire. It was one further attempt to unite the theatre and the people, which was one of the main aims of Unity Theatre.

(vii) *Pageants, 1937–9*

In 1937 I got another educational boost. I was invited to go to South Africa to produce a pageant. I'd never produced a pageant in my life before. I had always associated it with something like Lady Godiva riding about on a white horse. Anyway, because I had been in Russia, the organizers thought I must know about mass theatre. I did not disillusion them and accepted their offer. It was a pageant commemorating the fiftieth anniversary of the first gold field, so a lot of history had to be shown. It was purely and simply an historical pageant about the progress of South Africa from then until the thirties. I had a number of disagreements with the authorities about the use of black actors, but eventually we succeeded in ironing out our differences.

The experience in South Africa was a rewarding and instructive one for me, and was of immense value when I returned to England and produced, in 1938, a very different pageant – in Wembley Stadium – celebrating the founding of the Co-operative Movement. Alan Bush wrote the music, Montagu Slater the script, and I gathered together groups of co-operators from all over London to rehearse the various scenes. Margaret Barr directed the dancing, and we built an enormous stage in circular form in the centre of the stadium, with steps on all four sides and a centre rostrum. The pageant was written in a very declamatory kind of speech, which could be relayed through microphones. I had learnt from South Africa that it was vital to reduce the amount of speech to a minimum and concentrate on the visual impression.

We showed the whole growth of the Co-operative Movement, linked of course to the development of the working class as a whole. We started in feudal England, with the festivals around Jack o' the Green in the villages, traced the growth of the working class under capitalism, the machine wreckers, the gradual meeting of trade unionists and the founding of the Co-operative Society, coming up to the 1914–18 War and the subsequent desolation, with mourning women dancing on the central platform. Finally, we showed the emergence of the united working-class movement, demonstrating and celebrating around the striped flag of the Co-op Movement, and surrounded by massed dancers.

It was not a subtle performance, but simple, straightforward, and visually effective. Everything that was said was pertinent, but not said at too great length. This I found very impressive, a form of mass theatre which I and the actors could believe in. It is not an ideal form, because it does not go to any great depth; it shows only the broad outlines of human development. But living pictures do make an impression on the mind of an audience, and that was our aim. The theatre is a weapon, and we were using it in numerous forms. A film was made of the performance, mostly taken from the air so that you could look down and see the patterns made. I was pleased because the patterns made by the living people on this film reproduced exactly the coloured chalk marks I had made for the groups on the pre-rehearsal plans. And there you saw it live, worked out by thousands of living people!

The Co-op was enormously pleased with the 1938 pageant, so Alan Bush, Benn Levy and myself formed a deputation to try and persuade the London Co-op to set up a permanent co-operative workers' theatre. We showed that there were writers in America and Britain who could write plays for such a theatre, and we tried to get the Co-op to develop from the groundwork provided by the pageant, and from the broad interest in the theatre as an educational and inspirational force.

We did not succeed. The Co-op had the money, but was not interested in using it in that way. It had spent a lot on the Wembley pageant, of course; but it could have gone on to start a real professional socialist theatre then. I had made a whole list of actors ready to work with us for a moderate wage in a theatre which had social realism and played with a social conscience. But the Co-op refused; it did not feel it was its task.

I did two further pageants in 1939, both celebrating the hundredth anniversary of the Chartist Movement. One was for the London District of the Communist Party, *Pageant of Chartism*, and the other was a *Pageant of South Wales*, organized by the South Wales Miners' Federation in association with the Labour Research Department. The South Wales pageant was performed on the 1 May 1939, in three different places (Abertillery, Pontypool and Ystradgynlais) at the same time. Altogether 6,000 people took part, around 2,000 in each locality. They were all amateur actors from the local communities, and were joined by massed choirs – there were plenty of those in Wales.

The scenario was again written by Montagu Slater, and the music was arranged by Bamford Griffiths. Again it was a form of mass theatre I found tremendously satisfying, using the people themselves to play to the people, so linking theatre and audience in a very real way.

Pageants had a very general application, and worked in all kinds of contexts where mass movements, or specific groups, were celebrating their history, their victories and defeats. I used the pageant technique subsequently in a meeting commemorating the International Brigade in Spain, and on numerous other occasions. There were rarely professional actors in these performances, but of course we usually had fine singing and music. In the Welsh miners' pageant I was able to learn from my previous experience, simplifying, using visual strength and the shape of the groupings to strengthen the interior message.

The programme of the 1939 *Pageant of South Wales* contains the following words, which give a clear impression of the kind of atmosphere in which we were performing this kind of workers' theatre:

The British working class has a tradition it can be proud of, a tradition of fight after fight successfully fought and won for freedom. In attempting to revive the form of the pageant to express this tradition we are, I think, choosing the only form which can truthfully frame so large a canvas. It is a form which calls for the co-operation of all for the sake of all. It demands crowds and processions and fine, rousing music which stirs the memory and sets the heart pounding.

There is pain and dumb tragedy and burning indignation in the life of a working man – there is apathy and the struggle against apathy – there is religion and revolution. All of this we have tried to show with the means at our disposal – these means are the collective sacrifice and activity of 6,000 people from the hills and valleys of South Wales.

Agitprop and Unity Theatre: Socialist Theatre in the Thirties

JON CLARK

1. INTRODUCTION

British 'naturalistic' theatre in the first half of the twentieth century has often been criticized as sentimental, thematically dated and lacking in creativity. The plays of Galsworthy, Maugham, Priestley, Barrie and Coward are quoted in evidence to support such a dismissive evaluation: the works of Shaw (and in 'poetic drama' the works of Eliot and Yeats) are seen as the exception that proves the rule.

What is immediately striking about such assessments[1] is that they are based on highly restricted concepts of literature and theatre, and also a narrow, 'textual analysis' approach to literary and cultural criticism. However, the major mode of theatrical expression and communication, the main form of theatrical activity and creativity, is not the printed play-text, but the performance. In fact, every theatrical performance is a highly complex and uniquely creative process of interaction and tension between various component parts, including play-text, artists (actors, directors, producers, stage managers, and often musicians), 'technicians' (lighting, sound and make-up specialists) *and* audience. Each performance is also the result of a number of very important preliminary activities and decisions, including play-writing, adaptation and interpretation, rehearsals, administration, costume and set design, costume-making and set-building, ticket-selling and advertising and so on. It is only by ignoring most of these factors, and reducing the concept of theatre to the printed play, that it is possible for one commentator to conclude that, apart from the works of Shaw, there was 'nothing truly creative' and 'little of permanent interest'[2] in the 'naturalistic' and 'social' theatre in Britain in the first half of the twentieth century.

In fact, the British theatre between 1900 and 1939 was particularly rich in variety, experimentation and creativity, seeing as it did the growth of a national repertory theatre movement and numerous 'little theatres', an unprecedented expansion of amateur dramatic societies (1919–39) and, by the late thirties, the development of around 300 'Left' theatre groups performing plays and sketches to labour movement audiences all over Britain. Probably the best known of these socialist theatre groups was Unity Theatre (London).[3]

As Julian Symons has pointed out, the conception of theatre underlying all Unity's activities was essentially practical rather than aesthetic and formal and, despite his lack of sympathy with its 'political radicalism',[4] Symons pays tribute not only to its enthusiasm, but also to its originality.[5] The aim of this article is to reconstruct and explain the reasons for the founding and development of Unity Theatre, and to analyse the aesthetic and political significance of the different forms of theatrical production of this socialist theatre collective.[6]

2. WORKERS' THEATRE AND AGITPROP

In order to understand the reasons for the founding of Unity Theatre in 1936, it is necessary to examine the development of the Workers' Theatre Movement (WTM) in Britain, which was the immediate precursor of the experiments in 'Left' theatre between 1934 and 1939.

According to the pioneering study of L. A. Jones,[7] there were five distinct periods in the history of working-class and socialist theatre up until the outbreak of the Second World War. The first period pre-1926 saw the isolated beginnings of an independent socialist theatre of the British labour movement, often with close political and organizational links to the Independent Labour Party (ILP) and the Co-operative Movement.

The years 1926–9 are seen by Jones as the first major period of workers' theatre in Britain, with the founding of many small travelling theatre troupes committed to going out to the labour movement, performing wherever they could find an audience. This period also saw the founding of the Workers' Theatre Movement (WTM) and important attempts at stage drama, most notably the dramatization of Robert Tressell's *The Ragged Trousered Philanthropists* by Tom Thomas and the Hackney People's Players in 1927.[8]

Jones regards the period 1929–33 as the time when workers' theatre in Britain went radically wrong. The WTM was a product more of the Communist than the Labour Party wing of the British labour movement, and the move of the Labour Party and the official trade union movement to the right and of the Communist Party to the left in this period led to bitter divisions in the ranks of organized labour. Theatrically this led inside the WTM to a move away from stage drama to street drama and agitprop, a period of development which Jones characterises as an abandonment of the tradition of British and world drama, a one-sided emphasis on amateurism, collectivism and untheatrical sloganizing, and a concentration on didacticism and instruction to the detriment of entertainment. There was little or no contact with professional theatre workers.

Jones describes the years 1933–36 as a period of transition, both in the arena of politics and of theatre. In the political arena there was a growing emphasis on the *unity* of the labour movement in the fight against war and fascism, and in the theatrical field there was a growing co-operation between amateur workers' theatre groups and professional theatre artists such as André van Gyseghem. All these developments prepared the ground for the period 1936–9, which Jones identifies with the founding and activities of Unity Theatre and 'Left' theatre groups all over Britain and the generally successful blending of agitprop and stage drama – in short, the creation of a broadly based socialist theatre movement fighting against fascism and for left unity.

This periodization of the history of socialist theatre[9] in Britain shows how, between 1929 and 1933, the sectarian political strategy of the Communist wing of the labour movement exerted a major influence on the activities of the WTM, which were based largely on an exclusively agitational concept of theatre, what Raphael Samuel has called a 'cultural shock-brigade'[10] approach. There is no doubt that, as Jones argues, an exclusive concentration on the agitprop method loses much of what the theatre has to offer as a form of cultural expression, self-expression and communication. The danger in Jones's analysis, however, lies in his own understanding of the function of the drama, which contains certain underlying aesthetic presuppositions which come near to being as rigid and one-sided as he claims agitprop was. In counter-identification with the 'agitprop period' of the WTM, he goes to the other extreme and identifies drama with one particular form of theatre, namely the full-length play with finely drawn individual characters and complex plot. Agitprop is defined *ex negativo* as the opposite of this.[11]

In fact, one of the most significant features of the work of Unity Theatre between 1936 and 1939 was the tremendous diversity of dramatic forms and techniques which were used and developed, according to what the group wanted to achieve, the audience they were speaking to, the texts available, the time allotted to them for performance, etc. In certain cases, topicality was of vital importance: the living newspaper was the ideal form of theatre to achieve immediacy and intervene actively in ongoing campaigns and struggles. The revue and the sketch were additional 'small forms' which could be assembled, rehearsed and performed in a short space of time. In other cases, the aim was to show the broad contours of historical development: here the pageant, speech-choir or mass chant could be used, none of which shows clearly delineated characters or has a dramatic 'plot'. Such forms derived their validity and theatrical effectiveness from a simplified and stylized form of expression, making no attempt to tackle the subtleties and complexities of individual character development.

One of Unity's most successful and popular ventures, which achieved a mass audience reaching out beyond the labour movement, was the political pantomime. Here a popular, traditional form of music and theatre was employed, and refunctioned to become a highly topical and entertaining political satire. Probably the most widespread dramatic form used by 'Left' theatre groups in the late thirties was the one-act play, which cannot obviously achieve the psychological and political subtlety and depth of the full-length play, but is an ideal form for amateur dramatic groups.

How important, then, was 'agitprop' for the socialist theatre movement in Britain and the founding of Unity Theatre, and how can it be defined more adequately than in the work of L. A. Jones?

The term agitprop comes originally not from the theatre, but from labour movement politics and political organisation. Already in the early twenties the German Communist Party created an agitprop department: agitation referred to political activity in relation to day-to-day campaign demands, issues and struggles; propaganda referred to the broader and more long-term activity of winning people to the general aims of the labour movement, to education on the underlying reasons and purpose of the fight against capitalism and for socialism. The agitprop department was thus concerned with coordinating campaigns and distributing leaflets, with activities extending from local issues to national elections and referenda, from organizing public meetings to producing guides and handbooks on Marxist theory and the history of the labour movement.

Agitprop theatre in Germany in the twenties and early thirties has often been caricatured with some justification as primitive sloganising, the use of the 'hammer-method' approach to political theatre, which seemed more concerned to demonstrate the revolutionary credentials of the actors and the political organisation to which they belonged rather than to entertain and convince the audience. To paraphrase one of the leading participants in this movement, Maxim Vallentin, there was usually too much agit and not enough prop![12]

However, agitprop as a concept, method and practice can also be identified with such potentially positive attributes as theatrical mobility, with taking the theatre out to an 'untheatrical' audience, with adaptability, immediacy, topicality and popular forms of expression. There is no doubt that these elements in agitprop played no small part in the vitality, effectiveness and popularity of Unity Theatre, an assessment which finds powerful backing in a handbook on 'Left' theatre groups published in the late thirties. Referring to the Unity Theatre Club, London, the handbook stated:

... those actors who are still the backbone of the club spent five years rehearsing in attics and cellars, and giving performances at street corners, from the back of lorries, etc.; and it is my own belief that the quite remarkable strength and vigour of these actors is due entirely to this training. . . . What we strongly advise is that groups should concentrate for some months on short sketches, one act plays, burlesques, mass recitations, etc. . . In London there is a tremendous demand for short pieces to be included in political meetings, rallies, socials, dances, and so on. Groups affiliated to the old Workers' Theatre Movement used to do a considerable amount of work on these lines, and I repeat that I believe the present strength of the Unity Theatre Club to be entirely due to the tempering effect of five years of such performances.[13]

The guide did however also warn against an over-emphasis on the subject matter and political content and perspective of a text to the exclusion of theatrical considerations:

There are texts that live and texts that do not live when spoken aloud on the stage. Paragraphs from *Capital* . . . do not live on the stage merely by virtue of their excellent matter, and anything that does not live on the stage, however wise, witty, or wonderful it may be, will not only leave your audience unmoved: it may even antagonise them seriously. And you can only learn to tell the difference between dead and living texts by constantly hearing words read aloud, by reading them aloud yourself, and watching carefully what effect they make on anyone else who may be present listening'.[14]

Or, as Mordecai Gorelik wrote in a monumental survey of trends in world theatre in the twenties and thirties, 'theatre is not a weapon unless it is something better than a weapon'.[15]

3. THE FOUNDING OF UNITY THEATRE – ORGANIZATIONAL AND POLITICAL DEVELOPMENT, 1936–9

The gradual dissolution of the Workers' Theatre Movement in the mid-thirties and the founding of the Unity Theatre Club (London) at the beginning of 1936 signified both a break with, and a continuation of, the dramatic and political development of socialist theatre in Britain.

The elements of continuity were numerous. The core members of the new permanent amateur theatre group (at the outset there were sixty full and three hundred associate members of Unity Theatre Club) consisted of people who had already worked with the old WTM, particularly old members of the Rebel Players and individual professional theatre workers such as André van Gyseghem. In the first year of its activity Unity performed a number of plays which had previously been staged by Rebel Players, including Ramón Sender's *The Secret*, Ernst Toller's mass recitation *A Man and a Woman* and Clifford Odets's most popular play *Waiting For Lefty*,[16] which had received its first British performance on the 12 October 1935 and later became 'the play which made Unity's reputation'.[17]

Until mid-1937 the number of outside performances given by Unity far exceeded the number of performances given in its new premises at St Jude's Church Hall in Britannia Street, King's Cross, and it retained much of the mobility, flexibility, topicality and aggressiveness of agitprop. The overall political outlook and orientation of its work remained largely under the ideological influence of its Communist Party members – not, however, under the direct influence of the CP centrally, which made no major attempt to develop a detailed policy on art or the theatre.

Despite all these links with the tradition of the WTM, the founding of Unity Theatre signalled a number of breaks with this tradition. Historically, agitprop (in Germany from 1924 to 1932 or in Britain between 1927 and 1935 and 1968 and 1974, for example) has played a major role as a form of socialist theatre at times of heightened and overt industrial and political conflict, and has often represented an attempt consciously to break with the individual and pyschological orientation of traditional 'naturalist' or even 'social realist' theatre.[18] While the agitprop of the WTM had addressed almost exclusively an audience of the militant industrial working class and the unemployed, the 'Left' theatre groups of the middle and late thirties were operating at a time of declining unemployment and industrial militancy and yet increasing danger of fascism and war which demanded the creation of a broadly based movement.

The very name 'Unity' theatre announced the new political orientation towards the policy of a United or Popular Front against fascism and a break with the more sectarian goals of the WTM. Moves towards such a reorientation had been made by a number of WTM groups since 1933–4, and the desire of the Rebel Players and other groups to establish permanent amateur theatres with proper rehearsal facilities and technical equipment arose out of their recognition that winning a wider audience for the fight against fascism and for socialism demanded a more 'aesthetically convincing'[19] basis of theatrical performance. As Tom Thomas later wrote:

In 1934 there was a gradual change in the political direction of the WTM. It became clear that in Germany the political warfare waged between socialists and communists had been tantamount to political suicide, and that in the rest of Europe survival would depend on an alliance of everybody threatened by fascism. This wise attitude, when generally accepted, brought problems for the WTM. The whole of our work had been against the Labour Party and the ILP as well as against the National Government. . . . We had . . . treated Labour and Tory as the same. The new popular front line didn't lend itself as easily to popular theatre. In theatre terms, it's much more difficult to present an argument for a constructive line, like building a united front against fascism, than to write satires and attacks on the class enemy.[20]

The links between the socialist theatre movement and the broader cultural and political United and Popular Front movement in Britain were strengthened organizationally in April/May 1937 with the establishment of the Left Book Club Theatre Guild (LBCTG), a joint project of Unity Theatre (London) and Victor Gollancz's Left Book Club. The aim of the Guild, whose first national organiser was John Allen, was to encourage the formation of theatre groups similar to Unity throughout the country, advise on the organization and running of such theatres, issue recommendations and scripts of suitable plays, and so on.[21] The function of the theatre in mobilising support for the Popular Front was summed up by John Allen as follows:

The formation of the Left Book Club Theatre Guild has been made possible by the generosity and enterprise of Mr Gollancz. We follow, not out of lip-service, but because we believe in . . . the ideals, aims, and objects set out by Mr Gollancz in his editorials in the *Left News*. We believe that the fight against war and Fascism can best be conducted on the basis of a popular front, and we are convinced that the theatre gives as good, if not a better basis for such activity than the Left Book Club itself. This applies equally to actors and audience. An example of this is the Unity Theatre Club's production of *Waiting for Lefty*. The twenty or so actors who form the cast of this play number among them members of the Liberal, Labour, and Communist Parties, members of Co-operative Societies, trades unionists, and so on. The audiences who come to the Unity Theatre Club are even more varied, for they are not solely confined to members of the working class. A theatre such as this is continually presenting left-wing opinions and problems to people who would never dream of attending a political meeting; and if those ideas are presented in a way that is theatrically effective, they will have a considerable influence on those members of the audience.[22]

Apart from the founding of the LBCTG, the year 1937 also saw the reorganization of the Unity Theatre Club to become a registered co-operative society, the Unity Theatre Society Ltd,[23] and the securing of new premises, an old Methodist Church previously used as a doss-house, at 1 Goldington Street in the Somerstown district of North London. The hundred-seat auditorium at Britannia Street had proved to be far too small, and the new premises were soon converted into a theatre, largely due to the voluntary labour of club members and London trade unionists who gave up their spare time in the evenings and at weekends to build it. The cost of renovation, which had been assessed at between £3,000 and £4,000, was thereby reduced by over two-thirds.

The new theatre contained a large, well-equipped stage with an auditorium seating 323 people, rehearsal, dressing and club rooms, an office, a workshop, a bar and storage space. A review of the opening night on the 25 November 1937, which appeared in *New Theatre*, the journal of the LBCTG, conveys something of the atmosphere, the variety and the commitment of 'Left' culture in Britain in the thirties, as well as indicating one of its weaknesses:[24]

At eight o'clock the doors were opened, by eight-thirty the theatre was for the first time playing to a packed house. Here before an audience representing a cross-section of London's cultural and social forces, Unity, built by workers, was to give its first vital message through the medium of drama. . . .

The theatre programme opened with five songs by the London Labour Choral Union. These songs were put over with terrific vigour, and evoked an equally vigorous applause.

The Workers' Propaganda Dance Group then gave a performance of *A Comrade Has Died*. Here we saw the brutality and inhumanity of fascism and the inevitability of its overthrow in the workers' revolution. . . .

Paul Robeson was greeted with thunderous applause and . . . sang six songs of the Negro struggle. . . .

Alan Bush appealed for funds for the Unity Theatre Club, which were readily forthcoming – £78 being subscribed in ten minutes. . . . Next and last item was *Waiting for Lefty* with the original London cast.

Although already played by Unity Theatre over one hundred and fifty times, this performance was as vital as it had been on its first night.

Unity's opening night was in every way a triumph. The audience told us so, and what is far more important, the building itself showed that the workers for Unity had achieved all that they had striven for.[25]

In the summer of 1938 Robeson aroused a great deal of publicity in the national press by turning down more lucrative parts in the West End theatre in order to joint the cast of Unity in a number of performances, including a provincial tour, of an American play dealing with the fight for trade union recruitment, recognition and better working conditions. *Drama*, the official magazine of the British Drama League, sent a reporter down to Goldington Street, who reported rather incredulously:

Paul Robeson . . . has turned down several extremely tempting offers and is appearing . . . with a cast of amateurs at the Unity Theatre in St Pancras, for which he is receiving no salary whatever.

The play is *Plant in the Sun*, written by a young American playwright, Ben Bengal. There is not a star part in the play. Robeson is simply one of the cast – no more and no less. And he is very happy about it.

In spite of several difficulties, such for example as the fact that rehearsals can take place only in the evenings and on weekends since the members of the cast are at other times occupied in their several workaday tasks – carpentry, book-keeping, stenography, and so on – Robeson has thrown himself heart and soul into rehearsal, and it is certain that a salary of a thousand pounds a week could not have drawn from him greater effort or deeper conscientiousness.[26]

In the autumn of 1938 Unity staged the British première of Brecht's powerful anti-fascist play on the Spanish Civil War, *Señora Carrar's Rifles*: this was the first ever performance of a full-length Brecht play in Britain.[27]

Despite internal tensions in Unity from mid-1938, linked to the growing controversy inside the Labour Party over the Popular Front policy, and Victor Gollancz's dissatisfaction over the degree and form of CP influence in the LBCTG,[28] as well as to personal and political disagreements amongst members of the theatre itself, London's foremost socialist theatre continued to flourish and diversify its activities. In addition to the highly popular Summer schools and provincial tours, night classes were arranged under the auspices of the London County Council on acting, production, playwrighting and stage management, etc., moves were being made to enlist the co-operation of ballet and opera groups to create a broad front of all the performing arts, and plans were well advanced to establish a full-time, professional repertory Unity in the Kingsway Theatre, London.

In 1939 Unity won the Howard de Walden Cup in the annual national amateur drama competition of the British Drama League with *Plant in the Sun*, this time without Paul Robeson. By September 1938, over 250 Left theatre groups were affiliated to the LBCTG and by May 1939 Unity Theatre (London) had 7,000 individual members and over 250,000 affiliate members belonging to various labour movement organizations. Both from the subject matter and the quality of John Allen's production, the world première of Sean O'Casey's anti-fascist, pro-Communist play *The Star Turns Red* in March 1940 marked both a high point and an end of the first major period in the history of Unity.[29]

In the meantime, the impetus behind the anti-fascist Popular and United Front movement had received a number of setbacks. It had failed both to gain the official support of the Labour Party and the TUC and to prevent the defeat of Republican forces in Spain, and it had been disoriented over the controversy surrounding the political and military implications of the German/Soviet Non-Aggression Pact of August 1939. With the outbreak of the Second World War in September 1939 and the belated commitment of the National Government to fight German fascism, a fundamental change took place in political alignments in Britain which demanded a new response from the left.[30]

4. INTERNATIONAL INFLUENCES ON UNITY THEATRE

Between 1936 and 1939, in a period when the established and commercial theatre had shown little ability or desire to experiment artistically or intervene creatively in the social, political and economic crisis facing the British people, it was Unity Theatre which, in the words of Sybil Thorndike, was 'the most exciting movement in the theatre of our day'.[31] It was not only in Britain that socialist theatre proved to be the most vital and responsive movement in the face of the deep social crisis in the latter part of the inter-war years. During the late twenties and early thirties, it was the work of Erwin Piscator, Bertolt Brecht, Gustav von Wangenheim and Friedrich Wolf which was widely recognised, among others by the two leading Berlin theatre critics, Alfred Kerr and Herbert Ihering, as the most significant contemporary contribution to German theatre. The drama critic of the *New York Times*, Brooks Atkinson, complained in 1935 that Broadway had no comment to make in the midst of vast social upheaval, whereas the revolutionary theatre was becoming more dynamic and central to theatrical life as a whole.

American, German and Soviet theatre all exerted an influence on Unity's development, albeit in very different ways. The influence of Soviet theatre was felt mainly through the application by André van Gyseghem and Herbert Marshall of production techniques they had experienced during their work in Moscow. Herbert Marshall, who had studied with the film-maker Sergei Eisenstein and the theatre directors Meyerhold and Oklopkhov, was particularly instrumental in the introduction of 'method acting' techniques associated with the name of Constantin Stanislavsky.[32] He also directed a performance of Nikolai Pogodin's epic play *Aristocrats*, in December 1937 to celebrate the twentieth anniversary of the October Revolution, the most ambitious play yet attempted by Unity with more than twenty scenes and fifty characters and including the use of massive projections (a skyscraper and water for a canal project) super-imposed on the basic industrial set dominated by two large factory gates.

The most significant contribution of the American theatre to Unity undoubtedly came through one-act plays, which provided the main basis of the repertoire of most socialist theatre groups in Britain in the late thirties. The German influence, apart from productions of the plays and speech-choirs of Ernst Toller, seems to have been largely exerted indirectly via the USA, where such forms of agitprop theatre as the mass chant, speech-choir, living newspaper and revue had already been successfully developed in the late twenties and early thirties.[33] However, it should not be forgotten that many of these forms had been 'organic-ally' and 'spontaneously' developed by the old WTM, so that it would be wrong to attribute the creative diversity of Unity's theatrical productions solely to techniques, forms and plays 'borrowed' from abroad.[34]

5. THE UNITY REPERTOIRE, 1936–9

It is not possible in the framework of this short article to give an adequate account of the variety and diversity of Unity's repertoire between 1936 and 1939.[35] Mention has already been made of a number of productions, but without doubt the form which predominated was the one-act play, the ideal genre for 'lay' theatre groups with limited technical facilities, modest theatrical training and short rehearsal periods.[36]

The most celebrated one-acter was incontestably Clifford Odets's fifty-minute play about a New York taxi drivers' strike, *Waiting for Lefty*, which was performed over 300 times by Unity Theatre Club between 1936 and 1939 and received countless additional performances by 'Left' theatre groups in Britain and all over the world.[37] Its author was both a playwright and actor in the American Group Theatre company, and a director in the Theatre Union studio. This was typical of the international 'Left' theatre in the twenties and thirties in which professional artists were rarely just actors or writers or directors, but artistic 'organisers' who united many different functions and activities in one person. Examples abound not only in America, but in Britain (Miles Malleson, André van Gyseghem, Herbert Marshall, John Allen, and Barbara Nixon) and Germany (Maxim Vallentin, Gustav von Wangenheim, Friedrich Wolf).

Waiting for Lefty turns the theatre into a trade union meeting, with the audience as the rank-and-file members and the actors on the stage as the 'officials' conducting the meeting (Harry Fatt, the union boss with his gunman in support, and the six members of the local union committee). The play opens with Fatt addressing the audience, using every possible means to try and dissuade them from deciding to go on strike. He is heckled at various points by members of the audience, and one worker in particular shouts out 'Where's Lefty?', a cry taken up all round. Lefty Costello proves to be the chairman of the local branch committee, an avowed opponent of Fatt and the union 'bosses'. Clearly, the other members of the branch committee are lacking in confidence and direction, putting their trust and hope in Lefty and expecting that he will take the decision for them. All the main characters in the play, its action and its plot, are dominated by the figure of Lefty, who in fact never appears – a dramatic device used many years later with very different effect and purpose by Samuel Beckett in *Waiting for Godot*.

The major part of the play is composed of a series of flash-back episodes, showing how this particular point in time is crucial in the life of each of the very different members of the union committee. The main characters are Joe, whose wife Edna threatens to leave him for another man if he does not stand up for himself against the bosses and go on strike; Miller, who was sacked from his previous job as a laboratory assistant because he refused to spy on a research chemist involved in the manufacture of poison gas; Sid, who cannot marry the girl he loves because he hasn't got enough money; Philips, an out-of-work actor whose wife is expecting a baby; and Dr Benjamin, who lost his previous job because he is a Jew and a radical. All these people are at a point in their lives where their individual and collective identity, their domestic and job personality, are inextricably linked. Fatt continues to threaten and cajole the meeting, he even uses a company spy to try and manipulate the audience.

Finally, Agate Keller, an ex-factory worker with experience of trade unionism, gets up and addresses the meeting. At first he is bitter and cynical in his attitude towards trade unions, and he is only saved from being man-handled off stage by Fatt and the gunmen after some of the men from the branch committee come to his aid. Agate then immediately turns to the audience, dropping his previously flippant style and making a serious appeal to them to unite and fight. Throughout his long speech Agate is backed up by the other six committee members, so that it becomes clear that the whole group supports his words. In conclusion, he throws out a challenge to the audience:

AGATE: What are we waiting for. . . . Don't wait for Lefty! He might never come. Every minute –
(*This is broken into by a man who has dashed up the centre aisle from the back of the house. He runs up on stage, says*)
MAN: Boys, they just found Lefty!
OTHERS: What? What? What?
SOME: Shhh . . . Shhh . . .
MAN: They found Lefty . . .
AGATE: Where?
MAN: Behind the car barns with a bullet in his head.
AGATE (*crying*): Hear it, boys, hear it? Hell, listen to me! Coast to coast! HELLO AMERICA! HELLO. WE'RE STORMBIRDS OF THE WORKING-CLASS. WORKERS OF THE WORLD. . . . OUR BONES AND BLOOD! And when we die they'll know what we did to make a new world! Christ, cut us up to little pieces. We'll die

for what is right! put fruit trees where our ashes are! (*To audience*): Well,
. what's the answer?
ALL: STRIKE!
AGATE: LOUDER!
ALL: STRIKE!
AGATE(*and others on stage*): AGAIN!
ALL: STRIKE! STRIKE! STRIKE![38]

Although the realism of Odets's play is occasionally undermined by a
forced and romanticised form of expression, for instance in Agate's
description of the striking taxi drivers as 'stormbirds of the working
class', the effect of the play on the predominantly working-class
audiences at Unity Theatre was tremendous. The first production in
Britannia Street was staged 'naturalistically', with just a bare table and
chairs for the committee members. Strike leaflets were handed out to the
audience at the entrance to the theatre; as they entered the auditorium
there was continual activity as if in preparation for a large meeting. A
convincing impression was created that the audience was in fact
participating in a real strike meeting. The immediacy and emotional
power of the play, particularly at the end when Agate calls on the
audience to join in the call for a strike, was particularly well captured by
Herbert Kline, who attended one of the first American performances:

The quality that makes *Waiting for Lefty* so remarkable is this new
playwright's ability to achieve and maintain what might be described as
absolute audience identification. By combining the best quality of 'agitprop',
direct appeal to the audience – with realism, Odets succeeds in involving us
completely in the lives and struggles of his taxi-driver characters. By effective
use of a technical device – 'the flashback' – we are given, simultaneously, an
insight into the background of the individual strikers and the story of the strike-
meeting in progress.[39]

After attending a performance of *Lefty* at Unity Theatre, a London
taxi driver, Herbert Hodge, was inspired to write his first play, *Where's
That Bomb?*, which dealt with the difficulties facing an aspiring worker
poet and which was given its première at Unity in November 1936
under John Allen's direction.[40] Hodge followed this short two-act play
in 1937 with a less successful full-length 'theatrical cartoon' called
Cannibal Carnival, and subsequently joined John Allen, Montagu
Slater and a number of other Unity members in an ambitious collective
theatrical and political experiment, the living newspaper *Busmen*.
The production was concerned with the background, events and

lessons of the London busmen's strike of May 1937, one of the major
labour disputes in a decade not generally noted for its industrial
militancy. The basic 'text' of the living newspaper was written by a
collective under the chairmanship of John Allen, and then subsequently
modified during rehearsals. It included monologues and dialogues,
quotations from various meetings (House of Commons' debates, the
union/management negotiating committee, the Court of Inquiry as well
as the executive council of the Transport and General Workers' Union),
doggerel verses, various off-stage effects, projections and music as well
as a poetic ballet of the industrial speed-up. The twenty-four scenes
were linked by loudspeaker announcements from a chorus, the so-
called 'voice of the living newspaper'. *Busmen* ran for a two month
period in the spring of 1938, and was followed in the autumn of the
same year by a living newspaper on Czechoslovakia called *Crisis*,
which was conceived, written, rehearsed and premièred inside forty-
eight hours!

Probably the most immediately accessible of Unity's productions
pre-1939 was the 'pantomime with a political point', *Babes in the
Wood*, written by Geoffrey Parsons and Robert Mitchell, with music by
Berkeley Fase. It ran from the middle of November 1938 until the end
of May 1939, six performances a week played with two alternating
casts of 36 actors, in all 162 performances attended by over 40,000
people.[41] *Babes in the Wood* was a remarkable blend of political satire
and popular theatrical conventions and traditions (pantomime and
music hall), substituting contemporary political figures and groupings
for the well-known legendary characters (Austria and Czechoslovakia
were the babes, Hitler and Mussolini the robbers, and Neville
Chamberlain the wicked uncle), parodying familiar hymns (the
Clivedon Set sang: 'We own the press and scatter/Confusion in the
land./Reaction's fed and watered/By our exclusive band', and so on)
and even creating new songs like 'Love on the dole' which achieved
widespread popularity in their own right.

There could hardly be a greater contrast than that between the music
of the leading composer of the labour movement in Weimar Germany,
Hanns Eisler, and the music of the songs in Unity's political
pantomimes. While Eisler's music was a mixture of ostinato rhythms,
intense intellectual seriousness and bitter satire, strongly influenced by
the syncopations of jazz and the spartan unsentimentality of the
Viennese school of Arnold Schoenberg, the music for *Babes in the
Wood* was unashamedly derivative of Cole Porter and the big dance

bands. It was this 'popular' element in the music, together with the rough comedy, knock-about, sentimentality and humour of the political satire, which largely accounted for the tremendous success of Unity's pantomimes in the thirties and also in later years.

6. CONCLUSION

It would be easy to see the activities of Unity Theatre and the hundreds of other 'Left' theatre groups of the late thirties purely and simply as a reflection of the specific contemporary crisis in the (commercial) theatre and in economic, political and social life in Britain and internationally. In the meantime, it is not only social and political conditions that have changed. The advent of television has substantially altered the leisure habits of the broad mass of the population, theatre censorship by the Lord Chamberlain has been abolished, state and regional community arts' subsidy has been introduced. While socialist theatre in Britain in the thirties was largely an amateur movement, it is now almost exclusively professional.

And yet, if there is one aspect of the socialist theatre movement in Britain in the thirties which seems to be of particular relevance for the late seventies, it is the active participation of working people and important sections of the labour movement in running their own theatres (and other cultural activities), supported and advised by professional artists. For what was practically demonstrated by Unity and other 'Left' theatre groups was that theatre is not just a means of entertainment and professional artistic expression, but also a means of individual and collective self-expression, self-constitution and self-realisation. It is this factor which lies at the heart of the following passage from the handbook for 'Left' theatre groups published by the Left Book Club Theatre Guild in the late thirties:

Acting, dancing, mimicry, and singing are primitive instincts. They are the simplest means man ever invented for the purpose of expressing himself. And yet Capitalism has appropriated 'culture' to such an extent, that the right, or even the possibility of self-expression has become the exclusive property of the middle and upper classes. The fact of a man being obliged to work for eight or more hours a day at some back-breaking job at a factory bench is an argument that he has more rather than less need to express himself in what spare time he has, than the listless intellectual who can live all day with Beethoven quartets and Auden's poems. Malraux makes this very point in his preface to *Days of*

Contempt – that one of the highest functions of art is to help man in the increasingly difficult task of being man.

This the theatre can do predominantly well. In mass recitations a man can learn the simplest elements of theatrical technique. He can experience, even more vividly than if (he) were playing some considerably larger role, the exalting sensation of addressing an audience with words in which he passionately believes, and that of communion with other people on the stage; and for the more experienced actor, singer, dancer, or acrobat, there are opportunities always commensurate with the degree of his talent.

Nor is this the end. There is a place in the theatre for electricians, carpenters, painters, sempstresses, tailors, and designers to apply their talent to the work they have been taught to do, but which they can now practice with freedom and imagination for a cause in which they can believe. . . . Even those without specific gifts can find a good deal of interest and amusement in serving coffee in the bar, selling programmes in the auditorium, and officiating in the box office and cloak room. . . . All this activity, therefore, is a practical means of furthering the cause; and the tremendous amount of cooperation that is needed among the different people concerned in putting on a play is in itself a splendid lesson in practical socialism. . .

Few forms of activity can surpass the theatre for combining learning with entertainment and instruction with fun.[42]

NOTES

1. For a classic example of such a dismissive evaluation, see the article by T. R. Barnes, 'Shaw and the London Theatre' in *The Pelican Guide to English Literature*, vol. 7, *The Modern Age* (Penguin Books, 1973), pp. 224–35.
2. ibid., p. 231.
3. Unity Theatre (London) was not the only 'Left' theatre group to call itself by that name. By 1939 there were Unity Theatres in a number of towns and cities in England, and the London Unity was rivalled in its experimentation and the breadth of its activity by groups such as the Manchester Theatre of Action (with Joan Littlewood and Ewan MacColl) and the Merseyside Left Theatre Club. Henceforth, when we refer to Unity Theatre or Unity in the text, we mean Unity Theatre (London).
4. Julian Symons, *The Thirties – A Dream Revolved* (Faber & Faber, 1975), p. 82.
5. Symons actually goes as far to say that the Group Theatre of Doone and Auden and Unity Theatre 'embodied the only new ideas of dramatic production in Britain' (ibid., p. 81) in the thirties. He thereby ignores the work of other 'Left' theatre groups, of the repertory and 'little theatre' movements and of experiments like the professional theatre group, Left Theatre. See André van Gyseghem, 'An Autobiographical Record', pp. 214–15.
6. The main sources for this article have been: L. A. Jones, *The British Workers' Theatre 1917–1935*, unpublished dissertation (Halle, 1964); Ron Travis, *The*

Unity Theatre of Great Britain 1936–46. A Decade of Production, unpublished M. A. thesis (Southern Illinois University, 1968); Reiner Lehberger, *Das sozialistische Theater in England 1934 bis zum Ausbruch des Zweiten Weltkriegs* (Peter Lang, Frankfurt-am-Main, 1977). The two main archives of original material on Unity Theatre, on which the above studies were based, are to be found in London (private archive of Bram Bootman, secretary of the Rebel Players and a founder member of Unity Theatre) and in the USA ('Unity Papers' in the Morris Library of the Southern Illinois University, based on the private collection of Herbert Marshall). Marshall and Bootman have also had articles printed in the *Listener* (22 and 29 March, 5 April and 12 September 1973) on Unity Theatre. The Marx Memorial Library (London) has recently acquired the remaining papers of Unity Theatre, and has complete numbers of *Left Review* and *International Literature* as well as some plays, programmes, etc. Finally I would like to thank the three leading professional theatre artists associated with Unity in the 1936–9 period, John Allen, André van Gyseghem and Herbert Marshall, who have all read the first draft of this article and made many useful criticisms and suggestions. Reference should also be made to *History Workshop*, a journal of socialist historians, which has recently published a study of the *Workers' Theatre Movement* by one of its leading figures, Tom Thomas (Issue 4, Autumn 1977), and prefaced by a historical introduction from Raphael Samuel. The editors of this journal promise further articles on the issue in the future.

7. A condensed version of Jones's thesis, which is more accessible to the English reader and to which we shall refer in this article, appeared under the title of 'The Workers' Theatre in the Thirties' in *Marxism Today*, vol. 18, no. 9, September 1974, pp. 271–80. Cf. also on the history of the WTM, Raphael Samuel, 'Editorial Introduction' in *History Workshop*, Issue 4, Autumn 1977, pp. 103–12.

8. See Tom Thomas, 'A Propertyless Theatre for the Propertyless Class' in *History Workshop*, Issue 4, Autumn 1977, pp. 113–42.

9. The term 'socialist theatre' or even 'Left theatre' seems in general preferable to 'workers' theatre' in that it emphasizes the political aims rather than the social origins of the participants. One of the main reasons for the success of Unity Theatre was the cooperation between workers and professional theatre artists in the aim of creating a politically committed theatre. However, the term workers' theatre does emphasize the fact that the participants are amateurs and not full-time theatre workers, something which is not clear from the concept of socialist theatre.

10. Samuel, op. cit., p. 106. Samuel also describes the WTM as 'uninhibitedly – even exuberantly – sectarian' (ibid., p. 107).

11. Cf. L. A. Jones, op. cit., particularly p. 273, p. 278.

12. Cf. M. Vallentin, 'Prop' (1928), printed in L. Hoffmann and D. Hoffmann-Ostwald, *Deutsches Arbeitertheater 1918–1933* (Henschelverlag, Berlin, 1972), vol. 1, p. 311.

13. *Some Notes on the Formation of Left-Wing Amateur Theatre Groups* (LBCTG, 1937/8), p. 4, p. 5. This guide was written by John Allen.

14. ibid, p. 18, p. 19. .

15. Mordecai Gorelik, *New Theatres For Old* (Dennis Dobson, 1940), p. 409. The slogan 'Art is a weapon' was first popularized by the German Communist doctor and playwright, Friedrich Wolf, whose article 'Kunst ist Waffe' was published in 1928 by the German Workers' Theatre League.

16. *Waiting for Lefty* was published in a Left Book Club Edition in 1937. It will be analysed in more detail below.

17. Samuel, op. cit., p. 109.

18. For an assessment of agitprop in Britain post-1968 see David Edgar, 'Political Theatre', Part 1, in *Socialist Review*, no. 1, April 1978, pp. 16–19.

19. John Allen, 'The Socialist Theatre' in *Left Review*, vol. 3, no. 7, August 1937, p. 420.

20. Tom Thomas, op. cit., pp. 124–5.

21. For a more detailed study of the LBCTG see Lehberger, op. cit., pp. 194–237. Also John Lewis, *The Left Book Club. An Historical Record* (Gollancz, 1970), pp. 44–48, pp. 76–86, p. 124. The Left Book Club also organized a Professional Actors' Group numbering over 300 members and including Lewis Casson, Michael Redgrave, Sybil Thorndike and André van Gyseghem. In 1937 the TUC engaged a professional theatre group including Casson and Thorndike to tour with Miles Malleson and H. Brooks's play about the Tolpuddle Martyrs, *Six Men of Dorset*. The text was published by Victor Gollancz.

22. *Some Notes . . .*, op. cit., pp. 1–2 (cf. note 13).

23. Unity took the form of a 'club' or 'society' in order to avoid censorship. All commercial theatres selling tickets to the public on the open market had to submit their plays to the Lord Chamberlain at least seven days in advance of the first performance. The system of club membership also furthered the aim of building up a stable, permanent audience, and enabled members to participate in the annual election of a Management Committee which was responsible for the overall administration of the theatre.

 An indication of the broad political support enjoyed by Unity can be gauged by the composition of its advisory 'General Council', which included Stafford Cripps, George Strauss, Harold Laski, Victor Gollancz, D. N. Pritt, Sean O'Casey, Alan Bush, Michel Saint Denis, Miles Malleson, Tyrone Guthrie and Paul Robeson.

24. The mention in the review of the 'inevitability' of the overthrow of fascism by 'the workers' revolution' shows how a certain conception of political change which was widely held by the 'Left' in the late thirties found its expression in the 'Left' culture of the period. In his article in this book, James Klugmann refers to a number of 'weaknesses' of the Communist left in the thirties, including what he terms 'inevitabilism', 'voluntarism', 'over-simplification' and an idealization of the Soviet Union. All these could be found to a greater or lesser degree in the work of Unity.

25. Quoted from Travis, op. cit.

26. Haemi Scheien, 'Paul Robeson Becomes an Amateur', quoted from Travis, ibid. In order to emphasize the collective nature of their productions, Unity members decided not to print the names of the actors in their programmes. No exception was made to this rule before the Second World War, not even for Paul Robeson! A photograph of a scene from Unity's production of *Plant in the Sun*, including Paul Robeson and a young Alfie Bass, is printed in Symons, op. cit.

27. See Nicholas Jacobs and Prudence Ohlsen, *Bertolt Brecht in Britain* (London, 1977), p. 29 for more details of this production.

28. On the relations between the Labour Party and the CP in this period see Ralph Miliband, *Parliamentary Socialism* (Merlin Press, 1972), pp. 231–67, and Kingsley Martin, *Harold Laski* (Jonathan Cape, 1969), pp. 95–119. Cf. also Hugh Thomas, *John Strachey* (Eyre Methuen, 1973), pp. 109–97. While Thomas

provides some useful and detailed information on relations between Strachey, Gollancz, the Left Book Club and the Communist Party, his rather confused statements on Unity and the LBCTG (p. 173) in no way clarify the complex tensions between the political and theatrical development of the theatre in the years preceding the Second World War. This is an area on which more research is needed.

29. Cf. Lehberger, op. cit., pp. 171–88.
30. Cf. Miliband, op. cit., pp. 268–85.
31. Quoted from Lehberger, op. cit., p. 100. The quotation comes from Sybil Thorndike's introduction to the *Unity Theatre Handbook*, produced just before the outbreak of war.
32. For a detailed analysis of Russian theatre (1900–39) see Gorelik, op. cit., in particular pp. 313–77, André van Gyseghem, *Theatre in Soviet Russia* (London, 1943). Also the comments by Herbert Marshall and Bram Bootman in the *Listener*, op. cit.
33. Cf. Gorelik, op. cit., in particular pp. 378–450, Lehberger, op. cit., pp. 108–9, 147–9. Also Eberhard Brüning, 'Probleme der Wechselbeziehungen zwischen der amerikanischen und der deutschen sozialistischen und proletarisch-revolutionären Literatur' in *Literatur der Arbeiterklasse* (Aufbau-Verlag, Berlin and Weimar, 1971), pp. 420–41, in particular pp. 428–39.
34. Cf. Samuel, op. cit., Tom Thomas, op. cit., Jones (1974), op. cit., Lehberger, op. cit., pp. 108ff.
35. Cf. the detailed account of the Unity repertoire in Lehberger, op. cit., pp. 108–88.
36. J. W. Marriott, whose selections and editions of one-act plays appeared regularly from 1924 onwards, rightly linked the growing popularity of the one-act play to the revival of non-professional drama in the period after the First World War. 'The popularity of one-act plays to-day is due to three causes: the growing recognition of the importance of drama in schools and colleges, the annual tournaments arranged by the British Drama League and other organizations, and the amateur movement generally' (J. W. Marriott, Foreword to *The Best One-Act Plays of 1937* (Harrap, 1938), p. 5).
37. For an examination of *Lefty* see Jones (1964), op. cit., pp. 171–3, Jones (1974), op. cit., pp. 279–80, Lehberger, op. cit., pp. 118–20, and Symons, op. cit., pp. 83–4. A number of quotations from reviews of the first US performances are to be found in *International Literature* (organ of the IURW), in particular 1935, no. 3, p. 119, no. 4, p. 102. Barbara Nixon reviewed both a publication of three plays of Odets and a Unity performance of *Lefty* in *Left Review*, vol. 2, no. 8, May 1936.

To give an indication of the variety of performances of *Lefty* in the mid-thirties one only needs to quote two examples: first, the performance by a group of anti-fascist German professional actors in Prague in the spring of 1936; second, the performance by an English-speaking touring group of the Moscow Foreign Workers' Club under the direction of Herbert Marshall in front of American lumberjacks working in the Soviet-Finnish Republic of Karelia!
38. Clifford Odets, *Waiting For Lefty* (Left Book Club Edition, 1937), pp. 45–6.
39. Quoted from *International Literature*, no. 4, 1935, p. 102.
40. The play was mainly written by Herbert Hodge, who came to watch a Unity production of *Lefty* to review it for his union journal. At a later stage Hodge had some assistance from a colleague, Bob Buckland, and a number of meetings with

John Allen to discuss the text. It was published by Lawrence & Wishart in 1937 under the pseudonyms of Roger Gullen and Buckley Roberts (this information stems from John Allen).

41. Cf. Lehberger. op. cit., pp. 146–7. Branson and Heinemann capture well the kind of humour and satire of Unity's *Babes in the Wood* in the following passage: '. . . the wicked uncle resembled Neville Chamberlain, and Robin Hood saved the babes to the melody of "Affiliate with me" . . . The Cliveden Set sang their support for the Munich agreement in four-part harmony to the tune of "Land of Hope and Glory", and the Fairy Wish Fulfilment waved her tinsel wand, hoping with the sob-sisters of the press that all might turn out for the best' (Noreen Branson and Margot Heinemann, *Britain in the Nineteen Thirties* (Panther, 1973), p. 300).

42. *Some Notes* . . ., op. cit., pp. 2–3.

Cinema in the Thirties: Documentary Film and the Labour Movement

RALPH BOND

1. FACTS AND FIGURES

Despite unemployment ranging from between two and three million, and widespread poverty, the thirties could be described as golden years for the movies. Never had the cinemas been so prosperous, never had the queues for admission been so long and so persistent. This apparent paradox was really not so mysterious. For the great mass of the people housing conditions were abominable, and to get out of their homes to the warmth of a cinema and for a few coppers enjoy three hours of entertainment was luxury indeed. There was no other form of entertainment so cheap and so easily accessible.

I was 'signing on' at Camden Town Labour Exchange for some of these years, and if we had threepence in our pockets we went to the local cinema for the whole afternoon with often a cup of tea thrown in. Of course, for the unemployed this was highly improper. We were supposed to be 'genuinely seeking work' or be struck off benefit; but as there was no work to seek, and as officialdom could not follow everyone all the time, we thumbed our noses and only argued as to which cinema in the area would receive our valuable patronage.

In 1934 there were nine hundred and fifty-seven million admissions to British cinemas, an average of some eighteen million weekly. This represented an average of nearly twenty-two visits every year for each man, woman and child in the country. For those aged fifteen and upward the average worked out at nearly thirty visits every year. And to emphasize how cheap cinema-going was in those days, 42 per cent of the entire cinema admissions were for seats costing no more than seven old pence, including entertainment tax.

There were then some 4,300 cinemas in Great Britain, one for every ten thousand of the population and one cinema seat for every twelve persons.

Remarkable facts dealing with the visits of London schoolchildren to cinemas, their preferences and the moral and physical affects on them, were provided in a report issued by the London County Council in 1932. Out of every hundred children, nine went to the cinema twice a week, thirty went once a week, forty-eight at irregular intervals and only thirteen never went at all. Among the boys the most popular films were cowboy Westerns, war, adventure, mystery and detective films. Romance or love stories were definitely disliked by boys but much preferred by the girls, and both preferred English to American 'talkies'.

The moralists who feared young children would be contaminated by the movies had no cause to worry, said the report. 'The film is no worse than the old-time "blood" universally read by the boys only a few years ago, and no more falsely sentimental than many of the feminine equivalents of the "blood". Evil in the film never pays'. 'The one distinct evil,' the report adds, 'is the fear and bad dreams caused by films depicting acts of violence'.

The introduction of the 'talkies' led to some of the old fleapits closing – the cost of installing sound equipment was high – but we had then entered the era of the 'super cinema', great buildings with extravagant décor and all the refinements of comfort, if not of good taste.

A night out at a 'super' was indeed an event. The manager would be in evening dress, the attendants in smart uniforms, and you were welcomed as people whose patronage was esteemed. There would probably be a double feature, a few shorts, certainly a newsreel and in all probability a mighty Wurlitzer which appeared slowly from below ground, lights flashing and filling the whole auditorium with a great volume of sound.

It was sheer magic and the crowds loved it. Of course it was escape, escape into the dream-world so skilfully manufactured by Hollywood and copied by British studios when they had the chance. There is no question that films then were the popular culture of the mass of the people, as television is today. That generation of the thirties had unlimited choice, thanks to the mass production methods of Hollywood and the deliberate building of the star system. One week it would be Shirley Temple, Garbo and the Marx Brothers, the next James Cagney, Fred Astaire, Ginger Rogers and Janet Gaynor.

The talkies had captured all. Silent films were dead, much to the chagrin of the purists who believed that talking pictures were an artistic abomination, and that the silent film had scarcely begun to explore the infinite possibilities of the medium. But then, who the hell cared about 'Art' when profits were the yardstick for everything? And profits there were in abundance, not so much for the small exhibitor, but for the great circuits with unlimited financial backing which were more and more dominating not only exhibition and distribution but also production.

The largest of these circuits was the Gaumont-British,which started in 1927 with only twenty cinemas, but by 1935 owned 331 cinemas. Similarly, the Associated British Picture Corporation started business in 1928 with a small group of 32 cinemas, expanding to 225 by 1935.

Because so many of these circuit cinemas were situated in the main towns and in prime sites, they exercised considerable muscle with the film makers and distributors and were able to obtain exclusive first-run rights at the expense of the smaller independents who had to be satisfied with second and third runs when the circuits had skimmed off most of the cream. Because of the circuits, a proprietor who owned only one theatre was often able to show only the least attractive films – the larger companies through their greater booking power could demand the best pictures for themselves.

The developing monopoly power of the two major circuits in the production of films was achieved in a number of ways, firstly by acquiring the studios where films were made, and secondly by entering into contracts with American production companies for their product. Pinewood, Denham, Amalgamated, Shepherds Bush, Elstree, Welwyn and Gainsborough Studios were all under the control of the two giants, who also acquired laboratories, newsreels, and equipment manufacturing companies.

The 'independence' of British film production was largely illusory. Most of it was dependent on American finance, either directly from Hollywood, or through the American distribution companies operating in Britain. Of 162 British features films registered in 1938, no less than 116 were distributed by the nine major renters operating in this country and of these nine renters, seven were Americans. The long history of British films is really one long history of booms and slumps, with virtually no security for the thousands of employees. The Cinematograph Films Act of 1927 had imposed an obligation on the importers of foreign films to acquire a percentage of British product, and on cinemas to show a percentage of British films. The Act was grossly abused by some of the American companies, but it afforded at least some stability and enabled responsible producers to plan ahead.

It was also the era of what was known as the 'Quota Quickie' – cheap, shoddy films without merit, hastily thrown together in a few days, with their workers and technicians grossly overworked and underpaid, and made solely to satisfy the bare legal requirements of the Act.

The spectacular success of Korda's *Private Life of Henry VIII*

CHEEP CRAPPY FILMS

attracted a host of (mainly) foreign speculators who saw the prospect of quick and rich profits. Many of these people were totally lacking in any of the qualifications necessary for the making of good pictures, but they had the ability to induce banks and insurance companies to invest millions of 'idle' money.

This artificial boom soon collapsed at the time of the first crash; the city lost its millions, and thousands of technicians, craftsmen, writers and actors had to suffer the consequences. Months of unemployment were to follow. Savings slowly disappeared, houses and other personal possessions had to be sold up.

In the years following the crash, the industry slowly recovered. The crash did one good thing: it drove out many of the questionable characters who had infiltrated it.

Every year some six or seven hundred feature films – the great majority American – were shown in British cinemas. The Hollywood dream-factories were working all out to supply the world demand for their product. The theory behind it all can be summed up in one word – escapism. The masses, it was argued, wanted to escape from the drabness of their lives, wanted 'to get away from it all' and lose themselves for a few hours in a world that had nothing to do with reality. For the most part the heroes and heroines of their films were plastic figures involved in a lollipop, sugar-candy world. The carefully-nurtured star system created gods and goddesses who were worshipped and adored by millions. Happy endings were the order of the day.

For instance during one week in 1933, the cinema's contribution to the intellectual life of the nation included: (1) a Ruritanian princess who falls in love with a 'delicatessen' man only to discover that he is really a captain in the Imperial Guards; (2) a mannequin who falls in love with the son of a newspaper millionaire who much to the confusion of the poor girl conceals his identity in the disguises of a railway ticket inspector, a Channel boat inspector, and the owner of a luxury yacht; (3) a shop girl who has an affair on the French Riviera with a man whom she imagines to be a poor clerk but who is in reality an English lord; (4) a gang of crooks who play hide-and-seek with Scotland Yard, and (5) a shyster lawyer who fakes accident claims.

In a world full of troubles and difficulties, with poverty and unemployment on a scale never before encountered, in a world of dictatorships and revolutions and economic crashes, the film moguls churned out romances in settings bearing no conceivable relation to the lives of the great mass of people. The industry was convinced that when people went to the movies they did not want to see a reflection of their hum-drum existences, and this precious argument was made the excuse for every outrage on good sense and decency that Hollywood and the other producing centres cared to perpetrate.

The social purpose of the cinema was clearly to act as a drug, for it is just as much propaganda to prevent people thinking as to make them think in certain directions. So millions of dollars and pounds and francs and liras were invested for the primary purpose of keeping the great mass of humanity in a state of intellectual stupor, and to make great profits by doing so.

There were of course a few brave exceptions such as John Ford's *Grapes of Wrath*, and the Warner Brothers, for a time, challenged the conventions with the gangster and underworld films based on the 'hot' stories from the sensational newspapers. Cagney started a new cult when he smashed a grapefruit in his girl friend's face, and for a time the tough guy became the hero. But the dream-world remained predominant.

Then there were the newsreels, five of them with twice weekly editions. Without exception the events covered fell into a few clearly defined and monotonous categories – Sport, Royalty, Military, or Military, Sport, Royalty. The newsreels never covered the real issues of their time, for instance the emerging threat of Nazi Germany and all its implications for the peace of the world.

2. THE WORKERS' FILM SOCIETIES AND THE WORKERS' FILM AND PHOTO LEAGUE

For a long time the British Labour Movement had failed to realize the enormous influence of the cinema. Lenin had said: 'For us the cinema is the most important of the arts'. He was under no illusion as to the cultural and propaganda potentialities of the film medium, and with this encouragement a whole new generation of films directors – Eisenstein, Pudovkin, Dovshenko, Vertov, Shub and others – smashed through the bourgeois conventions and brought the realities of life to the screeens not only of the U S S R but to most of Europe.

But not to Britain! The censorship saw to that. None of this Bolshevik propaganda would be allowed here! Mr J. Brooke Wilkinson, our chief censor, would see to that. When a copy of Eisenstein's *Battleship Potemkin* was smuggled in and shown to Eton College students who cheered their heads off when the mutinous sailors threw their officers into the sea, the British Establishment was convinced that the end of their world had come.

Film censorship in the thirties was rigid, at times hilariously ridiculous, and above all politically reactionary. Things forbidden included the nude 'both in actuality and shadowgraph', orgy scenes, embraces which 'overstep the limits of affection', indecorous dancing and 'intention to rape'.

In one year some 254 films had scenes deleted by the censor. Among reasons given (and recorded at the time by Ivor Montagu in his booklet *The Political Censorship of Films*) were:

References to H.R.H. The Prince of Wales;
white men in a state of degradation amidst Far-Eastern and native surroundings;
equivocal situations between white girls and men of other races;
officers in British uniform shown in a disgraceful light;
reflection on the wife of a responsible British official stationed in the Far East;
police firing on defenceless population;
girls and women in a state of intoxication;
son falling in love with his father's mistress;
indecorous bathroom scenes;
men and women in bed together.

Today the mind boggles at such absurdities, but the reasoning was clear. Filmgoers in the mass were regarded as children who must be protected against evil thoughts and temptations and it was the duty of their betters (i.e. the Establishment) to make this their responsibility.

But it was the openly reactionary political censorship which was the most dangerous. Forbidden were subjects 'calculated to wound the susceptibilities of foreign people' and 'stories and scenes which are calculated and possibly intended to ferment social unrest and discontent'.

These designations were broad enough to ban any film with a political content unfavourable to the established order of things, and the censors had no hesitation in using them to prevent public showing of many of the new Soviet films, such as *Potemkin*, and Pudovkin's *Mother* and *Storm over Asia*. *Mother*, for instance was forbidden on the ground that its scene was Russia, that its action concerned a strike, and that forces of law and order were depicted firing on the mob.

The actions of the Censor aroused a storm of opposition and many public campaigns were mounted. Petitions were signed by thousands, but positive action was required, and it was found that one way of circumventing the censor was to form private film societies which came outside his jurisdiction.

The original London Film Society was launched in October 1925 and, no doubt partly because of the many distinguished intellectual figures among its sponsors, received permission from the London County Council to exhibit uncensored films. It was here that film enthusiasts saw for the first time films from the new revolutionary cinema of the Soviet Union. The films of Eisenstein and Pudovkin caused a virtual sensation, especially when at the performance of Pudovkin's *End of St Petersburg*, a large section of the audience rose from their seats and cheered the Bolshevik workman who called for 'All Power to the Soviets'!

But many of us felt that these films were not getting through to the audiences that would most appreciate them and so in 1929 a group of us, Emile Burns, John Grierson, A. L. Plummer, the present writer and some trade unionists, launched the London Workers' Film Society (with a subscription of thirteen shillings per season) for the purpose of 'facilitating the exhibition and production of films of value to the working class'.

At first difficulties were encountered in finding a suitable hall, and the London County Council denied us the privileges they had afforded the Film Society. Eventually after a prolonged campaign against this discrimination, the LCC amended their regulations to allow film societies to show films that had not been submitted to the Board of Film Censors, but maintained the ban on films that had been so submitted and rejected!

The immediate success of the Workers' Film Society was astonishing. Hundreds applied to join and soon the Scala Theatre was packed for two evening performances once a month.

Similar societies were formed in many parts of Britain and the problem arose as to how to obtain a sufficient supply of films to meet the requirements of all the societies.

We grouped the societies into a Federation and set up our own distribution organization – Atlas Films. We scoured Europe for suitable product and were helped by a similar organization in Germany – Welt-Film – which had produced a number of films specifically for working-class audiences. With these films, and a growing supply of Soviet films made available to us, the workers' films society movement flourished.

Atlas Films was not content to have the films shown only to society members; it wanted to break into the ordinary commercial cinemas. It was discovered that each local authority had the power to override the censor if it so wished, and fortunately a number of London boroughs and some in Scotland gave the necessary permission, and several of the Soviet films were shown in these areas.

The Federation of Workers' Film Societies decided that an attempt should be made to produce their own films, and production was commenced, on a small scale, of a number of newsreel type actuality films on various aspects of the current struggles, with emphasis on the problems of unemployment and the hunger marches of the time. The films were made on a shoe-string, but were warmly welcomed wherever they were shown.

We regarded film as a valuable weapon in the class struggle. Any film that challenged the *status quo*, that widened horizons of thinking and understanding, was welcome and the workers' film movement did its best to bring it to as wide an audience as possible. Progressive films were few, apart from those coming from the new Soviet cinema, but some did emerge from Germany, France and other European countries and we gladly exhibited them.

In 1932 the supply of new films virtually ceased. Sound films, or 'talkies' as they were popularly described, had swept the board and the day of the silent film was finished. The Soviet Union at first lagged behind and took some time to adjust its film industry to the new techniques. Atlas Films did acquire the first Soviet sound film – *The Blue Express* – and secured a long run for it at the Academy Cinema in London's West End, but this was an exception, and slowly the workers' film society movement dissolved, solely due to the lack of films.

In some three years it had achieved much. Working-class audiences throughout the country had the opportunity of seeing films that would never be accepted by the commercial cinemas, and the foundations had been laid for an even more exciting period. This was made possible by the reduction of films from the standard 35 millimetre size to 16 millimetre. This meant that the censorship's dead hand could no longer apply, for the films were then on non-flammable stock and censorship only applied to the old nitrate flammable stock.

Welt-Film in Berlin acquired the 16 millimetre rights to all the Soviet films, and in Britain a new company, Kino Films, was established in 1933 to distribute them for viewing in ordinary halls and meeting-rooms.

In 1934 Kino Films acquired its first print of Eisenstein's classic, *The*

General Line, and the Royal Arsenal Co-operative Society gave a hundred performances of this film to 40,000 cooperators in twelve months.

By 1935 Kino Films had acquired some of the best Soviet and German films, fifteen short films of which a number had been made in England by the newly-formed Workers' Film and Photo League.

The League was, at first, an ancillary production group for Kino but in 1936 it decided to become an independent group and renamed itself the Film and Photo League. It declared its aim to be 'the production of films of a definite social value'. For some time, despite the usual chronic financial situation, the League produced films recording various aspects of the current struggles. Several of these were of the newsreel type and covered such diverse events as the international workers sports' festival in Paris, the Gresford colliery disaster, Mosley's Hyde Park fiasco and the anti-fascist counter-demonstration, the May Day procession in London, the visit of the Soviet folk dancers to London, the ILP summer school, and Tom Mann at a Pioneers' Camp.

Another short film made by the league had a slight story element. An unemployed man on the Means Test had his benefit stopped at the Labour Exchange and, his family being on the edge of starvation, he steals a loaf of bread. He is arrested, tried and sent to prision, whereas a gang of students who have been upsetting a coster's barrow are discharged with a caution. But the film stressed that stealing is not the way out of poverty, and that the correct solution was to organize, demonstrate, and build the united front of employed and unemployed to demand a better living.

The league also encouraged the formation of local groups who could make their own films, or shoot local material that could be incorporated into complete films, such as *National Hunger March* (1934) and *March Against Starvation* (1936).

The League sought close links with the Left Book Club and coproduced with it a film called *Red Right and Blue,* which included shots of the Club's conference, featuring Victor Gollancz and John Strachey.

Meanwhile Kino established its own production group, but was chiefly engaged in developing its distribution network. It also published an occasional broadsheet – *Kino News* – and by 1936 was able to announce at its annual conference that during the previous year film shows had been given to over a quarter of a million people. Its catalogue of films had greatly extended and now included some of the social documentaries made under the auspices of John Grierson's GPO Film Unit and similar professional documentary Units.

3. THE DOCUMENTARY MOVEMENT

The documentary movement was without doubt the most exciting and stimulating development in British films during the late twenties and the thirties. It was begun by John Grierson under the auspices of the Empire Marketing Board and later transferred to the General Post Office. Grierson himself described the movement as 'an adventure in public observation'. The basic force behind it was, he insisted, social, not aesthetic.

Documentary was from the beginning an anti-aesthetic movement. . . but we had the good sense to use the aesthetes. . . we were reformers open and avowed, concerned with bringing alive the new materials of citizenship (*Documentary Newsletter,* June 1942).

He coined the phrase 'the drama of the doorstep'. This was indeed a revolutionary concept. British feature films had never been interested in the drama of the doorstep, or indeed any form of drama that bore the remotest relation to real life. And the British working man had certainly never been put on the screen as anything but a servile comic relief. Grierson's intention was to dramatise the undramatic and honour the unhonoured and to bring to the screen the affairs of our time 'in a fashion which strikes the imagination and makes observation a little richer than it was'.

Grierson himself was a man of extraordinary talent and incredible energy. His vision was combined with an infinite skill of manoeuvre within the bureaucratic channels of the civil service. He insisted on full creative freedom for his Unit. I recall that a film of mine was criticized by a senior civil servant. Grierson turned to him and said: 'You look after the money, I'll take care of the art.'

To some people the phrase 'drama of the doorstep' conjured up visions of gloom and disaster, of hopelessness and despair, and indeed some of the German workers' films of the time did have a strong element of pessimism. Grierson's concept was contrary to this. 'The ordinary affairs of people's lives,' he said, 'are more dramatic and more vital than all the fake excitements you can muster.'

It was Grierson's one and only personally directed film – *Drifters* (1929) – that started the documentary movement. Here was a film that dared to show in the most graphic detail the skills and the 'braveries' (Grierson's favourite word) of ordinary working people in an environment full of hardships and dangers. The social implications were subtly indicated – when the fishing fleets returned to harbour their catch (and their income) was totally dependent on the market place, and auctioned to the highest bidder.

The success of *Drifters* critically and with a wide public was immediate. A new era of film making was opened, and Grierson had no difficulty in attracting to his film unit a number of dedicated young film makers. On the whole the people who joined the unit, whatever their backgrounds – some public school – were 'socially aware', and grasped the opportunity to make films that would have something positive and critical to say about the world around them.

Some newspaper hacks accused us of being Reds and Marxists, but this cut very little ice. Grierson certainly understood the fundamentals of Marxism – the economic base and the superstructure, the theory and methods of dialectical materialism, and so on, and our evening discussions in the pub often reached high intellectual standards, much to the bewilderment of the plain-clothes CID man who had been deputed to keep an eye on us, and whom we occasionally bought a drink in sympathy for his boring occupation.

As the GPO Film Unit grew in numbers and output other units dedicated to the same ideas and principles sprung up – the Realist Film Unit, Strand Films, Film Centre and others, and they rapidly extended the horizons of sponsorship far beyond the GPO.

It was mainly by these commercial units that the great social documentaries were made. One of the first was Edgar Anstey's *Housing Problem* (1935), commissioned by the British Commercial Gas Association – a devastating indictment of the slums in which millions of working people lived. The camera and the sound recorder were taken right into the alleyways and homes, and the people told their own stories. This was unheard-of and the film created a sensation. More important than that, its wide distribution did compel some local authorities to do something about the situation in their areas.

Another film, Edgar Anstey's *Enough to Eat* (1936) examined the question of nutrition in Britain and came out openly and honestly with some terrifying facts and figures. The film was narrated by Julian Huxley, then in charge of the London Zoo. One of his most devastating remarks was that if he subjected his animals to a diet similar to that 'enjoyed' by millions of British people, he would be imprisoned for cruelty. Basil Wright's *Children at School* (1937) was another powerful exposé of a national disgrace.

My own *Today we Live* (1936–7) was filmed in the South Wales coalfields at a time of massive unemployment. The pits had closed, the mining villages were almost deserted. Unemployed miners collaborated with me on the script for the film, which was promoted by the National Council for Social Services who gave money for the building of a community centre in one of the villages. In one of the film's scenes, a miner pointed out that there was money to build centres, but not for providing work.

Most of these social documentaries were made outside the GPO Film Unit because this Unit had to concentrate on the manifold and widespread activities of the postal services. It might have been supposed that this would have led to a long series of humdrum films, but the creative imagination of Grierson and his collegues succeeded in making dramatically exciting not only the daily routines of postal sorting and deliveries, but the wider services of cable ships, weather forecasting, broadcasting, and the ship to shore radio services for the fishing fleets. This last aspect of the GPO's work was outstandingly portrayed in Harry Watt's *North Sea* (1938). But the undoubted classic of the GPO Film Unit was Basil Wright's and Harry Watt's *Nightmail* (1936), with music by Benjamin Britten and a verse script by Auden.

These social documentaries were of course a minority of the total documentary output. As official and commerical sponsorship of films developed, the subject became more specific, offering fewer opportunities for social observation and comment. Some directors claimed that they had hidden away some profound social message in their films, but it was generally so well hidden that no one else could detect it.

The documentary movement had a permanent influence on the whole future of British film making, both in the commercial area, and for the independent progressive groups who were seeking new forms of communication, whether it be straight reporting or 'agit-prop'.

Commercially, its greatest impact came in the war years. The British public became increasingly disgruntled with the American product, with war themes which bore no relation to its own reality. Errol Flynn winning the war in Burma single-handed got booed off the screen, but those documentary-trained directors who moved into the feature world brought a freshness of vision and a *rapport* with public feeling that at last brought British films to a standard of excellence that continued right through the war years and many years afterwards. The drawing rooms and stately mansions, the vapid meanderings of the idle rich, the affected accents of the public schools were left behind. For the first time a feeling of honesty and objectiveness was discernible. Real people, real situations and real, instead of synthetic, emotions became the rule, not the exception. British films found an integrity that the public responded to. This was the direct legacy of the documentary movement.

4. THE LABOUR MOVEMENT AND THE CINEMA

From the middle of the thirties onwards the political use of film by left-wing and other progressive organizations developed considerably. This was particularly so in the case of the Co-operative movement. The Co-operative Wholesale Society was using films for advertising purposes, and the London Co-operative Society made a number of documentaries. The big breakthrough came when Joseph Reeves, general secretary of the Co-operative Film Committee, persuaded four London Co-operatives to finance a five year film plan aiming to produce one new film each year. I was entrusted with the first in the series, *Advance Democracy* (1938).

Bert Hogenkamp, who has undertaken research on the use of film by the British labour movement for the Dutch magazine *Skrien*, describes what we portrayed in this film:

The central characters in *Advance Democracy* [he writes] are a docker and his wife, the latter active in the Co-operative Movement. The husband doesn't really see the point, but the wife persuades him to listen to a speech on the radio by A. V. Alexander, one of the leaders of the Parliamentary Co-operative Party, who recounts the history of the movement from the first Co-op in Rochdale to the present world-wide organisation. Alexander points out that fascism is threatening to destroy the movement and its ideals, and calls on all democratic forces to unite in the fight against it. The husband gains a deeper understanding of his own union activities in the docks and now also fully appreciates his wife's work for the Co-op. The end of the film shows them both marching in a huge May Day demonstration with socialist songs heard in the background.

The second film was *People with a Purpose* which showed the wide range of cultural and educational activities within the Co-operative Movement. Benjamin - Britten conducted a Co-op choir in a lively rendering of 'The Red Flag' for this film.

Apart from the Co-operative Movement, the official labour

Movement – the Labour Party and the TUC – showed little awareness of the value of film, and while individual members of both played an active role in the Workers' Film Societies, Kino and the Film and Photo League, the leadership was apathetic and indifferent.

However, in 1936 the Labour Party, jointly with the TUC, did announce an intention to create their own film service. They suggested the setting up of local film societies and by 1937 they had got around to deciding that they would collaborate with the Co-operative Film Committee to avoid duplication. From this emerged the Workers' Film Association, with the energetic Joseph Reeves as general secretary. Most of its performances were with films acquired from Kino, and at the TUC Congress of 1938, *Advance Democracy* and *Spanish Earth* (directed by Joris Ivens) were shown to the delegates. Plans made for production by the Workers' Film Association were cancelled with the outbreak of war.

The Communist Party, after making a short ten-minute film of its 1938 Congress, later commissioned a more ambitious film to propagate the policy of the Party as decided by the Congress. Ivor Montagu offered to undertake the production with a number of colleagues. The result was *Peace and Plenty*, a devastating political analysis and exposure of the National Government under Chamberlain.

Montagu used cartoons, animation puppets and graphics, as well as newly-filmed material and archive records to make this film, which skilfully combined the political message with humour and 'entertainment values'. Earlier in the thirties, Ivor Montagu had founded the Progressive Film Institute, whose first film was *Free Thälmann* (1935) (Ernst Thälmann was the imprisoned leader of the German Communist Party).

But the films for which the Insititute became famous were those they made of the Spanish Civil War. Montagu gathered round him a team of professional film technicians whose sympathies were wholly with the Republicans (among them were Sidney Cole, Thorold Dickinson, and Alan Lawson). Their first film was *Defence of Madrid* (1937), which included shots of the bombing of Madrid and of the International Brigade, as well as dealing with the pre-history of the civil war and the intervention of Germany and Italy.

The film was widely shown here and raised some £6,000 for medical aid. It was followed by *News from Spain* and *Crime against Madrid*.

Still more films were made in 1938 as a result of further visits by the groups of technicians to Spain and financial support from the Republican Government. The best known of these were *Spanish ABC* and *Behind the Spanish Lines*. If anyone had ever doubted the tremendous value films could have for the progressive movement, these films were the answer. Their impact on public opinion was enormous and was a vital part of the great national campaigns in Britain on behalf of Republican Spain.

While in the thirties, the commercial cinema of Hollywood and its British imitations remained all-powerful, the 'alternative cinema', as it would now be called, found its roots in the working-class movement and with very limited resources made a considerable impact where it was most needed.

Among the many groups who devoted their energies to the production of films showing some aspects of the real world of unemployment, struggle, the menace of fascism, there were naturally differences of opinion, not of principle but of methods.

There were some who argued that film propaganda had to be conducted via the commercial cinema, since screenings at film societies and political and trade union meetings simply meant preaching to the converted.

This idealistic view ignored the plain fact that in no way would the powerful groups controlling the big circuits and most of the independent cinemas permit the type of film that our movement was prepared to make. Even if some cinemas were amenable, the censor's rigid rules on what was described as political propaganda would have precluded the exhibition of such films.

There was also a fallacy in the argument about 'preaching to the converted', as if this was a waste of time. The 'converted' are not robots. They need stimulation and encouragement to fortify their faith, and there is no question that many of the films made by the workers' film societies, Kino, the Film and Photo League, the Progressive Film Institute and others were received with enormous enthusiasm despite their technical imperfections.

It was in the thirties that films were used for the first time as a weapon in the class struggle in Britain, and their impact and importance should not be underestimated. For the audiences we attracted, the documentary and the newsreel were the most practical to make and the most urgently required. When action was needed, as in the case of Spain, the Spanish films proved invaluable.

Not all the films made in those years have survived; some were lost or destroyed in the London blitz. But many have been preserved, and they are available in the archives – vivid reminders that what could be accomplished then could be achieved on an infinitely greater scale today.

Making Films with a Purpose: Film-making and the Working Class

BERT HOGENKAMP

In the first issue of *Kino News* (Winter, 1935), a four-page newspaper published by the leftwing film distribution company Kino, three key articles are printed – two written by Ralph Bond, and one by Ivor Montagu – on the production of films for the working-class movement, the foundation of worker's film societies and the limitations of film censorship in Great Britain. Both Bond and Montagu were 'veterans' of the worker's film movement in the early thirties and their articles in *Kino News* were based on experiences gained in this movement. They offered a set of recommendations for people as yet inexperienced in the use of film. In the following article I shall examine, after a short general introduction, the production of films for the working-class movement in the mid-thirties. I shall use Ralph Bond's article in *Kino News*, 'Making Films With A Purpose', as a guideline, and test the application of its recommendation on two films produced at that time for the working-class movement: *Construction* (1935), made by a group of London builders and edited by the Film and Photo League, and *Hell Unltd* (1936), made by two students at the Glasgow School of Art. The crucial part played by Kino and its offshoot the (Workers') Film and Photo League in the 'life' of these two films will be examined in detail.

(i) *Kino*

Kino (the Russian word for Cinema) was founded in December 1933 by some members of the Workers' Theatre Movement (WTM)[1]. One of them was 'Charlie Mann, son of the veteran Tom Mann' who 'along with several enthusiasts, first used a toy projector to give an experimental exhibition of the Russian film *Potemkin* ... in the backyard of an old garage in Bloomsbury'[2]. Kino was the outcome of a partial reorientation within the International Union of Revolutionary Theatre (IURT). During the International Theatre Olympiad in May 1933 in Moscow the Cinema Buro of the IURT organized a cinema conference. At this conference it was decided that the national workers' theatre associations had to be the bodies that would breathe new life into the ailing workers' cinema movement. This had been crippled by the closing of Weltfilm – the Berlin film distribution agency founded by Willi Münzenberg that took care of the supply of workers' films to organizations in Germany and abroad. It was recommended to the delegates at the conference that they should use sub-standard (16mm and 9·5mm) film.[3] The smaller size of the equipment required for this meant that crews were more mobile and projection easier to organize. In addition, the fact that such film was on non-inflammable stock meant that it was not such an easy target for the authorities to restrict it under safety regulations. The Japanese film organization, Prokino, used such film with great success and was able to continue its activities under fascist repression as a result.

Shortly after the Moscow conference a film section of the WTM was founded. It started its activities with an open-air exhibition of *Soviet Russia: Past and Present* – a film that could be hired via the *Daily Worker* – in the East End of London on a Sunday evening in August 1933. This event was described as 'Pioneer work which will lead to big developments'.[4] It took the group about half a year to organize properly, but then Kino started with a smash-hit, a 16 mm print of *Potemkin*, Eisenstein's film about mutiny on a tsarist battleship. The British Board of Film Censors (BBFC) had not shared the admiration for Eisenstein's masterpiece expressed by leading artists, intellectuals and film critics in Western Europe, and had forbidden its public exhibition. The London County Council had upheld this decision, although it had the power to override the decisions of the BBFC under the 1909 Cinematograph Act, which only applied to inflammable (i.e. nitrate) film stock. As we have seen, the stock used for sub-standard film was non-inflammable, in other words it was not subject to the 1909 Cinematograph Act and its censorship regulations. Legally this meant that Kino's print of *Potemkin* could be shown everywhere without interference from any authority. Even the Quota Act which decreed the percentage of British films that had to be produced, distributed or exhibited by a British firm – an act which had hastened the end of Kino's predecessor, Atlas Film Company, in 1932[5] – did not apply to non-inflammable stock.

When in December 1933 and January 1934 Kino and its supporters booked various unlicensed halls in London for the exhibition of *Potemkin*, the LCC brought pressure to bear on the owners to cancel these bookings. The LCC threatened the owners with proceedings under the 1909 Cinematograph Act, even though this Act did not apply.[6] If

these threats did not succeed, the arrival of policemen on the date of the
exhibition of *Potemkin* could be expected. In this way the LCC helped to
make the '*Potemkin* case' a matter of national interest, and Kino was
obliged to order extra-prints so that the rising demand could be met.[7]
Alarmed by the failure of the LCC to ban the screening of *Potemkin* the
Government intervened. Ivor Montagu wrote in the first issue of *Kino
News*: 'Not so long ago, the then Home Secretary, Sir John Gilmore,
declared that all films were inflammable and consequently, that all films
were subject to fire-protection laws. He proposed not to make stricter
laws for inflammable film (nothing so undemocratic), but to relax the
rules for "slow-burning" films. *Relax* rules that had never been applied.
Very kind of him.'[8]

Montagu was an expert on censorship. He had fought many a battle
with the LCC about the exemption of the Film Society from censorship
regulations. In 1929 he published a pamphlet, *The Political Censorship
of Films*, based on these experiences. His expertise must have been
extremely valuable to Kino, but the decisive turn came when the
National Council for Civil Liberties (NCCL) took the matter in hand.
The NCCL was able to mobilize educational circles, for whom the
government measure would have been a disaster. Referring to reports
from authoritative laboratories, the NCCL was able to prove that sub-
standard film stock was completely non-inflammable.[9] The
Government had to give up its plans. A battle of utmost importance had
been won. As Montagu resumed it: 'If you use small-size film you are
exempt from the power of the Board of Trade. If you use non-
inflammable film you are exempt from the power of the police. If you
use an unlicensed hall (a private house or hall without any sort of
licence) you are exempt from the power of the magistrates and county
councils.'[10]

After winning this battle, Kino could direct its attention towards the
acquisition of more films for its distribution library and, even more
important, the production of its own films. An East End group had
produced a short fiction-film, *Bread*, about the distressed situation of
the unemployed, ending with the call to organize in the National
Unemployed Workers' Movement. This film was distributed by Kino,
as was *Hungermarch 1934*, a 10-minute documentary.

In the summer of 1934, Kino organized its own production group. It
was severely handicapped by the lack of proper equipment: as the *Daily
Worker* reported, they 'are dependent on the use of one camera'.[11]

Nothing is known about the composition of this group, which produced the first two issues (August and September 1934) of *Workers' Newsreel*. These newsreels are conspicuous for their militancy, juxtaposing in a Russian montage style images of capitalist destruction (bombing practice at Hendon aerodrome) with images of the peaceful intentions and constructive work done by the workers. The net result of the group's activities was a deficit of more than £12.[12] This loss may well have lead to the split between Kino-Production and Kino-Distribution in November 1934.[13] The financially more vulnerable production group merged with the Workers' Camera Club to form the Workers' Film and Photo League (WFPL). This move enabled Kino-distribution to change itself into a limited liability company, Kino Films (1935) Ltd.

In 1935 Kino extended its distribution library with a great number of films, the prints of which had to be imported from as far as Paris or New York. Most of the Soviet films were purchased in close cooperation with the Friends of the Soviet Union (FSU). The FSU were Kino's best customers: 30 per cent of the screenings of Kino's films were organized by its branches.[14] Titles included *The General Line* (purchased in February 1934), *Son of a Soldier* and *Little Screw* (November 1934), *New Babylon* and *Shadow of the Mine* (January 1935), *Storm over Asia* and *Mother* (March 1934), *Heroes of the Arctic* (May 1935), *The Ghost that Never Returns* (September 1935), *Ten Days that Shook the World* (November 1935), *The End of St Petersburg* (early 1936) and *In the Land of the Soviets* (February 1936).

The WFPL produced a number of short films that were handed over to Kino for distribution. Some of these films were made by its own WFPL-crew, others were sent in by other bodies, for which the WFPL acted as an agency. Among the WFPL productions in 1935 were a third and fourth issue of *Workers' Newsreel*, *Jubilee* (a film produced by the North London Film Society contrasting the extravagance of the Silver Jubilee celebrations with the poverty of working-class life), *Winter* (demanding extra relief for the unemployed during the winter months), and *Construction*.

Late in 1935 the League dropped the prefix Workers', hoping to attract a broader membership as the Film and Photo League. By that time it had a membership of about sixty but still remained a voluntary body. Compared to the professionalised Kino, the League seems to have been ill-equipped to cope with all the difficulties inherent in the production of films.

Early in 1936 Kino decided to set up its own production department. Its aims were: (1) to discuss and determine themes and treatments for films of social significance; (2) to form units throughout the country for their production, on sub-standard stock, and to act as coordinating body to all such units and give assistance in every possible way; (3) to offer existing units a source of distribution for suitable productions in the sub-standard market, and to assist and advise them on scenarios; (4) to undertake production for any organization which felt that a film illustrating its work from a particular angle would aid it in its own sphere.[15] These aims were hardly different from the ones set by the F P L. However, Kino invited the F P L to join its production section, this move seems to have been vehemently opposed by a group of FPL-members for political and organization reasons. Kino and the F P L remained two different bodies. Ironically Kino Production was, like the F P L, unable to fulfill its aims. The very ambitious Frank Jackson led its first production, 'the first working-class comedy',[16] *Touch Wood*. As far as is known the film has never been released. It was Ivor Montagu's Progressive Film Institute that would fill the gap by producing a number of important documentaries (like *Defence of Madrid* on the Spanish Civil War) for Kino.

Shortly before Kino had set up its own production group, Ralph Bond's article 'Making Films With A Purpose' was published by *Kino News*. Bond had been responsible for the production of the first workers' films in Great Britain in the early thirties (*Workers' Topical News*, a series of three newsreels, *Glimpses of Modern Russia* and *1931 – The Charter Film*).[17] Based on these experiences and on his close knowledge of the Kino- and WFPL-productions, Bond wrote this article, outlining 'the reason and purpose for Kino making films'.[18] Everybody has a purpose for making films, Bond argued: the movie moguls because they want to make profits, the Conservative Party for getting more votes for their candidates, and Shell for selling more petrol. What has Kino to sell? 'Yes, we are trying to sell working-class ideas and working-class politics through a medium that is popular in every town and village.' However, this 'powerful form of propaganda . . . is under the control of vested interests who use it not only to make profits but to put across propaganda for their own class-interests'. Kino had been able to break this monopoly by producing some 16 mm films, notwithstanding 'the expense involved in any sort of film production . . . because of its dependence on costly technical equipment'. Bond demands that future Kino-films should be 'real':

— films that 'dramatize the lives and struggles of the workers' with subjects like 'unemployment, victimization, housing, children, strikes, hunger marches, war'. No 'melodrama or false heroics and the message or lead must grow naturally out of the material'.

— films that are 'positive in the sense that they must indicate the subjective factor of revolt and struggle against existing conditions'.

— films that 'have unity and lead up to its motivating point in such a way that the audience will be carried with it naturally and logically'.

— 'the documentary type is . . . the one most suited to our aims . . . We can take our cameras out into the streets, and at the expense of little more than filmstock, patience and infinite capacity for taking trouble, photograph our material as it actually exists.' In this way 'the stupidity and false values of the commercial film' would be exposed.

In his argument Bond covers the whole field of film production: the choice of the subject-matter, the 'tendency', the dramatic construction and the actual shooting of the film in the documentary way. Were Bond's recommendations realistic? After so many years it is very hard to form a judgement. Some (not all) of the films have survived – as have some of those who were involved in making them. This makes it possible to reconstruct the production of some films from their inception to the impact of their screening. I have chosen two 'inside-stories' of rather contrasting (and less known) films of the thirties, which have in common that their makers sought to fulfill Bond's aim and make a film with a purpose.

(ii) *Construction*

Frank Jackson (no relative of Kino's Frank Jackson), a trade unionist of long standing,[19] got a job as foreman-carpenter at a building-site, Exeter House, in Putney, London, in 1934. Jackson recalls that it was 'a 100 per cent T.U. job'.[20] In October 1934 a nine-day strike took place at Exeter House. The sacking of a labourers' steward was the immediate cause of the strike, but there had been 'an accumulation of small grievances over a long period that caused the men to take drastic action'.[21] In the end the steward was reinstated, even though the workers had been let down by the higher trade union officials. Strengthened by the result of the strike, Jackson and his comrades extended their trade union activities. At lunchhours Jackson and others

led discussions on evolution and on current political topics, very much
like Owen in Robert Tressell's *The Ragged Trousered Philanthropists*
(of the abridged version of this book that was then available, more than
two hundred copies were sold on the site after the strike). At one of
these lunch meetings Alf Garrard, carpenter and amateur film-maker,
'suggested the making of a film showing actual work on the job in
progress'.[22] Garrard 'was a fanatic on this film business. He used to take
everything he could with his hand camera. He got so used to it, he could
walk around with it quite naturally.'[23] According to Jackson, Garrard
had been involved with Kino's early production activities. Jackson
arranged that Garrard could move freely on the site by taking over a
general maintenance job.[24] There remained the question of how
Garrard could hide his hand camera. Jackson recalls that Garrard put
on 'a large sackcloth apron, instead of the usual white linen one, cut a
hole in it and took a number of photos. This resulted in some pictures
coming out OK, but also many of them just showing the fibres of the
sack. It took several weeks, and I don't know how many feet of film was
lost.'[25] Garrard went around the job and 'took all the process of it:
carpentering, sawing, weighing, plumbing, fitting in doorways,
plastering and bricklaying'.[26] However, Garrard did not have the
facilities to edit this film material and it was only much later, long after
the job at Exeter House had been finished, that the FPL intervened and
helped to finish the film. After the final version of the film had been made
(its release must have been early 1936), it was shown with much success
to various building trade union branches in London. Kino took care of
its national distribution.

The surviving print of *Construction* (10 mins, silent, black and white)
shows a slightly changed re-enactment of the October 1934 strike at
Exeter House. The title-card reminds the spectators that they are
looking at a film 'made by the men on the job'. The film shows the
different aspects of the building-work (as the title-card says: 'All trades
at work'). Some of the shots are blurred (for reasons described above).
One of the men opens his pay packet (total: £2 12s 6d) and goes home
to a slum tenement. Title-card: 'Only 100 per cent trade union will
improve our conditions.' A 12 o'clock meeting with trade-union
agitation is shown, which leads to the dismissal of the 'agitator'. All the
builders strike for the reinstatement of the dismissed. The strike is
successful. 'Unity wins' (last title-card).

In the 1935–6 FPL production notes, two builders (Alf Garrard and
Hugh-Campbell) and two members (Bill Megarry and Alf Pizer) are

mentioned as 'persons engaged in production'. In the same document *Construction* is described as 'shot by a builder on the job. His group asked the League for help with finance and cutting, scenario, etc. Cutting was done by a League member, with the aid of the Builders.'[27] This would mean that Bill Megarry did the cutting of *Construction*. Megarry became Ivor Montagu's closest assistant at the Progressive Film Institute and edited *Defence of Madrid* and other PFI-productions.

In the second issue of *Kino News*, *Construction* is praised as a film that 'shows more than volumes of talk'. According to this same article the film would have cost 'under £8'. After the exhibition of *Construction* to delegates from the Building and Transport Unions, Kino presented *Construction* as a model for the future trade union films. However, no other Kino trade union film was ever made. Various reasons can be given for this. In April 1936 the TUC, in cooperation with the Labour Party, published a circular, *Labour Cinema Propaganda*, revealing the intention to produce its own films. This plan was not realized until 1938 when the Workers' Film Association was founded, but the circular made it less urgent for Kino to produce trade union films. Moreover, as we have seen, Kino was far from successful with its productions in 1936. Still other reasons may have determined the cancellation of the project. *Construction* was an extremely effective propaganda film, if shown to builders or trade union organizers. Its appeal to a more general public – the kind of public that would pour in by hundreds to see Kino's documentaries on the civil war in Spain – was restricted: it was crudely made, contained a long sequence on the various crafts of the building trade, and had an unsophisticated story. Kino became more interested in films that appealed to large audiences.

Perhaps more important were the conditions under which *Construction* had been made (and other trade union films would have to be made). Alf Garrard was an amateur cameraman, who as Frank Jackson put it 'got so used to it, he could walk around with it quite naturally'.[28] Jackson recalls that one of Garrard's cherished projects was the filming of *The Ragged Trousered Philanthropists* and that he even got as far as presenting parts of the book on slides! This was the opposite of what Kino (perhaps for propaganda purposes) said in *Kino News*, No. 2: 'The photography is by one of the building workers, who learnt to use the camera in a few days.' Furthermore Jackson has stressed how the shooting on the site had to be thoroughly organized by having men switch jobs. At Exeter House this could be done relatively easily because of the presence of 'experienced militants'.[29] The making of *Construction* was only one of the activities of this group. It included, besides lunch discussions and the sale of *The Ragged Trousered Philanthropists* on the job, the launching of a paper, *The New Builders Leader* (from October 1935 onwards), and assistance to alterations being carried out in a disused church, which was to become Unity Theatre's new theatre in Britannia Street. A production like *Construction* was only possible with the presence of such a well-organized group of trade-union activists like Jackson, Garrard, Campbell and comrades. Even then, the technical difficulties of filming indoors (for example in a factory) would have been insurmountable with the kind of equipment available.

(iii) *Hell Unltd*

When Kino started to extend its activities to regions outside London, it encountered enormous difficulties. Only one print was available of most of the films, and the projection equipment had to be transported over long distances. Kino decided to improve this situation by setting up a network of local agencies in the most important provincial centres. Early in 1936 there were Kino groups in Manchester, Doncaster, Bradford, Birmingham and Glasgow.[30] These groups acted as agencies for the distribution of Kino films in their region. It was even hoped that they would be able to extend their activities and, in the end, produce their own films, but as Kino's *First Annual Report* (April 1936) said: 'We had to start from scratch in the provinces, and . . . were not in a position to provide the very necessary capital for provincial development.' Notwithstanding the lack of (financial) support from the London headquarters, some of these groups managed to produce their own films, Glasgow Kino being one of them.

Glasgow had a tradition of showing films to working-class audiences through special workers' film societies. In November 1932 the Scottish USSR Society and the New Art Cinema Movement had organized a season of Soviet films. The Scottish USSR Society in particular had a large working-class following. However by the end of 1932 the Glasgow authorities found an excuse to ban the showing of films by both organizations. Nevertheless, two years later, a Workers' Film Society in Glasgow was able to finish a season of film shows without interference from the authorities, for like everywhere else in Great Britain, the exemption of sub-standard film from censorship regulation changed the situation drastically. In 1935 Glasgow was able to begin its own Kino group.

Despite her diminutive height and hunchback (due to early spinal injuries), the sculptress Helen Biggar was clearly an outstanding personality among Glasgow's left wing artists. A graduate of the Glasgow School of Art, she kept in close touch with events at the School and so met Norman McLaren – the famous film animator who subsequently moved to Canada. Helen Biggar was very impressed with McLaren's *7 till 5* (1933) and helped him on his next film, *Camera Makes Whoopee* (1935). By the end of 1935 both became members of Glasgow Kino and early in 1936 the two developed a project on health and environment. As the Glasgow Corporation refused to permit the shooting inside a hospital, McLaren and Biggar had to give up this project. The night after they had received this sad news, McLaren wrote an enthusiastic letter to Biggar outlining a new project.[31] This film, *Hell Unltd*, was made in about a month with help from students and was in no way a Glasgow Kino production.

Hell Unltd was an anti-war film, or to be more precise an anti-arms trade film. Peace campaigns had been recurring events in Britain in the thirties and it is therefore not surprising that McLaren and Biggar chose to make a film on this theme. They managed to make a very original film, using documentary, fiction and animated footage in various combinations. Norman McLaren later became known all over the world for some of the techniques used in *Hell Unltd* (for example, scratching directly onto celluloid, done with the word 'War' in this film).

The story of *Hell Unltd* is quite simple. Mr Hell (played by Ian Fleming) is an arms' dealer. The film depicts world history from 1900 onwards featuring Mr Hell. The first three title-cards say: 'This film is addressed to all who are made to pay each day for their own and other people's destruction. / To all who are taxed just now to pay for the future murder of millions of men, women, and children, / and especially to those who sit back and say, 'We can do nothing about it.' On each of these title-cards the message is also embodied in an image projected onto the background (respectively a growing heap of coins, devastated houses, and a man with his hands in his pockets).

This method is characteristic for *Hell Unltd*: McLaren and Biggar were evidently unconvinced of the effectiveness of the written word (i.e. title-cards and newspaper headlines) and tried to drive home the message by images as well. In the same way, combinations of fiction, documentary and animated material serve to reinforce the message expressed in the preceding image. For example: (1) a display-poster of the *Herald*, saying 'Advance In Steel Prices'; (2) Mr Hell smiles; (3)

animated cartoon of three school-girls slowly fading into three bombs. This method of embodying one message into two, or more, images/sequences of images, juxtaposing various filmic codes (fiction, documentary, animation, written texts) makes *Hell Unltd* exciting to look at and easy to understand. After having shown the double-dealing of the armaments' business (selling weapons both to Hitler Germany and to Great Britain) and the destruction wrought by weaponry, the film ends with the call 'Stop It'.

Hell Unltd shows three ways of doing this: (1) by writing to one's MP; (2) by demonstrating, if the first has failed; (3) by mass strike, if other means have failed. With images reminiscent of Eisenstein's *Strike* (a film that McLaren and Biggar could not have seen) the effects of such a mass strike are shown. Mr Hell falls to the ground like a modern Dracula. The film ends with an animation sequence: a circle of dancing puppets who become dancing human beings.

Compared to Paul Rotha's *Peace Film*, a three-minute film against rearmament made about the same time, *Hell Unltd* seems more politically conscious. Rotha ends with the call to the audience to write to their MPs. McLaren and Biggar realize that they have to show other means, in the (very likely) case that writing to MPs fails. The two Glasgow film makers even anticipate the distinctive feature of warfare in the Second World War: the bombing of densely populated areas (Rotterdam, London, Coventry, etc.).

Hell Unltd was finished with the assistance of Willie McLean, a tutor at the Glasgow School of Art. In August 1936 Helen Biggar went down to London to show the film at Kino headquarters. Kino suggested some changes, one of which, the omission of the caption 'Strike Now', McLaren refused to carry out arguing: 'Other means have been failing for years. We need one-day strikes to protest against the present policy of governments and to show what resistance will have to be met with, in the case of the outbreak of war.'[32] The film was a considerable success. Glasgow Kino acquired a print of it, as did London Kino.

Late in 1936 McLaren and Biggar parted company. After a trip to Spain with Ivor Montagu to film the siege of Madrid (*Defence of Madrid*), Norman McLaren joined the John Grierson documentary group in London. Helen Biggar stayed in Glasgow, where she helped build up Glasgow Kino which was able to produce its first film in 1938, *Challenge to Fascism* or *Mayday 1938*. This film, financed by Glasgow Kino itself, proved that it was possible to produce workers' films outside London.[33]

(iv) *Conclusions*

The stories of *Construction* and *Hell Unltd* seem very disparate. One may even be inclined to consider them as 'untypical' for the production of workers' films in the thirties.

Let us return to Ralph Bond's directives in 'Making Films With A Purpose'. In this article Bond never indicates where the money can be found to make the films. Neither does he indicate who should make the films (i.e. workers, or professional film makers, or a combination of both). In this context it is worth noting that here were two films made without finance, one by workers, the other by students, which – thanks to Kino – received national distribution which they would not have had otherwise.

Generally speaking *Construction* and *Hell Unltd* were made in accordance with Bond's recommendations. Of course *Hell Unltd* has fiction and animated sequences besides documentary, recommended by Bond, but this film exposes the 'false values of the commercial film' by deliberately breaking the dominant filmic codes (i.e. a documentary film is a documentary film, etc.). In the choice of their subject-matter, their 'tendency', and their dramatic construction, both films can be categorized as 'films made with a purpose'.

By presenting these two stories I hope to have clarified some aspects of the production of films for the working-class movement in the thirties.

I would like to thank Peter Latham and Anna Shepherd for giving me access to their research work, Frank Jackson for allowing me to interview him, and Norman McLaren and Anna Shepherd for allowing me a print of Hell Unltd.

NOTES

1. *First Annual Report, Kino Films (1935) Ltd*, in Film and Photo League Archive; Tom Thomas, 'A Propertyless Theatre for the Propertyless Class', in *History Workshop*, no. 4 (Autumn, 1977), p. 124.
2. *Reynolds News*, 3 October 1937, p. 9.
3. Maria Baker, 'Film Conference', in *New Theatre*, September/October 1933, pp. 24-5.
4. *Daily Worker*, 3 August 1933, p. 4.
5. *Daily Worker*, 21 December 1931, p. 6.

6. *Daily Worker*, 9 January 1934, p. 4.
7. *Daily Worker*, 21 February 1934, p. 4.
8. Ivor Montagu, 'On Film censorship', in *Kino News*, Winter, 1935, p. 2.
9. Montagu, art. cit.; *'Non-Flam' Films*, London n.d. (1934), a 20-page pamphlet published by the National Council for Civil Liberties.
10. Montagu, art. cit.
11. *Daily Worker*, 24 August 1934, p. 4.
12. In Film and Photo League Archive (statement of account of 29 October 1934).
13. *Daily Worker*, 27 November 1934, p. 4.
14. *First Annual Report, Kino Films (1935) Ltd*, in Film and Photo League Archive.
15. *Film Production*, Kino Manifesto, in Film and Photo League Archive.
16. *Daily Worker*, 6 August 1936, p. 3.
17. See Bert Hogenkamp, 'Workers' Newsreels in the 1920s and 1930s', *Our History*, no. 68, pp. 11–14.
18. Ralph Bond, 'Making Films With A Purpose', in *Kino News*, Winter, 1935, p. 1.
19. See Peter Latham, *Theories of the Labour Movement. A Critique in the Context of an Empirical Study of Building Trade Unionism*, London Ph.D., 1978; Peter Latham, 'Rank and File Movements In Building 1910-1920', *Our History*, no. 69.
20. Frank Jackson, letter to the author, 21 November 1977.
21. Peter Latham, *Theories of the Labour Movement*, op. cit., p. 195.
22. Frank Jackson, letter cit.
23. Frank Jackson, interview with the author, 7 March 1978.
24. Ibid.
25. Frank Jackson, letter cit.
26. Frank Jackson, interview cit.
27. *Production during 1935-36*, in Film and Photo League Archive.
28. Jackson, interview cit.
29. Peter Latham, *Theories of the Labour Movement*, op. cit., p. 195.
30. *First Annual Report, Kino Films (1935) Ltd*, in Film and Photo League Archive.
31. Anna Shepherd, 'Helen Biggar and Norman McLaren. Based on an MS "Helen Unlimited"', in *New Edinburgh Review*, no. 40 (February 1978), p. 25.
32. Anna Shepherd, art. cit., p. 26.
33. The factual information for this section was provided by Anna Shepherd's *Helen Unlimited*, unpublished MS, London, 1975, 'A Little Biggar', unpublished article, London, 1976; 'Helen Biggar and Norman McLaren', art. cit.

Notes on Contributors

Ralph Bond was a founder member of the London Workers' Film Society and the Federation of Workers' Film Societies in 1929. From 1931 he was production manager for the GPO Film Unit under John Grierson. He subsequently wrote, directed and produced many documentary films for different companies, and was later appointed supervisor for ACT Films Ltd. He served on the General Council of the Association of Cinematograph Technicians (later ACTT) from 1936 and was the union's vice-president from 1942 to 1974. He now teaches documentary film at the London International Film School.

Jon Clark is Lecturer in the Department of Sociology and Social Administration at Southampton University. He graduated in German at the University of Birmingham and has written a Ph.D. thesis on German workers' theatre in the Weimar Republic.

Margot Heinemann studied English at Cambridge from 1931 to 1935, associating there with contemporaries including John Cornford and James Klugmann and other members of the Left like Maurice and Kitty Cornforth. Active in the Communist Party since 1934, she worked in the Birmingham city organization and later in the St Pancras branch, twelve of whose members were killed in the Spanish Civil War. She taught in Birmingham in a day-continuation school for young factory girls, then worked from 1936 to 1949 at the Labour Research Department, and after that as a teacher and lecturer in schools and at Goldsmith's College, London. Now Fellow and College Lecturer at New Hall, Cambridge, her books include *Britain's Coal* (1933), *The Adventurers*, a novel about coalmining (1960), *Britain in the Nineteen Thirties* (with Noreen Branson) (1971), and *Puritanism and Theatre: Thomas Middleton and Opposition Drama* (forthcoming, 1980).

Bert Hogenkamp is a Dutch film critic and historian currently working on the Dutch edition of the works of Sergei Eisenstein. He has published numerous articles on the history of workers' cinema in Europe and is the author of *Workers' Newsreels in the 1920s and 1930s* (*Our History* booklet, 1977).

Arnold Kettle went to Cambridge in 1934 and read History and English. He joined the Communist Party in 1936 and became secretary, then president of the Cambridge University Socialist Club (which by 1938 had 1,000 members out of a total of 4,000 students). He served in the army in Italy, Yugoslavia and India during the war, after which he taught English literature at the University of Leeds and in Dar es Salaam. Now Professor of Literature at The Open University, his books include *An Introduction to the English Novel* (1952) and *Poetry and Politics* (Open University Course Unit, 1976).

James Klugmann, who died in 1977, played a leading part in the international student movement in the thirties, having joined the Communist Party in 1933 when a student at Trinity College, Cambridge. He served in the army in the Middle East and Yugoslavia during the war, after which he worked for the party as lecturer, editor and writer. He was the editor of *Marxism Today* from 1962–77 and was the author of two volumes of the history of the British Communist Party – *Formation and Early Years, 1918–1924* (1968) and *The General Strike, 1925–1926* (1969).

David Margolies lectures in English at Goldsmiths' College, London. He is the author of *The Function of Literature: A Study of Christopher Caudwell's Aesthetics* (1969).

Betty Reid worked, from 1937 until its disbandment in 1940, for the Left Book Club Groups' Department, of which her husband John Lewis was National Organizer. During the war she was secretary of the National Council for Democratic Aid, an organization concerned with the welfare of anti-fascist refugees in Britain. Since 1942 she has worked full-time in the Organization Department of the Communist Party.

Carole Snee is Research Assistant at Thames Polytechnic, London. She is currently writing a Ph.D. thesis entitled 'Documentary Expression in Britain in the 1930s'.

André van Gyseghem, director and actor, has been active in the theatre and television since the thirties. He worked as a director at the Embassy Theatre, Swiss Cottage, and was the first president of Unity Theatre and founder-director of the Library Theatre, Manchester and of the Nottingham Playhouse. He is the author of *Theatre in the Soviet Union* (1943), and currently works as an actor, mainly in television.

Peter Widdowson is Principal Lecturer in English at Thames Polytechnic, London. He is the author of *E. M. Forster's 'Howards End': Fiction and History* (1977) and an editor of the journal *Literature and History*.

Iain Wright is a Fellow of Queens' College, Cambridge, where he lectures in English Literature.

Name and Title Index

Numbers in bold type indicate main references

MacNeice, Louis—*cont.*
Strings are False, 110, 115; 'The
Sunlight on the Garden', 92–3
McGonigle, Dr, 30
McLaren, Norman, 266–7; *Camera
Makes Whoopee*, 266; *Hell Unltd*,
266–7; *7 till 5*, 266
McLean, Willie, 267
Madge, Charles, 70
Malleson, Miles, 214, 230, 237n
Maltz, Albert, *Black Pit*, 214; *Peace on
Earth* (co-author with George Sklar),
214
Mann, Charlie, 257
Mann, Tom, 249
Marriott, J. W., 238n
Marshall, Herbert, 229–30, 236n, 238n
Maugham, Somerset, 209, 219
Megarry, Bill, 263, 264
Mendelson, Edward, 85, 131n
Menen, Aubrey, 211, 213
Meyerhold, Vsevolod, 229
Mill, John Stuart, 162
Montagu, Ivor, 254, 257, 259, 261, 264,
267; *Free Thälmann*, 254; *Peace and
Plenty*, 254; 'The Political Censorship
of Films', 246, 259
Morton, A. L., 34, 55, 58, 72, 129; *A
People's History of England*, 201; 'So I
Became', 129–30
Mosley, Oswald, 33, 249
Münzenberg, Willi, 258
Mussolini, Benito, 17, 233

Nash, Ogden, 112
Nixon, Barbara, 214, 230, 238n

O'Casey, Sean, 209, 228, 237n; *The Star
Turns Red*, 228
Odets, Clifford, 232; *Waiting for Lefty*,
224, 230
Oklopkhov, Nikolai, 213, 229
O'Neill, Eugene, *All God's Chillun Got
Wings*, 210
Orwell, George, 10, 103, 131n, 133, 144,
149–51, 162, 164n; *Animal Farm*,
133, 149, 151; *Burmese Days*, 149;
Coming Up for Air, 149, 151; *Keep the
Aspidistra Flying*, 149–50; 'Inside the

Whale', 103; *1984*, 133, 149, 151; *The
Road To Wigan Pier*, 149
Owen, Wilfred, 16, 89, 91, 107, 118

Pageant of Chartism, 218
Pageant of South Wales, 218
Pinter, Harold, 100, 145
Piscator, Erwin, 210, 213, 229
Pizer, Alf, 263
Plant in the Sun (Ben Bengal), 227
Pogodin, Nikolai, *Aristocrats*, 229
Pollitt, Harry, 195
Porter, Cole, 233
Pound, Ezra, 9, 59n
Powell, Anthony, 133
Plummer, A. L., 247
Priestley, J. B., 219
Pritt, D. N., 237n
Proust, Marcel, 144
Pudovkin, Vsevolod, 20, 245, 247; *End of
St Petersburg*, 247

Rathbone, Eleanor, 30
Reeves, Joseph, 253–4
Redgrave, Michael, 237n
Remarque, Erich Maria, *All Quiet on the
Western Front*, 16
Renn, Ludwig, 16
Richards, I. A., 43–4, 46–9, 56, 62n;
Practical Criticism, 46
Rickword, Edgell, 10, 35, 58, 61n, 67–8,
70–2, 106, 108, 162n
Roberts, Michael, 67
Roberts, Wilfred, 195
Robeson, Paul, 195, 210, 212, 213,
227–8, 237n
Rosen, Tubby, 30
Rotha, Paul, *Peace Film*, 267
Rudé, George, 34

Saint Denis, Michel, 237n
Samuel, Raphael, 221
Sassoon, Siegfried, 16
Schoenberg, Arnold, 233
Sender, Ramón, *The Secret*, 224
Shakespeare, William, 71, 76–7
Shaw, G. B., 219
Shaw, Irwin, *Bury the Dead*, 210, 214–16